More Praise for Emotional Intelligence in Action

"Creating the metrics necessary to measure emotional intelligence was a daunting task. But teaching others how to change their behavior is an altogether different challenge. This book is an able teacher for the serious learners and leaders of the field."

—Esther M. Orioli, author, *Essi Systems' EQ Map"*

"Emotional Intelligence in Action is an important contribution to the field of applied emotional intelligence, particularly for its contribution in helping individuals improve their skills so that they can unlock their potential and live at a level more commensurate with their true capability."

—Rich Handley, coauthor, *EQ 360*™ and
Benchmark of Organizational Emotional Intelligence

"The authors provide a suite of well-designed tools for increasing emotional intelligence and then invite practitioners to apply these to respond to individual development needs. This is a needed addition to the field of emotional intelligence. The gift that these practitioners have given is they have helped to make EQ development a faster and more efficient process for both coaches and clients. Advanced practitioners will find these tools useful for sharpening their practice."

—Geetu Bharwaney, founder and managing director, Ei World

"Emotional Intelligence in Action is a very practical tool organizations can use to help employees anticipate, understand, and accept change and thrive in a fast-moving business environment."

—Tad Deering, Sr., director of strategic change, Time Warner Telecom

"Emotional Intelligence in Action is a must read for anyone serious about improving personal and professional relationships, while gaining greater self-knowledge."

—Richie Fontenot Hunter, vice president of marketing,
Anthem Blue Cross and Blue Shield, West Region

"A pioneering book for a cutting edge field! The authors have pulled together thoughtful and useful tactics and strategies for trainers and consultants that will enable audiences to understand and act on EQ concepts. The cross references with numerous resources enables the reader to quickly identify additional material for workshop use."

—Roger R. Pearman, president, Qualifying.org, Inc.

"*Emotional Intelligence in Action* delivers whether you are an EI newcomer or a seasoned professional with its refreshing 'workouts' and totally engaging approach. EIA passes my test; it is both fun to read and easy to implement. Hughes, Patterson, and Terrell make a significant contribution to EI and more importantly, will help you make a significant contribution to your organization."

—Scott Cawood, SPHR, vice president,
Global Talent Management, Revlon; founder, Modern Think

"*Emotional Intelligence in Action* is a valuable resource that is loaded with exercises and experiential learning scenarios ('workouts') that all of us can profit from as we seek to understand more clearly what moves us and motivates us. More accurate, realistic information, in turn, allows us to reason with emotions and emotional signals. The ability to do that serves as a valuable foundation for creating real change."

—Wayne Cascio, US Bank Term Professor of Management,
University of Colorado

"In all the training and developmental work I have done lately, I have seen repeatedly the importance of interactive experiences. To have tools to help people learn by experience is so valuable and clearly, the best way to promote learning. I am excited to have this excellent handbook to help individuals and teams strengthen their emotional intelligence. 'Hands On' is the best!"

—Kathy Yeager, SPHR, vice president, human resources,
The Medical Center of Aurora

About This Book

Why is this topic important?

Exploring and developing emotional intelligence not only makes us happier and more successful, but it helps us motivate ourselves, manage stress more effectively, and resolve conflict with others. It gives us the skills to be able to encourage, comfort, discipline, and confront different kinds of people appropriately in different situations. It determines how effectively we express our emotions within the cultural contexts of our family, our workplace, and our community. It determines how well people listen to us and how well we are heard.

What can you achieve with this book?

As an easy-to-use informational reference to the key components of emotional intelligence, this book is unsurpassed. The forty-six cross-referenced exercises serve as an invaluable resource for trainers, coaches, facilitators, HR professionals, managers, and anyone who needs to build emotional intelligence competencies in their work with individuals, teams, or groups.

Several books are available that discuss this topic, but very few provide exercises and learning scenarios to help build emotional intelligence skills. This book breaks new ground in providing a cross-reference matrix that maps the exercises to the four leading emotional intelligence models—the EQ-i® or EQ-360™, ECI 360, the MSCEIT™, and EQ Map®—making it easy to use with all the models.

How is this book organized?

This book is organized into three parts. Part One provides an overview of using emotional intelligence to create real change. It includes sections on why emotional intelligence is important and how to best use this book. It also contains the cross-reference table that maps the exercises to the four leading emotional intelligence models. Last, it discusses the integral connection between thinking and emotions. Part Two gives a synopsis of fifteen components of emotional intelligence. Part Three features forty-six exercises to help build effective emotional skills. Each exercise includes a purpose statement, summary, description of the outcome/ desired results, estimated time, intended audience, skill level needed by facilitator, step-by-step instructions, and reproducible handout sheets for participants.

About Pfeiffer

Pfeiffer serves the professional development and hands-on resource needs of training and human resource practitioners and gives them products to do their jobs better. We deliver proven ideas and solutions from experts in HR development and HR management, and we offer effective and customizable tools to improve workplace performance. From novice to seasoned professional, Pfeiffer is the source you can trust to make yourself and your organization more successful.

Essential Knowledge Pfeiffer produces insightful, practical, and comprehensive materials on topics that matter the most to training and HR professionals. Our Essential Knowledge resources translate the expertise of seasoned professionals into practical, how-to guidance on critical workplace issues and problems. These resources are supported by case studies, worksheets, and job aids and are frequently supplemented with CD-ROMs, websites, and other means of making the content easier to read, understand, and use.

Essential Tools Pfeiffer's Essential Tools resources save time and expense by offering proven, ready-to-use materials—including exercises, activities, games, instruments, and assessments—for use during a training or team-learning event. These resources are frequently offered in looseleaf or CD-ROM format to facilitate copying and customization of the material.

Pfeiffer also recognizes the remarkable power of new technologies in expanding the reach and effectiveness of training. While e-hype has often created whizbang solutions in search of a problem, we are dedicated to bringing convenience and enhancements to proven training solutions. All our e-tools comply with rigorous functionality standards. The most appropriate technology wrapped around essential content yields the perfect solution for today's on-the-go trainers and human resource professionals.

Pfeiffer
www.pfeiffer.com   *Essential resources for training and HR professionals*

This book is dedicated to all those who help others enhance the quality of life by developing deeper, more profound business and personal relationships. Their actions, which add richness, strength, and meaning to life, resonate throughout the world and transform our lives.

Emotional Intelligence in Action

Training and Coaching Activities for Leaders and Managers

MARCIA HUGHES

L. BONITA PATTERSON

JAMES BRADFORD TERRELL

Pfeiffer

A Wiley Imprint

www.pfeiffer.com

Copyright © 2005 by Marcia Hughes, L. Bonita Patterson, and James Bradford Terrell.

Published by Pfeiffer
An Imprint of Wiley.
989 Market Street, San Francisco, CA 94103-1741 www.pfeiffer.com

For additional copies/bulk purchases of this book in the U.S. please contact 800-274-4434.

Pfeiffer books and products are available through most bookstores. To contact Pfeiffer directly call our Customer Care Department within the U.S. at 800-274-4434, outside the U.S. at 317-572-3985, fax 317-572-4002, or visit www.pfeiffer.com.

Pfeiffer also publishes its books in a variety of electronic formats. Some content that appears in print may not be available in electronic books.

ISBN: 0-7879-7843-4

Library of Congress Cataloging-in-Publication Data
Hughes, Marcia M.
Emotional intelligence in action: training and coaching activities for leaders and managers/
Marcia M. Hughes, L. Bonita Patterson, James Bradford Terrell.
p. cm.
Accompanied by a CD-ROM.
Includes bibliographical references and index.
ISBN 0-7879-7843-4 (alk. paper)
1. Executives—Training of—Handbooks, manuals, etc. 2. Leadership—Study and teaching—Handbooks, manuals, etc. 3. Executive coaching—Handbooks, manuals, etc. 4. Counselors—Training of—Handbooks, manuals, etc. 5. Group facilitation—Handbooks, manuals, etc. 6. Personnel departments—Employees—Training of—Handbooks, manuals, etc. 7. Emotional intelligence—Handbooks, manuals, etc. 8. Active learning—Handbooks, manuals, etc. I. Patterson, L. Bonita II. Terrell, James Bradford III. Title.
HD30.4.H824 2005
658.4'071245—dc22
2005004205

Acquiring Editor: Martin Delahoussaye
Director of Development: Kathleen Dolan Davies
Developmental Editor: Susan Rachmeler
Production Editor: Dawn Kilgore

Editor: Rebecca Taff
Manufacturing Supervisor: Becky Carreno
Editorial Assistant: Laura Reizman

Printed in the United States of America
Printing   10 9 8 7 6 5 4 3

Contents

Foreword by Reuven Bar-On   xv

Acknowledgments   xvii

Introduction: Getting the Most
from This Resource   1

PART ONE   Using Emotional Intelligence
to Create Real Change   7

CHAPTER 1   The Case for Emotional Intelligence   9

CHAPTER 2   How Everyone Can Use the Workouts:
Cross-Reference Matrix   17

PART TWO   Exploring Fifteen Competencies
of Emotional Intelligence   37

1 Self-Regard   41

2 Emotional Self-Awareness   45

3 Assertiveness   49

4 Independence 55

5 Self-Actualization 59

6 Empathy 65

7 Social Responsibility 71

8 Interpersonal Relationships 77

9 Stress Tolerance 81

10 Impulse Control 87

11 Reality Testing 91

12 Flexibility 95

13 Problem Solving 101

14 Optimism 105

15 Happiness 111

PART THREE Emotional Intelligence Workouts
to Build Effective Skills 115

1 Self-Regard

WORKOUT 1.1 Of Thine Own Self Be Aware 119

WORKOUT 1.2 Reconciliation 123

WORKOUT 1.3 Toot Your Horn and Scratch Your Back 129

2 Emotional Self-Awareness

WORKOUT **2.1** Are You in Touch? 133

WORKOUT **2.2** It Just Bubbles Up 139

WORKOUT **2.3** Moving Toward, Moving Away 145

WORKOUT **2.4** Grow Your Personal Power 153

3 Assertiveness

WORKOUT **3.1** Ramp It Up 157

WORKOUT **3.2** Dial It Back 163

WORKOUT **3.3** Getting Your Point Across 167

4 Independence

WORKOUT **4.1** Cut the Apron Strings 171

WORKOUT **4.2** Solitary Effort 175

WORKOUT **4.3** Going Along with the Group—Or Not 179

5 Self-Actualization

WORKOUT **5.1** The Scavenger Hunt 183

WORKOUT **5.2** Becoming All That You Can Be 193

WORKOUT **5.3** Applying Inspiration 201

6 Empathy

WORKOUT **6.1** Connect Feeling with Meaning 207

WORKOUT **6.2** Mixed Emotions 211

WORKOUT **6.3** Do As the Empathic Do 219

7 Social Responsibility

WORKOUT **7.1** Reflect the Best 223

WORKOUT **7.2** Who Do I Work for? 229

WORKOUT **7.3** The Value of Volunteering 235

8 Interpersonal Relationships

WORKOUT **8.1** You've Got Good News 239

WORKOUT **8.2** Making New Friends 245

WORKOUT **8.3** Fun and Meaningful Relationships 251

9 Stress Tolerance

WORKOUT **9.1** 'Cause You've Got Personality 255

WORKOUT **9.2** Water Off a Duck's Back 265

WORKOUT **9.3** Deep Center Breathing 269

10 Impulse Control

WORKOUT **10.1** To Impulse or Not to Impulse   275

WORKOUT **10.2** The Urge to Splurge   287

WORKOUT **10.3** Hot Buttons   293

11 Reality Testing

WORKOUT **11.1** Feel, Hear, See—Is It Reality?   297

WORKOUT **11.2** Visit Their Reality   301

WORKOUT **11.3** Using All Three of Your Minds   305

12 Flexibility

WORKOUT **12.1** No More Shutdowns   311

WORKOUT **12.2** Yes, No, Maybe So   317

WORKOUT **12.3** Flex Time   321

13 Problem Solving

WORKOUT **13.1** Using the MasterSolve Model for Teams   325

WORKOUT **13.2** Win-Win Negotiating   333

WORKOUT **13.3** Let's Cover Our Bases   337

14 Optimism

WORKOUT **14.1** Be Solution-Focused   343

WORKOUT **14.2** See a Positive Resolution   347

WORKOUT **14.3** The Optimistic Explanation   351

15 Happiness

WORKOUT **15.1** Growing My Happiness   359

WORKOUT **15.2** Pay It Forward with Gratitude 363

WORKOUT **15.3** Attitude of Gratitude   367

Resources   371

References   375

About the Authors   379

Index   383

How to Use the CD-ROM   391

Pfeiffer Publications Guide   393

Foreword

Everyone can profit from enhancing his or her emotional intelligence, because this important construct has a positive impact on human performance, leading to personal effectiveness and eventually to overall well-being.

The activities in this book are designed to be applicable to those who favor any one of the three major approaches to the emotional intelligence construct. The authors have focused on the Bar-On approach in defining and measuring emotional intelligence as the backbone of this book, but the activities are easily applicable to the Salovey-Meyer and Goleman/Boyatzis models as well. In addition, they are also readily applicable to a wide range of EI assessment tools, including Esther Orioli's EQ Map and other closely related instruments. This wide applicability across the major EI conceptual and psychometric models makes this workbook unique.

This method supports what I have referred to as "the multi-modal approach" in describing, assessing, and enhancing this construct. When this specific approach within emotional intelligence is combined with factoring in the impact of cognitive styles and personality traits, as the authors have uniquely suggested, the ability to assess, predict, and improve human performance is expanded exponentially.

Although the authors have targeted primarily organizational trainers, facilitators, executive coaches, and other closely related practitioners, these activities can be used by a wider range of individuals in a variety of settings. Those who are involved in parenting children at home, educating students at school, or counseling patients in clinical settings can all benefit from this workbook.

Emotional Intelligence in Action is well-written, interesting, and enjoyable to work with. The read is not merely a passive experience, but rather actively engages the reader from beginning to end. The activities and experiential learning scenarios ("workouts") are easy to understand and fun to do.

This workbook fills an important niche in developing emotional intelligence, representing a genuine contribution to the field. I would like to express my gratitude to Marcia Hughes, Bonita Patterson, and James Terrell for making this important contribution to emotional intelligence. I have thoroughly enjoyed reading the didactic material, experimenting with the activities, and noticing the effect that they have had on me. I highly recommend *Emotional Intelligence in Action* to all those who are interested in enhancing this vitally critical component of human intelligence and performance.

Reuven Bar-On
November 7, 2004

Dr. Reuven Bar-On holds a research position at the University of Texas Medical Branch and is affiliated with the Collaborative for Academic, Social, and Emotional Learning (CASEL) and the Consortium for Research on Emotional Intelligence in Organizations. He is the author of the Bar-On EQi, the co-author of EQi-YV, EQ360, EQ-Interview, and *Optimizing People* and the co-editor of the *Handbook of Emotional Intelligence.*

Acknowledgments

The authors wish to acknowledge and thank:

Reuven Bar-On, Peter Salovey, John D. Mayer, David R. Caruso, Daniel Goleman, Richard E. Boyatzis, Esther Orioli, Robert Cooper, Cary Cherniss, and Marilyn K. Gowing, for their pioneering emotional intelligence work, Robert Carkhuff for his substantial contribution to the field of interpersonal communication.

Lois Hart, Ed.D., for guiding us down the publishing path; Elaine Biech for opening the door; Martin Delahoussaye, senior editor at Pfeiffer, for being there to welcome us in and guide us with such good cheer; and Susan Rachmeler, Kathleen Dolan Davies, Laura Reizman, Dawn Kilgore, Jeanenne Ray, and Karen Warner at Pfeiffer, for guiding us with gentle insistence to the quality we most desired to achieve. Our thanks also go to Ken Hultman for valuable input.

Michael Snell, our agent, for creating an excellent interface with our publisher, orchestrating a win-win process, and continuing down the publishing path with us.

Danielle Hughes, Sherrol Horner, and Jake York for their much-needed assistance in editing and document preparation.

All of our parents, families, teachers, mentors, clients, and adversaries, and the grace and pluck that have gotten us each this far along the crazy paths we call our lives.

Introduction

Getting the Most from This Resource

PURPOSE

Emotional intelligence research and experience validate its importance as a critical factor in personal and business success. The Consortium for Research on Emotional Intelligence in Organizations provides a business case for emotional intelligence that lists nineteen success stories that resulted from developing or expanding emotional intelligence skills. They note:

> "Optimism is an emotional competence that leads to increased productivity. New salesmen at Met Life who scored high on a test of 'learned optimism' sold 37 percent more life insurance in their first two years than did pessimists." (www.eiconsortium.org)

The need for emotional intelligence increases with higher levels of responsibility, such as management or parenthood, and becomes even more important with groups, such as work teams. Recognizing the importance of emotional intelligence is a great starting place, but how do we develop competencies in the actual skills that empower us to function more effectively at work, at home, and in the community? The Guidelines for Best Practices for training and development in EI created by the EI Consortium emphasize the critical need for experiential practice to learn and enhance EI competencies. This book addresses that need by providing experiential learning scenarios drawn from real life to enhance emotional intelligence competencies.

AUDIENCE

This book is designed for coaches, trainers, facilitators, HR professionals, managers, and anyone who wants to help others improve their emotional intelligence. The in-depth description of key elements of emotional intelligence is supported by easy, practical, and impactful exercises, which we call "workouts."

For individual coaching, the primary audiences are leaders, managers, supervisors, and employees whose job success requires improved interpersonal skills. The exercises will also be useful in clinical applications with clients who need to develop emotional intelligence to achieve therapeutic goals.

For group development, the primary audiences are management teams, intact teams at any level, and cross-functional teams. The exercises will also be an important resource for those providing public workshops for people interested in developing competencies in social and emotional intelligence, improving relationships, and expanding their career development opportunities.

ASSESSMENTS

The exercises contained in Part Three of this book may be used with or without assessments. For those who use assessments, we urge you to consider using multiple assessments whenever possible. No one measure can tell everything about a person. Multiple data sets provide the opportunity to corroborate results, to better understand the feedback, and to understand the interrelationships among multiple factors. Dr. Cary Cherniss, professor, author of pivotal books on EI and co-founder of the EI Consortium, stated in his presentation at Collaborative Growth's 2004 EQ Symposium that many organizations are increasingly requesting the use of multiple assessment tools and finding more validity in results when they do so.

Assessments one might consider using in accompaniment with any of the four EQ measures discussed in this book include the Myers Briggs Type Indicator® (MBTI), Emergenetics®, FIRO-B®, the Center for Creative Leadership's Benchmarks, the Disc®, and the Campbell Interest and Skills Inventory. One interesting explanation of the combination of assessment interests is found in Pearman (2002), where he discusses MBTI and emotional intelligence.

HOW THIS BOOK IS ORGANIZED

This book is organized into three parts. Part One, Using Emotional Intelligence to Create Real Change, explains the rationale for developing emotional intelligence (EI) and highlights four key EI measures. The first section outlines the case for emotional intelligence. It explains why EI has such a powerful impact on personal effectiveness. The next section introduces the four most significant emotional intelligence measures and presents a matrix for cross-referencing the individual exercises (what we call workouts) in this book with the specific competencies for which each measure provides instruction. If you are working with one of the four major measures—the EQ-i® or EQ-360™, ECI 360, the MSCEIT™, or EQ Map®—you can look up your measure of choice in the cross-reference matrix and find the workouts that apply. These workouts will help you develop the competencies important to you for whichever measure you use.

Perhaps the best part is that you don't have to be working with a measure at all! You can use these workouts independently to strengthen any competency that is needed. For example, if you wanted to work with a team or individual to help him or her develop flexibility, you would look in Part Two for the in-depth description of the competency and then go to Part Three, where, under the heading Flexibility, you would find your three choices—Workouts 12.1, 12.2, and 12.3. Just choose the one that is best suited to your situation.

Part Two, Exploring Fifteen Components of Emotional Intelligence, provides an in-depth description of each of fifteen emotional competencies to help you and your clients become thoroughly familiar with the dimensions of each skill.

Part Three, Emotional Intelligence Workouts to Build Effective Skills, contains the experiential learning scenarios we call workouts. The first three sections of each workout—Purpose, Thumbnail, and Outcome—explain the following: Purpose answers WHY you would have the people do this workout; Thumbnail tells you HOW participants will engage with the instructional material to generate the learning experience; and Outcome explains WHAT your target is—the desired results that can be achieved. The workouts and the companion CD contain reproducible handouts that you may copy for your participants.

The book closes with a list of resources for finding additional useful information.

Note to coaches: Most of the exercises can be used in individual coaching situations as well as with intact teams and groups. The thumbnail summaries and instructions usually are written for the team and group experience. If you are coaching an individual, simply reframe the instructions for the one-on-one environment and the workouts will be effective for you and your client.

KEY TERMS

EI is an acronym for emotional intelligence.

EQ (emotional quotient) is a measure of the degree of emotional intelligence development, similar to IQ. The term was coined by Reuven Bar-On.

Workout is what we call the exercises, activities, and experiential learning scenarios included in Part Three.

ICONS

We have developed a set of icons to highlight specific parts of each chapter to which you may want to give special attention. They are meant to be fun and informative landmarks that help you navigate the material efficiently and make the best use of it.

The treasure chest icon is the first one you will encounter. It appears in the in-depth description of each specific competency, where it highlights a helpful tip or insight about that skill, how to develop it, qualities that make it important, or how applying it effectively can make a difference in the quality of your life.

The star performer icon indicates a biographical note about someone in real life who is an excellent model of that specific competency. Martin Luther King, Gandhi, Hans Blix, and Oprah Winfrey are among the examples you will find.

There are many excellent examples of emotionally intelligent behavior in the movies, so we have done our best to utilize some of the more popular films to illustrate each of the competencies. You will find *Lilies of the Field, Remember the Titans, Erin Brockovich, Whale Rider,* and *The Wizard of Oz* among our favorites.

The purpose of the thumbnail is to let the coach or trainer quickly know how long he or she will need to allow for the workout and what sort of an experience he or she will be facilitating.

The CD-ROM icon indicates a full-size version of the material is available on the accompanying CD-ROM.

FACILITATOR COMPETENCIES

This section is designed to show the coach or trainer how skillful he or she will have to be in order to successfully conduct the workout. There is generally also a significant relationship with how sophisticated the learning experience will be for the participants. If participants' skills tend to be less developed in an area, then starting with an easier workout will provide better results.

Three levels of facilitator skills are identified:

○ EASY

◑ MODERATE

● ADVANCED

FACILITATOR GUIDELINES

Preparation

- Read the "Introduction: Getting the Most from This Resource" section to familiarize yourself with the icons used in this book.
- Review the appropriate section in "Part Two—Exploring Fifteen Components of Emotional Intelligence" to better understand the emotional intelligence aspect on which you will be working.
- Read applicable material from the Resources list and the References at the back of the book.
- Ensure the room size and table arrangement are conducive to the type of workout you will be leading.

- Make sufficient copies of the reproducible participant handouts that are included in the workouts (full-size versions are available on the enclosed CD) and gather other needed materials.
- Consider playing music during the reflective phases of the exercises when participants are asked to think about their behaviors and responses. We recommend calming instrumental music that is played at a soft volume. (If you do use music, be sure to abide by any copyright restrictions.)

Materials

- The "Materials" section of each workout contains a list of materials you will need.
- Reproducible participant handouts are included in most workouts.
- Full-size versions of the handouts are available on the enclosed CD.

Debriefing and Reflection

- Debriefing is one of the most important phases of the workout. It gives participants a chance to reflect on and synthesize their experiences and to share what they have learned. It provides one of the best opportunities for introverts to be heard.
- Ask questions that help the participants uncover what they learned and surface any "aha's." Your mission is to lead them on a journey of self-discovery. The learning is more powerful when they recognize for themselves how they benefited from the workout, versus having you tell them what they learned.

Selection

- Refer to the cross-reference matrix in Part One of this book to identify the workout(s) you want to use.
- Look up the potential workouts you identified from the cross-reference matrix, and refer to the purpose, thumbnail, outcome, audience, estimated time, and facilitator competency information to help you identify the best workout(s) for your situation.

Using Emotional Intelligence to Create Real Change

In Part One we explain the rationale for developing emotional intelligence (EI) and highlight four key EQ measures. In the first section we outline the case for emotional intelligence and explain why EI has such a powerful impact on effectiveness. In the next section we introduce the four most significant emotional intelligence measures and present a matrix for cross-referencing the individual exercises (workouts) in this book with the specific competencies in which each measure provides instruction.

If you are working with one of the four major measures—the EQ-i® or EQ-360™, ECI 360, the MSCEIT™, or EQ Map®—you can look up your measure of choice in the cross-reference matrix and find the workouts that apply. These workouts will help you develop the competencies important to you for whichever measure you use. The first three measures are reviewed in the newly released *Encyclopedia of Applied Psychology* (Cherniss, 2004).

Perhaps the best part is that you don't have to be working with a measure at all! You can use these workouts independently to strengthen any competency that is needed. For example, if empathy is your focus, go to Workouts, 6.1, 6.2, and 6.3 and choose the one that is best suited to your situation.

CHAPTER 1

The Case for Emotional Intelligence

Would you like to be more effective in your work and in your personal life? Would you like to be able to better understand what you are feeling and why? Would you like to be able to participate more consciously in what you feel and how you respond, rather than just reacting in the same old patterns that you always have? Would you like to have more friends or be able to be closer and more open with the friends you have now? Would you like to be able to better monitor and motivate your progress toward your short- and long-term goals? Then you'll *Love* exploring the world of emotional intelligence!

Exploring and developing our emotional intelligence not only makes us happier, it makes us able to motivate ourselves, manage stress in our lives, and resolve conflict with others. It gives us the skills to be able to encourage, comfort, discipline, and confront different kinds of people appropriately in different situations. It determines how effectively we express our emotions within the cultural contexts of our family, our workplace, and our community. It determines how well people listen to us and how well we are heard.

EMOTIONS: WHAT ARE THEY?

To effectively introduce the topic of emotional intelligence we need to start by talking a little bit about emotions and what they are. We like to say that emotions are about what we touch . . . not just what we touch with our fingers or our skin, what we touch with our eyes and ears, what we touch with our taste buds and the olfactory nerves in our noses. Emotions are how we feel about what we touch with our imagination, from the dread of a loud scary noise in the dark to those fifteen minutes of fame when you know you're at the top of your game and everyone else gets to see. Emotions are what move us and motivate us. All three of these words—*emotion, move,* and *motivate*—share the Latin root *emovare,* which means *to move.* Emotions are what sustain us through our struggles and crown us in our victories. In fact when you really think about why we do anything that we do, there is always a feeling involved—something that we are avoiding and moving away from or something that we want and are moving toward. Fear and desire are two of our strongest emotions and have long been considered the most powerful motivators in the animal kingdom.

Research at the National Institute of Mental Health by Candace Pert has shown that emotions are very closely associated with neuro-peptides, long chain protein molecules that circulate throughout the organs of the body and act like "messenger molecules," conveying information about what is happening in one part of the body throughout the entire system. In her book, *Molecules of Emotion* (1997), Pert considers emotions to be a transformative link between mind and body, the mysterious quantum mechanical interface where information turns into matter and our bodies synthesize the chemicals of consciousness.

Recognizing that our feeling responses are grounded in our biochemistry is an important understanding. Emotional states such as anger, sorrow, depression, and joy can be influenced and even directed by us, but this does not mean they can be turned on and off like a light bulb. It takes our body time to metabolize these chemical components—such as the adrenaline that is released when we feel frightened. The chemistry of emotions can help us change our viewpoint and see the world through different attitudinal lenses depending on how we are feeling. When we create and maintain positive thoughts about ourselves and our world through our self-talk, we support positive emotional states such as resourcefulness, optimism, and motivation.

A good way to imagine emotions is as an invisible link that connects people with each other and to some extent with all living creatures—they constitute a field of specific information that we sense and decode using the ancient instinctual languages of facial expression, smell, body posture, and the whole realm of nonverbal language. On top of all that, human beings are able to add another layer of sophisticated interpretation. Through our use of cognitive intelligence and semantic language, we are able to label our feelings and give them a wide variety of symbolic meanings with subtle degrees of texture and nuance.

Intelligence

Early in the 20th century psychologists began to devise tests for measuring cognitive ability and intellect in human beings. The eventual result was what we know today as the standardized IQ test. As research into human intelligence continued along these lines, it began to appear as if it was an inherited capacity and was not greatly influenced by any amount of educational effort. Adults did not necessarily have higher IQ scores than children, and over the course of their lifetime they didn't seem to develop more. The view that intelligence was what was measured by IQ tests and that it was controlled by genetics generally prevailed into the 1970s. Yet when Weschler developed the IQ measure, he stated that there are other forms of intelligence besides the IQ he addressed.

Other scientists agreed with Weschler and were not satisfied with a static, one-dimensional definition of intelligence or the way in which it was measured. In the 1980s Howard Gardner published research that validated his work on "multiple intelligences," demonstrating the importance of expanding that definition, and Reuven Bar-On coined the term "emotional quotient" in an attempt to differentiate emotional competencies from intellect. Leading research by John Mayer and Peter Salovey was instrumental in developing a theory of emotional intelligence that consists of four domains: *perceiving emotions, facilitating thought, understanding emotions,* and *managing emotions.* They were joined in their efforts by David Caruso and together developed the MSCEIT (Mayer-Salovey-Caruso Emotional Intelligence Test), a reliable, valid, ability-based assessment of emotional intelligence with a normative database of five thousand people.

Their definition of emotional intelligence emphasizes "intelligence" and differs significantly enough from others that we will include it here:

"'Emotions' refer to the feelings a person has in a relationship. For example, if a person has a good relationship with someone else, that individual is happy; if the person is threatened, he or she is afraid. Intelligence, on the other hand, refers to the ability to reason with or about something. For example, one reasons with language in the case of verbal intelligence, or reasons about how objects fit together in the case of spatial intelligence. In the case of emotional intelligence, one reasons with emotions, or emotions assist one's thinking. That is, emotional intelligence, as measured by the MSCEIT™, refers to the capacity to reason with emotions and emotional signals, and to the capacity of emotion to enhance thought." (Mayer, Salovey, & Caruso, 2001, p. 2)

For more information on their description of intelligence within the concept of emotional intelligence, see the discussion of the "concept of an intelligence that processes and benefits from emotions" in Mayer, Salovey, and Caruso (2000, p. 105).

The idea of having an ability-based emotional intelligence test with right and wrong answers may seem foreign to those who think emotions are too subjective to be quantified, but here is a simple explanation of how it works:

"Emotional skills can also be measured in an objective way through the use of ability, performance, or knowledge tests. Such tests would ask a series of questions like these:

- What is the cause of sadness?
- What is an effective strategy for calming an angry customer?

The MSCEIT™ (pronounced mess-keet) asks people to solve emotional problems, and the correctness of the answers is evaluated. In turn, a person's scores are compared to a large, normative database to compute a sort of emotional intelligence quotient, or EI score." (Caruso & Salovey, 2004, p. 75)

The Brain

Processing emotion is a non-conscious event. It is something we do intuitively that allows us to anticipate others' behaviors in a more direct, immediate fashion than language can. Emotional intelligence is all about immediacy. The circuitry in our brains is set up to process emotional responses without having to consider them rationally. How am I feeling right now? How are you feeling right now? How are our feelings affecting each other and the actions we are choosing to take in this moment? These are the kind of critical comparisons that the limbic system, or emotional brain, is making for us constantly, most of it below the threshold of conscious awareness.

When sensory input enters our brain, it first is processed in the thalamus, which scans information for familiar patterns that may have been especially significant to us in the past. Such patterns are then forwarded to the hippocampus, which further screens them for threatening content before the amygdala's final decision as to whether it should trigger the fight-or-flight response. If it turns out there is no precedent for fear, the information is then passed along to the neo-cortex, which is able to analyze it for meaning in a rational process.

The emotional circuits in the brain also regulate the balance of two critical hormones throughout the body, cortisol and DHEA. Cortisol plays many positive roles in bodily functions; however, it is often known as the "stress hormone" because stressful situations cause it to be secreted in excess, and then it can have very negative effects on many aspects of our health. DHEA, on the other hand, is sometimes known as the "anti-aging hormone" because it counteracts the negative effects of cortisol that tend to wear the body out and cause it to age.

The Heart

But the brain is not alone in governing our emotional intelligence. In fact, recent research at the Institute of HeartMath (Childre & Martin, 1999) has revealed the heart to be a major player in the process of understanding and responding to our world. Our heart communicates chemically to the rest of our body by producing mood-enhancing hormones. Perhaps even more remarkably, the electromagnetic signal it sends to the brain (and every other cell as well) is the most powerful signal in the entire body! It produces an electromagnetic field that can be detected several feet away from the body in all directions. The heart also communicates mechanically with the rest of the body through pressure waves that are conducted through the vascular system. What is it sending in all these different channels of communication? It is giving the entire body feedback about how the whole system is functioning.

Research by Antonio Damasio (2003) has determined that human beings cannot make any cognitive decisions without also processing emotional information that incorporates how we feel about the situation. It turns out that emotional intelligence is actually the synthesis of both heart and brain functions, weaving together thought and feeling into the marvelously rich fabric of human experience.

EMOTIONS AND IDENTITY

Emotional intelligence also plays a critical role in conflict resolution. In their fundamental book, *Getting to Yes*, Fisher and Ury (1981) characterize the process of resolving conflict as one of helping people move from "No" to "Yes." What makes this difficult is that we tend to identify with our position, so in order for us to change it there has to be a change in our identity. In other words, if we think that we are the ones who deserve the promotion and the corner office because of our length and quality of service, we will have to change our sense of who we are and what those rewards mean to us symbolically in order to be able to accept another (equally good) solution. That change in identity may also come from the process of working through a deep disappointment and discovering that our competencies in flexibility and reality testing can truly help us transform.

Emotions play a critical role in identifying ourselves—in knowing who we are in the world and distinguishing "self" from "other." In addition to governing the fight-or-flight process, the limbic system also manages our immune system. The critical task of the immune system is to be able to distinguish what is part of us and what is foreign. Even the process of understanding who we are once again turns out to be grounded in our biochemistry. Our cells have self-receptors that are "read" by immune cells to determine whether or not they are part of the self or invaders that pose a threat to the health, wholeness, and integrity of our system.

My very sense of "I-ness" comes from recognizing familiar sensory patterns in the environment and experiencing the same emotional responses that were originally generated throughout my body/mind and recorded in my memory. After enough memories have been stored (generally around age two), this sense of familiarity undergoes a profound transformation. The billions of bits of data crystallize and initiate the advent of self, the recognition that it is "I" who is having this experience—"I" who is hungry and wants to eat, "I" who feel safe, or threatened, or curious, "I" who is powerful and can make things happen in the world!

Over time, sophisticated menus of preference and aversion come to be developed through this same process of associational memory. "I" discover that

I know what I like and dislike and, depending on my level of confidence, am able to express that effectively to the people whom I depend on for survival. If I have lived in a cooperative environment, family, or culture that requires me to get the approval of others for my decisions and actions at every level, then my need for interdependence will tend to overshadow my need for independence. If I have lived in a competitive environment in which I am only able to satisfy my desires through continuously creating and asserting new behavioral strategies which satisfy but the letter of the law, my need for independence will tend to overshadow my need for interdependence.

My ability to remodel, update, and even upgrade my identity, to resolve problems and conflicts, and consequently my ability to move myself and others from "No" to "Yes" will be dependent on how consciously or unconsciously I process my emotions. If I am unconsciously embedded in the automatic sequence of stimulus-response conditioning, I will tend to be a creature of habit and be liable to perceive myself as a victim of the world. If, through self-reflective processes, I have been able to lengthen the amount of time between stimulus and response, in other words to make my self more conscious of the processes that determine my behavior, then I will be more flexible and tolerant, and have available to me a more robust repertoire of behaviors and be able to generate better decisions and more creative solutions to the problems I encounter in my daily life. This is perhaps the truest measure of our emotional intelligence.

EMOTIONAL POWER

So as you begin the adventure of exploring new ways to develop your own emotional competence, as well as that of your clients, through the "workouts" in this book, we urge you to learn the distinctions and relationships among the fifteen skills defined in the Bar-On EQi®. They combine to provide a tremendously powerful lens through which human behavior and motivation can be seen and understood as never before. Significant examples of this can be found in the work of Geetu Orme (2001) where she exposes some of the popular myths about emotional intelligence and then develops the three strategic components that are critical for building quality in our relationships: tuning in, understanding, and taking action.

It is because our culture has conditioned us to perceive the world and measure the quality of life in terms of objective acquisition that we misunderstand our interpersonal relationships and fail to value them appropriately. Consequently, we need all the help we can get in learning how to develop, enhance, and care for our connectedness in ways that counteract this fragmentation. Fortunately, the methods for developing emotional intelligence have arrived on the scene in the nick of time and begun to re-weave the fraying strands of postmodern civilization. Whether we avail ourselves of such healing or not, the world will continue to grow more and more complex, and the quality of our lives will be impacted more deeply on a daily basis by the feelings and decisions of people we have never met or even seen before.

In a way, we each live at our own center of the World Wide Web, and in order to make all the connections in our network as secure and beneficial as possible, we have to be very skillful in the way we generate and broadcast our emotional power—too much and people avoid us or set up defenses that block communication; too little and they take advantage of us or we never break through the barriers to intimacy or develop enough energy to achieve the very dreams that give our lives their meaning.

CHAPTER 2

How Everyone Can Use the Workouts

Cross-Reference Matrix

Emotional intelligence is well established as a critical aspect of successful leadership. The greater the leadership responsibility, the more important our emotional intelligence competencies. Of the many emotional intelligence models and assessment instruments, four have risen to prominence because of their validity, reliability, and market acceptance—each uses a different approach, but all seek to foster skill development along the lines addressed by the workouts in this book. The four are

- Bar-On's EQ-i® and EQ-360™
- Goleman and Boyatzis' ECI 360
- Mayer, Salovey, and Caruso's MSCEIT™
- Orioli and Cooper's EQ Map®

In this chapter we discuss each model's unique approach to emotional intelligence and present a matrix that cross-references the workouts to all four models. The matrix enables you to quickly identify workouts relevant to the model you are using. It helps increase your awareness of the emotional intelligence field by providing a perspective on the interrelationship of the different models. The bottom-line positive intention of the authors for each of the four models was to create a useful instrument for facilitating greater awareness, thus leading to positive change. The workouts in this book were developed to provide specific learning experiences for each of the basic emotional skills and can be used to support whichever instruments you are using to assist your clients in developing their emotional intelligence. It can also be very helpful even if no assessments are given.

The following discussions are brief overviews of the models. We strongly encourage you to gain even more information about any specific model you are using by reviewing the materials distributed by the publisher of the model and its authors.

BAR-ON EMOTIONAL QUOTIENT INVENTORY® (EQ-i AND EQ-360)

The Bar-On EQ-i® is a thoroughly researched self-report measure of social and emotional intelligence capabilities developed over the course of nearly twenty years by Dr. Reuven Bar-On. The EQ-360™ is a multi-rater format. The EQ-i and EQ-360™ utilize a 1 -5 -15 method of scoring in which there is a single overall emotional intelligence score called the "Total EQ." This is broken down into the five composite scales: Intrapersonal, Interpersonal, Stress Management, Adaptability, and General Mood. These five scales are each made up of two to five specific factors, for a total of fifteen competencies. It is these fifteen factors that give the user the real "meat." Following are the five scales and fifteen factors (these are also referred to as components or competencies):

Intrapersonal EQ
- Self-Regard
- Emotional Self-Awareness
- Assertiveness
- Independence
- Self-Actualization

Interpersonal EQ
- Empathy
- Social Responsibility
- Interpersonal Relationships

Stress Management EQ
- Stress Tolerance
- Impulse Control

Adaptability EQ
- Reality Testing
- Flexibility
- Problem Solving

General Mood EQ
- Optimism
- Happiness

Each individual who completes the measure receives a report, approximately ten pages long, showing how strong his or her scores are in each of the areas and usually receives a thirty- to sixty-minute debriefing with someone who is certified to administer the measure. A skilled interpreter of the EQ-i® and EQ-360™ helps the client understand the relative meaning of each score, as well as providing insight into the relationships between the scores. For instance, it might turn out that a person with a very high score in reality testing and a significantly low score in optimism might want to explore how his or her perspective on life might change if he or she did not automatically devote so much attention to making critical evaluations. Might the person feel more optimistic? Similarly, can you imagine what might happen if someone is high in assertiveness and low in impulse control?

The composite Intrapersonal scale includes the following subscales: Self-Regard, Emotional Self-Awareness, Assertiveness, Independence, and Self-Actualization. These are the capabilities that are necessary to develop, maintain, and assert one's self effectively within a social context.

The Interpersonal scale looks at how effectively we interface and engage those five competencies within the social milieu. It is composed of Empathy, Social Responsibility, and Interpersonal Relationships.

The Stress Management scale measures how well we feel we do at coping with the tension, disappointment, and pain that come from living in a less-than-perfect world. It is that discrepancy between what we desire and what we are able to obtain that constitutes the essence of stress. Stress Management is composed of two factors: Stress Tolerance, which looks at how well we protect ourselves from the injurious effects of stress, and Impulse Control, which looks at how likely we are to project it as anger toward others or attempt to self-medicate with tobacco, food, alcohol, and other drugs, or to distract ourselves with sex, shopping, television, and so on.

The Adaptability scale is composed of three factors that explore our relationships with reality and change. The Reality Testing subscale tells us how well we are in touch with objective consensus reality. Flexibility tells us how resiliently we adapt when that reality changes—especially when it does so unexpectedly. Problem Solving evaluates how effective we are at causing that reality to change when we want something new or different.

The final composite scale, General Mood, includes the factors of Optimism and Happiness. Optimism shows us how hopeful we are about the quality of the future we expect, and Happiness shows how satisfied we feel in the present moment.

Our descriptions of these factors are merely summaries; we suggest you refer to the *Technical Manual* (Bar-On, 2002, pp. 112–117)* and similar data, especially articles by the author, for more detailed information. The elegance of the EQ-i and EQ-360™ is that its simple, straightforward presentation belies the rigor of its design. The scores can be normed for age, gender, and numerous populations. It has been published in many different languages and is in use worldwide. Developmental strategies for improving the three lowest scores are included in the individual report. After six months, the test can be retaken to assess progress in specific areas and the overall development of emotional intelligence.

EMOTIONAL COMPETENCE INVENTORY— ECI 360 (GOLEMAN & BOYATZIS)

Richard Boyatzis and Daniel Goleman developed the ECI 360. Boyatzis is professor and chair of the Department of Organizational Behavior at Case Western Reserve University, and co-author of *Primal Leadership* (Goleman, Boyatzis, & McKee, 2002). Goleman is co-director of the Consortium for Research on Emotional Intelligence in Organizations (www.eiconsortium.org) at Rutgers University and author or

---

*EQ-i: Copyright ©1997, 2002 Multi-Health Systems Inc. All rights reserved. 3770 Victoria Park Ave., Toronto, ON M2H 3M6., Reproduced with permission.

co-author of books such as *Primal Leadership* (2002), *Working with Emotional Intelligence* (1998), and *Emotional Intelligence* (1995).

The ECI 360 is a seventy-two-question multi-rater assessment that includes input from self, manager, direct reports, peers, customers/clients, and others. Its purpose is to measure the key competencies that contribute to outstanding performance in the workplace. It is based on Goleman's Emotional Competence Framework. An accredited ECI 360 practitioner provides access to the assessment and provides a report feedback to the subject.

The assessment measures personal competence (how people manage themselves) and social competence (how people manage relationships). It is composed of four domains, each of which has associated competencies. The ECI 360 was originally composed of five domains and twenty-five competencies. It was later streamlined to include four domains and eighteen competencies (Goleman, Boyatzis, & McKee, 2002, p. 39):

Personal Competence
- A. Self-Awareness
  - Emotional self-awareness
  - Accurate self-assessment
  - Self-confidence
- B. Self-Management
  - Emotional self-control
  - Transparency
  - Adaptability
  - Achievement
  - Initiative
  - Optimism

Social Competence
- C. Social Awareness
  - Empathy
  - Organizational awareness
  - Service
- D. Relationship Management
  - Inspirational leadership
  - Influence

- Developing others
- Change catalyst
- Conflict management
- Teamwork and collaboration

THE MSCEIT™ (MAYER, SALOVEY, & CARUSO)

The Mayer-Salovey-Caruso Emotional Intelligence Test, known as the MSCEIT (mes-keet), is unique in that it undertakes to measure actual intelligence rather than the behavioral competencies and social skills that are associated with individual workplace success. The authors define emotional intelligence as the "ability to perceive emotions, to access and generate emotions so as to assist thought, to understand emotions and emotional knowledge, and to regulate emotions so as to promote emotional and intellectual growth (Mayer, Salovey, & Caruso, 2002, p. 17). Their test is designed as an ability measure with objective "right and wrong" answers in contrast with the more subjective competency measures that rely on self-report.

Some examples of the abilities that the MSCEIT undertakes to measure include the ability to label emotions and understand the relationships between words and feelings, the ability to distinguish between authentic emotional expressions and those that are inauthentic or feigned, and the ability to manage emotions by strengthening positive ones and reducing negative ones. Although not all the abilities they seek to measure correspond with specific emotional skills, one can easily see that those listed above have significant correlations with such competencies as emotional self-awareness, empathy, optimism, and impulse control.

As shown in Figure 1.2.1, the authors group these abilities in a $1 - 2 - 4 - 8$ hierarchy so the individual taking the test receives fifteen different scores in the report. The first score is a total emotional intelligence score and is composed of two area scores for Experiential and Strategic emotional intelligence. Experiential refers to the basic human ability to respond emotionally—feeling, processing, recognizing, and classifying emotions. Strategic refers to the higher-level, more conscious processing of emotions, reasoning about them, understanding how they originate and develop over time, and how human beings can manage them to enhance social relationships.

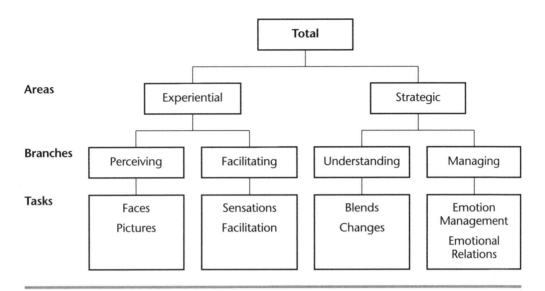

Figure 1.2.1. Abilities Hierarchy*

Each of the area scores is composed of two branch scores. Experiential includes the scores of Perceiving Emotion and Facilitating Thought. Perceiving Emotion measures the ability to recognize what you and others are feeling. This entails accurately detecting, decoding, and responding to the emotional signals of our own internal states, as well as our nonverbal communication, most of which is unconscious. Facilitating Thought is the ability to engage the feeling content of our experience on behalf of improved reasoning, decision making, and problem solving. This is the ability to emotionally activate cognitive processes and creatively utilize the variety of viewpoints that we experience as our moods change.

The Strategic score is also composed of two branch scores, Understanding Emotion and Managing Emotions. Understanding Emotion measures the ability to label emotions appropriately and reason with them in an understandable and effective manner. This includes our ability to recognize how our emotions combine and change over time and how well we are able to symbolically represent this complex process. Managing Emotions is the ability to remain open to emotional information when it will enhance our experience and the ability to limit and control that information when it might cause us to react impulsively. Managing emotions is the ability to appropriately balance their significance in our intellectual outlook and behavior, our general ability to cope with life in an emotionally effective manner.

Each of these four branch scores is composed of two task scores that measure eight specific emotional intelligence abilities, such as reading emotion accurately in faces and pictures, understanding how basic emotions combine to produce more complex feelings, and understanding the sequence that emotions go through as they change from one to another. These scores are to be used more hypothetically than predicatively (that is, for developmental suggestions), inasmuch as the reliability for some of the eight task scores is lower than that of the composite scores to which they give rise (Mayer, Salovey, & Caruso, 2002).

THE EQ MAP® (ORIOLI & COOPER)

Developed jointly by Esther Orioli, president and CEO of Q-Metrics and Essi Systems, and Robert Cooper, consultant and author of books such as *The Other 90 Percent* (2001), the EQ Map® is designed for individuals. It is normed on the North American workforce and is a self-report, self-score measure. People compile their own results on an interpretation sheet. It is designed strictly for developmental purposes and not for hiring or selection.

Each person who takes the measure will score his or her results and then turn to the Interpretation Guide for understanding. EQ is defined in the guide as: "The ability to sense, understand, and effectively apply the power and acumen of emotions as a source of human energy, information, trust, creativity, and influence" (Cooper & Q-Metrics, 1996, p. 1).

The Interpretation Guide describes the EQ Map as a "multidimensional guide, [which] helps you discover the many facets that make up your personal emotional intelligence and its relationship to your performance, creativity, and success. This landscape is about you and your life experiences, plotting the various twists and turns that symbolize your life events, unique strengths, work passions, pressures, and challenges" (Cooper & Q-Metrics, 1996, p. 1).

In comparing it with other EI assessments, Marilyn Gowing (2001, p. 118) wrote that, "Unlike [other] measures of emotional intelligence, the EQ Map attempts to capture information on the current environment of the respondent, in terms of Life Pressures and Life Satisfaction, as well as the effects of the EQ profile on a variety of outcomes, including General Health, Quality of Life, Relationship Quotient, and Optimal Performance."

The EQ Map is composed of two Current Environmental Scales, fourteen EQ Dimensions, and four Outcomes. The specific scales as further described in Cooper and Q-Metrics (1996) are

Part 1: Current Environment
- Scale 1: Life Pressures
- Scale 2: Life Satisfactions

Part 2: Emotional Awareness
- Scale 3: Emotional Self-Awareness
- Scale 4: Emotional Expression
- Scale 5: Emotional Awareness of Others

Part 3: EQ Competencies
- Scale 6: Intentionality
- Scale 7: Creativity
- Scale 8: Resilience
- Scale 9: Interpersonal Connections
- Scale 10: Constructive Discontent

Part 4: EQ Values and Attitudes
- Scale 11: Outlook
- Scale 12: Compassion
- Scale 13: Intuition
- Scale 14: Trust Radius
- Scale 15: Personal Power
- Scale 16: Integrated Self

Part 5. Outcomes
- Scale 17: General Health
- Scale 18: Quality of Life
- Scale 19: Relationship Quotient
- Scale 20: Optimal Performance

Additionally, there are three context factors, known as the Q-Metrics Approach™, which pull these twenty scales together for another perspective. The three areas are increasing effectiveness under pressure, building trusting relationships, and creating the future.

CROSS-REFERENCE MATRIX

The following matrix has been designed for easily cross-referencing the forty-six learning activities we call "workouts" to the relevant content areas for each of the four instruments. For instance, if you were using the EQi® and wanted to help your client develop assertiveness, you can see that Workout 3.3 would be a good choice. It would also be a good choice for helping a client using the EQ-Map® to improve his or her skills in emotional expression. If you had chosen to use the MSCEIT™, this same workout would be useful for developing skills in the Managing Emotions branch. Similarly, if the ECI 360 has been chosen, Workout 3.3 could be used to expand skills in the competency area of teamwork and collaboration.

Table 1.2.1. Cross-Reference Matrix

Workout	Page	EQ-i (Bar-On)		ECI 360 (Goleman, Boyatzis)		MSCEIT (Mayer, Salovey, Caruso)	EQ Map (Orioli, Cooper)	
		Composite	Factor	Domain	Competency	Branches	Scale	Dimension
1.1	119	Intrapersonal	Self-Regard	Self-Awareness	Self-Confidence	Understanding Emotions	Awareness	Emotional Self-Awareness
				Self-Awareness	Accurate Self-Assessment			
1.2	123	Intrapersonal	Self-Regard	Self-Awareness	Self-Confidence	Managing Emotions		
				Self-Awareness	Accurate Self-Assessment			
1.3	129	Intrapersonal	Self-Regard	Self-Awareness	Self-Confidence	Managing Emotions	Awareness	Emotional Self-Awareness
				Self-Awareness	Accurate Self-Assessment			
2.1	133	Intrapersonal	Emotional Self-Awareness	Self-Awareness	Emotional Self-Awareness	Perceiving Emotions	Awareness	Emotional Self-Awareness
						Managing Emotions		
2.2	139	Intrapersonal	Emotional Self-Awareness	Self-Awareness	Emotional Self-Awareness	Perceiving Emotions	Awareness	Emotional Self-Awareness
						Understanding Emotions		
2.3	145	Intrapersonal	Emotional Self-Awareness	Self-Awareness	Emotional Self-Awareness	Perceiving Emotions	Awareness	Emotional Self-Awareness
						Understanding Emotions		
2.4	153	Intrapersonal	Emotional Self-Awareness				Awareness	Emotional Expression

Workout	Page	EQ-i (Bar-On)		ECI 360 (Goleman, Boyatzis)		MSCEIT (Mayer, Salovey, Caruso)	EQ Map (Orioli, Cooper)	
		Composite	Factor	Domain	Competency	Branches	Scale	Dimension
3.1	157	Intrapersonal	Assertiveness	Relationship Management	Influence	Facilitating Thought	Awareness	Emotional Expression
				Self-Management	Initiative	Managing Emotions		
3.2	163	Intrapersonal	Assertiveness	Self-Management	Emotional Self-Awareness	Managing Emotions	Awareness	Emotional Expression
				Relationship Management	Influence			
				Relationship Management	Conflict Management			
3.3	167	Intrapersonal	Assertiveness	Relationship Management	Teamwork and Collaboration	Facilitating Thought	Awareness	Emotional Expression
				Relationship Management	Conflict Management	Understanding Emotions	Competencies	Constructive Discontent
				Relationship Management	Influence			
4.1	171	Intrapersonal	Independence	Self-Management	Initiative	Facilitating Thought		
				Relationship Management	Change Catalyst	Managing Emotions		
				Self-Management	Transparency			
4.2	175	Intrapersonal	Independence	Self-Awareness	Accurate Self-Assessment	Facilitating Thought	Values & Attitudes	Personal Power
				Self-Awareness	Self-Confidence	Managing Emotions		

| Workout | Page | EQ-i (Bar-On) | | ECI 360 (Goleman, Boyatzis) | | MSCEIT (Mayer, Salovey, Caruso) | EQ Map (Orioli, Cooper) | |
		Composite	Factor	Domain	Competency	Branches	Scale	Dimension
4.3	179	Intrapersonal	Independence	Relationship Management	Teamwork and Collaboration	Facilitating Thought	Competencies	Constructive Discontent
				Relationship Management	Inspirational Leadership	Understanding Emotions		
				Social Awareness	Organizational Awareness			
				Social Awareness	Service			
5.1	183	Intrapersonal	Self-Actualization	Relationship Management	Teamwork and Collaboration	Facilitating Thought	Values and Attitudes	Personal Power
			Self-Actualization	Self-Management	Achievement		Values and Attitudes	Integrated Self
5.2	193	Intrapersonal	Self-Actualization	Self-Management	Achievement	Understanding Emotions	Outcomes	Optimal Performance
				Self-Management	Transparency		Outcomes	Quality of Life
5.3	201	Intrapersonal	Self-Actualization	Relationship Management	Inspirational Leadership	Perceiving Emotions	Outcomes	Quality of Life
						Managing Emotions		
				Self-Management	Achievement	Understanding Emotions		
6.1	207	Interpersonal	Empathy	Social Awareness	Empathy	Facilitating Thought	Awareness	Emotional Awareness of Others
				Social Awareness	Service	Understanding Emotions	Values and Attitudes	Compassion

Workout	Page	EQ-i (Bar-On)		ECI 360 (Goleman, Boyatzis)		MSCEIT (Mayer, Salovey, Caruso)	EQ Map (Orioli, Cooper)	
		Composite	Factor	Domain	Competency	Branches	Scale	Dimension
6.2	211	Interpersonal	Empathy	Social Awareness	Empathy	Facilitating Thought	Awareness	Emotional Awareness of Others
						Perceiving Emotions		
						Understanding Emotions	Values and Attitudes	Compassion
6.3	219	Interpersonal	Empathy	Social Awareness	Empathy	Perceiving Emotions	Awareness	Emotional Awareness of Others
				Relationship Management	Teamwork and Collaboration	Understanding Emotions	Values and Attitudes	Compassion
				Relationship Management	Developing Others	Managing Emotions		
7.1	223	Interpersonal	Social Responsibility	Self-Management	Optimism	Facilitating Thought		
				Social Awareness	Organizational Awareness	Understanding Emotions		
				Social Awareness	Service	Managing Emotions		
7.2	229	Interpersonal	Social Responsibility	Self-Awareness	Emotional Self-Awareness	Facilitating Thought		
				Relationship Management	Developing Others	Understanding Emotions		
7.3	235	Interpersonal	Social Responsibility	Social Awareness	Service	Facilitating Thought		
						Understanding Emotions		
						Perceiving Emotions		
						Managing Emotions		

Workout	Page	EQ-i (Bar-On)		ECI 360 (Goleman, Boyatzis)		MSCEIT (Mayer, Salovey, Caruso)	EQ Map (Orioli, Cooper)	
		Composite	Factor	Domain	Competency	Branches	Scale	Dimension
8.1	239	Interpersonal	Interpersonal Relationships	Relationship Management	Developing Others	Facilitating Thought	Compentencies	Interpersonal Connections
				Relationship Management	Teamwork and Collaboration	Perceiving Emotions	Outcomes	Relationship Quotient
8.2	245	Interpersonal	Interpersonal Relationships	Relationship Management	Inspirational Leadership	Managing Emotions	Compentencies	Interpersonal Connections
						Perceiving Emotions	Awareness	Emotional Awareness of Others
							Values and Attitudes	Trust Radius
							Outcomes	Relationship Quotient
8.3	251	Interpersonal	Interpersonal Relationships	Relationship Management	Conflict Management	Facilitating Thought	Compentencies	Interpersonal Connections
				Relationship Management	Teamwork and Collaboration	Understanding Emotions	Awareness	Emotional Awareness of Others
				Relationship Management	Influence		Values and Attitudes	Trust Radius
							Outcomes	Relationship Quotient
9.1	255	Stress Management	Stress Tolerance	Self-Management	Emotional Self-Control	Perceiving Emotions	Current Environment	Life Pressures
				Self-Management	Initiative	Managing Emotions		

Workout	Page	EQ-i (Bar-On)		ECI 360 (Goleman, Boyatzis)		MSCEIT (Mayer, Salovey, Caruso)	EQ Map (Orioli, Cooper)	
		Composite	Factor	Domain	Competency	Branches	Scale	Dimension
9.2	265	Stress Management	Stress Tolerance	Self-Management	Adaptability	Perceiving Emotions	Current Environment	Life Pressures
						Managing Emotions		
9.3	269	Stress Management	Stress Tolerance	Self-Awareness	Emotional Self-Awareness	Perceiving Emotions	Current Environment	Life Pressures
				Self-Management	Emotional Self-Control	Managing Emotions		
10.1	275	Stress Management	Impulse Control	Self-Management	Emotional Self-Control	Facilitating Thought	Competencies	Intentionality
						Understanding Emotions	Competencies	Constructive Discontent
10.2	287	Stress Management	Impulse Control	Self-Awareness	Emotional Self-Awareness	Perceiving Emotions	Competencies	Intentionality
				Self-Management	Emotional Self-Control	Managing Emotions	Competencies	Constructive Discontent
				Self-Awareness	Accurate Self-Assessment	Understanding Emotions		
10.3	293	Stress Management	Impulse Control	Self-Awareness	Emotional Self-Awareness	Managing Emotions	Competencies	Intentionality
				Self-Management	Emotional Self-Control	Perceiving Emotions	Competencies	Constructive Discontent
11.1	297	Adaptability	Reality Testing	Relationship Management	Teamwork and Collaboration	Facilitating Thought		
				Relationship Management	Conflict Management	Perceiving Emotions		
				Relationship Management	Developing Others			

Workout	Page	EQ-i (Bar-On)		ECI 360 (Goleman, Boyatzis)		MSCEIT (Mayer, Salovey, Caruso)	EQ Map (Orioli, Cooper)	
		Composite	Factor	Domain	Competency	Branches	Scale	Dimension
11.2	301	Adaptability	Reality Testing	Relationship Management	Conflict Management	Understanding Emotions		
				Relationship Management	Teamwork and Collaboration			
				Relationship Management	Developing Others			
11.3	305	Adaptability	Reality Testing	Self-Awareness	Emotional Self-Awareness	Facilitating Thought	EQ Values and Attitudes	Intuition
				Self-Management	Transparency	Perceiving Emotions		
12.1	311	Adaptability	Flexibility	Self-Management	Adaptability	Facilitating Thought	Competencies	Resilience
				Self-Management	Optimism	Managing Emotions		
				Social Awareness	Service			
12.2	317	Adaptability	Flexibility	Self-Management	Adaptability	Facilitating Thought	Competencies	Resilience
				Social Awareness	Empathy	Managing Emotions		
						Understanding Emotions		
12.3	321	Adaptability	Flexibility	Self-Management	Adaptability	Managing Emotions	Competencies	Resilience
				Self-Management	Emotional Self-Control	Understanding Emotions		

		EQ-i (Bar-On)		ECI 360 (Goleman, Boyatzis)		MSCEIT (Mayer, Salovey, Caruso)	EQ Map (Orioli, Cooper)	
Workout	Page	Composite	Factor	Domain	Competency	Branches	Scale	Dimension
13.1	325	Adaptability	Problem Solving	Self-Management	Adaptability	Facilitating Thought	Competencies	Constructive Discontent
				Self-Management	Achievement	Managing Emotions		
				Relationship Management	Inspirational Leadership			
				Relationship Management	Change Catalyst			
13.2	333	Adaptability	Problem Solving	Relationship Management	Conflict Management	Understanding Emotions	Competencies	Constructive Discontent
				Relationship Management	Influence	Managing Emotions		
13.3	337	Adaptability	Problem Solving	Self-Management	Adaptability	Managing Emotions	Competencies	Constructive Discontent
				Self-Management	Achievement	Facilitating Thought		
				Relationship Management	Change Catalyst			
14.1	343	General Mood	Optimism	Self-Management	Optimism	Facilitating Thought	Competencies	Resilience
				Relationship Management	Conflict Management	Understanding Emotions	Competencies	Constructive Discontent
							Values and Attitudes	Outlook
14.2	347	General Mood	Optimism	Self-Management	Optimism	Facilitating Thought	Competencies	Resilience
						Managing Emotions	Values and Attitudes	Outlook

Workout	Page	EQ-i (Bar-On)		ECI 360 (Goleman, Boyatzis)		MSCEIT (Mayer, Salovey, Caruso)	EQ Map (Orioli, Cooper)	
		Composite	Factor	Domain	Competency	Branches	Scale	Dimension
14.3	351	General Mood	Optimism	Self-Management	Optimism	Facilitating Thought	Competencies	Resilience
				Self-Management	Achievement	Understanding Emotions	Values and Attitudes	Outlook
15.1	359	General Mood	Happiness	Self-Management	Optimism	Perceiving Emotions	Outcomes	Quality of Life
				Self-Management	Emotional Self-Control	Managing Emotions	Outcomes	Optimal Performance
15.2	363	General Mood	Happiness	Relationship Management	Teamwork and Collaboration	Facilitating Thought	Outcomes	Quality of Life
				Self-Management	Optimism	Understanding Emotions	Outcomes	Optimal Performance
15.3	367	General Mood	Happiness	Relationship Management	Inspirational Leadership	Facilitating Thought	Outcomes	Quality of Life
				Self-Management	Optimism	Understanding Emotions	Outcomes	Optimal Performance
				Social Awareness	Organizational Awareness			

Exploring Fifteen Competencies of Emotional Intelligence

Part Two provides a description of each of the fifteen emotional competencies that combine to make up social and emotional intelligence according to the Bar-On model (the other models are similar, and their list of competencies can be found in the Cross-Reference Matrix in Chapter 2). We provide an overview of each of the fifteen below.

The descriptions of each competency begin with a section entitled What Is It?, in which we define the competency. Following that is a section called Why Should We Care About It? Here we point out both the advantages that strength in this competency gives and the disadvantages we may experience if it is a weaker area. Next we provide a section called How Can We Build It? This starts with a tip to help develop the competency or appreciate what makes it valuable and provides the specific instruction necessary for increasing skillfulness in this area. In the section called Transformational Benefits, we discuss how building this particular competency into a strength can transform one's experience of life, increasing the level of satisfaction and effectiveness.

A BRIEF OVERVIEW OF THE FIFTEEN COMPETENCIES

Self-Regard is the skill of liking ourselves just the way we are. It includes the strength of our self-confidence and self-respect and is directly related to other competencies such as self-actualization, optimism, and happiness.

Emotional Self-Awareness comes from how familiar we are with our emotional response patterns. Do we know what we're feeling and why? Can we accurately assess how strong a particular feeling is? Did we notice when it first started, or did it sneak up on us? The stronger this skill is for you, the more accurately you can fill in the blanks for the following statement: "I feel _____ because _____."

Assertiveness is the emotional strength that allows us to confidently tell others what we like and want more of, what we dislike and will not accept, and what we stand for.

Independence shows up in the ability to make decisions based on your own best-informed assessment and understanding of a situation without having to satisfy the perceived emotional needs of everyone who has an opinion about the matter.

Self-Actualization is the competency of being able to set goals for oneself and then meet those goals. It is our own measure of how successful we feel, thus its close relationship to self-regard.

Empathy is the ability to listen and pay attention so we understand how other people are feeling and why, and even how their feelings might be likely to change. The stronger this skill is for us, the more accurately we can fill in the blanks for the following statement: "You feel _____ because _____."

Social Responsibility is the competency of being able to care and discipline our work efforts to serve the interests of individuals and groups that lie outside the field of our personal needs, goals, and concerns.

Interpersonal Relationships is the competency we demonstrate in being able to initiate and sustain lasting friendships.

Stress Tolerance is the coping skill we use to keep the unavoidable pains, threats, and intrusions of life from weakening our physical and emotional health.

Impulse Control is the ability to regulate the buildup of nervous energy that accompanies stress without projecting it as anger, anesthetizing it through self-medication, or distracting ourselves from it with TV, shopping, and so forth.

Reality Testing is the competency that enables us to correctly evaluate the nature of our current situation (or pending situations) according to objective criteria. If this is difficult to do, we may be in denial, "checked-out," or fooling ourselves.

Flexibility is the skill that allows us to change direction rapidly without resistance and protest, and needing to be convinced when our reality changes.

Problem Solving is the process through which we solve problems in the world and thus are able to change it to better correspond with our needs and desires.

Optimism is the skill of positive expectancy that faithfully holds the vision for potential improvement in the future.

Happiness is the emotional skill of being more or less consistently content and satisfied in the present moment.

STARS AND MOVIES

To illustrate how powerfully these competencies can influence success in life and our relationships, we include an example of an historical figure who demonstrates the transformational benefits of the skill as well as a character from a movie example.

Table 2.1 is the complete list of the star performers and reel performers (movie examples) we use to illustrate emotionally intelligent behaviors.

Table 2.1. Examples of Emotionally Intelligent Behaviors

Emotional Intelligence Skill	Star Performer	Movie Example
Self-Regard	Dalai Lama	*The Good Girl*
Emotional Self-Awareness	Oprah Winfrey	*The Manchurian Candidate*
Assertiveness	Dr. Martin Luther King, Jr.	*Erin Brockovich*
Independence	Mahatma Gandhi	*The Matrix* *Norma Rae*
Self-Actualization	Viktor Frankl	*Whale Rider*
Empathy	Sherrol Horner Lawrence "Chick" Patterson	*Terms of Endearment*
Social Responsibility	George Washington Carver	*Remember the Titans*
Interpersonal Relationship	Jan Eller Phoebe from "Friends"	*Something's Got to Give*
Stress Tolerance	Rudolph Giuliani	*The Negotiator*
Impulse Control	Anita Hill	*To Kill a Mockingbird*
Reality Testing	Hans Blix	*Matchstick Men*
Flexibility	Thomas P. "Tip" O'Neill, Jr.	*Lilies of the Field*
Problem Solving	William Ury	*GI Jane*
Optimism	Nelson Mandela	*Wizard of Oz*
Happiness	Jimmy Carter	*Love, Actually*

Self-Regard

WHAT IS IT?

Simply defined, self-regard indicates how good we feel about ourselves. It also reflects our ability to accept ourselves warts and all. Webster's (1993) dictionary defines self-regard as "consideration of oneself or one's own interests." In contrast, it defines self-esteem as "a confidence and satisfaction in one's self: self-respect."

All of these definitional considerations figure in the meaning of self-regard according to the *Bar-On Emotional Quotient Inventory® Technical Manual* (2002, p. 15), where self-regard is defined as, *"the ability to respect and accept oneself as basically good* . . . essentially liking the way one is . . . . Feeling sure of oneself is dependent on self-respect and self-esteem, which are based on a fairly well developed sense of identity. A person with good self-regard feels fulfilled and satisfied with himself/herself. At the opposite end of the continuum are feelings of personal inadequacy and inferiority."

WHY SHOULD WE CARE ABOUT SELF-REGARD?

This is obviously a bit like asking, "Why should I care about myself?" Self-regard is a critical competency because, without a well-integrated identity that allows you to know and respect yourself, there is no way you can ever participate authentically in life, be truly reliable in work or love, or fully express all the gifts you have to give. A lack of self-regard often indicates feelings of uncertainty and insecurity, an unwillingness to venture out into one's own world and explore it with appropriate reality testing.

In his research, Bar-On (2000, p. 374) found that self-regard emerged "as one of the most powerful predictors of competent behavior."

HOW CAN WE BUILD SELF-REGARD?

Stand in front of the mirror. Look deep in your eyes. Call your name out loud with authority three times, then be silent and feel yourself show up! Now clap wildly and bow.

How worthy or unworthy you feel about receiving good in your life results from a blend of ingredients that includes your experiences, values, attitudes, behaviors, and expectations. You will perceive these conditions more or less accurately, depending on how honest and self-aware you are.

Where emotional self-awareness reflects how well you know your feelings, think of self-regard as how well you know, and like, the whole constellation of features that combine to make up who you are. This is determined to a large degree by how congruently you express your values and desires through your external behavior. Because much of your motivation to move toward some things and away from others is unconscious, building healthy self-regard must include a process of ongoing self-exploration so that you can continue to discover more of your full self and give more complete expression to the whole you.

The overlap with emotional self-awareness demonstrates the deep integration of all fifteen factors of the EQi®. Other examples that illustrate this deep interconnectedness between factors include the way in which self-regard relates to problem solving and assertiveness. It is not possible to hold oneself in the highest regard if one is unsuccessful in solving problems in one's life or unable to assert one's desires with sufficient strength to satisfy them. Reciprocally, as one strengthens his or her self-regard, his or her problem-solving and assertiveness skills may also strengthen.

TRANSFORMATIONAL BENEFITS

As self-regard is one of the most powerful predictors of competent behavior, then the benefits of its development will include an expanding knowledge of identity that is richer, more flexible, more confident, and more secure. As we continue to build increasingly positive self-regard, we expand our capacity to enjoy our lives and be of service to others.

 ## STAR PERFORMER

The Dalai Lama is a Buddhist monk as well as the spiritual and political leader of all Tibetan people. His life's work is to enable his people, a large number of whom are living in exile, to maintain the high spiritual, ethical, and artistic values of their ancient culture. He is an excellent model of self-regard because he is able to assert his intelligence and authority effectively in the world without the self-importance that sometimes makes others come off as arrogant and egotistical.

 ## REEL PERFORMER

Jennifer Aniston in *The Good Girl* presents a remarkable example of the development of self-regard. As a young high school graduate, she's married and working in a chain discount store. Her life is predictable and boring. She undertakes self-exploration in part by developing a relationship with a young man who is very "out there" for this conservative small town. Through challenges, including her pregnancy and the young man's suicide, she begins to come into herself, becoming much more alive and whole. She becomes more aware and accepting of herself.

Emotional Self-Awareness

WHAT IS IT?

Emotional self-awareness is a foundational element of emotional intelligence. It is the ability to understand what we are feeling and why, as well as to understand what caused those feelings. It enables us to connect with our underlying beliefs, assumptions, and values and to know what drives us. Emotional self-awareness is key to our ability to communicate our feelings to others. It helps us *keep our eye on the ball* and stay aligned with our true motivations.

Have you ever had a gut feeling, just known when something felt right or wrong, or had a hunch about something? If so, you were experiencing emotional self-awareness. Emotional self-awareness enables us to be more strategic and effective in interacting with our environment. When this skill is well developed, we can easily recognize when something is emotionally draining or energizing, identify the reason why, and make an informed decision about our continued involvement with a person, activity, or organization.

Emotional self-awareness is considered by many to be the centerpiece of emotional intelligence, because it is requisite for the successful development of other areas. Stein and Book describe it as "the foundation on which most of the other elements of emotional intelligence are built" (2000, p. 55). Empathy, "the ability to be aware of, to understand and to appreciate the feelings of others"

(Bar-On, 2002, p. 16), requires that one understand his or her emotions in order to understand those of others. Lane purports, "One's ability to empathize cannot exceed one's ability to monitor one's own emotional states"(2000, p. 173).

Goleman, Boyatzis, and McKee agree that "self-awareness means having a deep understanding of one's emotions, as well as one's strengths and limitations and one's values and motives. . . . Self-aware leaders also understand their values, goals, and dreams" (2002, p. 40).

Webster's defines self-awareness as "an awareness of one's own personality or individuality" (1993, p. 2059).

Bar-On's definition is *the ability to recognize one's feelings . . . to differentiate between them, to know what one is feeling and why, and to know what caused the feelings. Serious deficiencies in this area are found in those with alexithymic [the inability to express feelings verbally] conditions*" (2002, p. 15).

WHY SHOULD WE CARE ABOUT EMOTIONAL SELF-AWARENESS?

Emotional self-awareness is valuable because it is at the very core of being human! The person over whom one has the most influence is oneself. Understanding ourselves is the first step in putting the world in context. Emotional self-awareness allows us to know how we are responding to our environment and what we are feeling. It is important for us to know when we feel happy, sad, loving, angry, ambivalent, apathetic, or impassioned. Emotional self-awareness provides the springboard for the positive development of the other emotional intelligence skills.

HOW CAN WE BUILD EMOTIONAL SELF-AWARENESS?

We can consciously tune in to our emotions and ask ourselves questions about our current emotional state and identify the reasons for our emotions. Did a particular event trigger the feeling? Are our feelings the result of something that has been simmering for a period of time? Consider how long we've been feeling those emotions and when we first began to notice them. This can also help us to begin to gauge the intensity of what we are feeling.

MOOD SHIFTS

- Check to see whether your client's moods shift during the course of a day.
- Every half hour have your client write a sentence or a phrase about how or what he or she is feeling.
- At the end of the day or early the next day have him or her analyze what he or she recorded.
- Ask clients to identify points at which their moods shifted.
- Have them recall what happened to cause the shift and how it impacted their thoughts and behavior.

TRANSFORMATIONAL BENEFITS

Being aware of our emotions is key to successfully interacting with our environment. People typically project onto others what they feel inside. To improve our interactions and relationships, it is necessary to examine what is going on inside ourselves. Once we are in tune with our emotions we can develop strategies to eliminate or mitigate the emotions that are bringing us down. This will enable us to become happier and more expansive and increase our capacity to relate to others.

 STAR PERFORMER

Oprah Winfrey, the supervising producer and host of the award-winning "Oprah Winfrey Show," has overcome adversity and attained dizzying success. One of her strengths is her ability to stay in touch with herself and understand what she is feeling, when she is feeling it, and why she is experiencing a specific emotion. Her emotional self-awareness strengthens the empathetic capabilities for which she is renowned. Oprah's ability to connect with people and make them feel safe, comfortable, and understood is enhanced because she "listens" to her own emotional self.

Emotional self-awareness has fortified her connection to her own underlying beliefs and values of encouraging people to expand their horizons and lead happier lives. This has enabled her to restructure her show away from sensationalism and toward personal enrichment at a time when sensationalism is generating very high ratings.

REEL PERFORMER

In the original version of *The Manchurian Candidate,* Sergeant Raymond Shaw (Laurence Harvey) is a brainwashed Korean War hero who has been programmed to assassinate a presidential candidate. During the war, his troop is captured by the Koreans and brainwashed. They return home from the war with a "planted" memory of the incident that omits the brainwashing aspects. One of the men involved was Captain Bennett Marco, played by Frank Sinatra. Marco begins to have nightmares about the brainwashing experience. Rather than trying to put them out of his mind, he strives to unravel the secret. One aspect of the brainwashing is that every soldier in the troop uses the exact same complimentary phrase to describe Shaw. They say they feel that way now, but the truth is they all hate him because he is a cold and repulsive man. In one pivotal scene when Marco is trying to convince his Army superiors that something is amiss, he repeats the line they all use to describe Shaw and then says that it just doesn't feel right and that somehow he knows it isn't true. Ultimately disaster is averted because Marco heeds his feelings and keeps digging until he uncovers the sinister plan.

Assertiveness

WHAT IS IT?

Assertiveness is the ability to express feelings, beliefs, and thoughts and defend one's rights in a nondestructive manner. Stein and Book (2000, p. 66)* present the following definition:

> "Assertiveness is composed of three basic components: (1) the ability to express feelings (for example, to accept and express anger, warmth, and sexual feelings); (2) the ability to express beliefs and thoughts openly (being able to voice opinions, to disagree, and to take a definite stand, even if it is emotionally difficult to do so and even if you have something to lose by doing so); and (3) the ability to stand up for personal rights (not allowing others to bother you or take advantage of you). Assertive people are not over-controlled or shy—they are able to express their feelings (often directly), without being aggressive or abusive."

Assertiveness, which requires directness, finesse, and consideration of others, is described by Weisinger (1998, p. 122) as

---

"the ability to stand up for your rights, opinions, ideas, beliefs, and needs while at the same time respecting those of others."

The concept of negative space can help us understand the difference between assertiveness and aggressiveness. Artists and designers use the concept of negative space to gain clarity about the shape, contour, and contextual meaning of an object. This is accomplished by looking at the space surrounding the object. For example, if you are drawing a pear, shift your eyes slightly away from the pear to see how it blocks and shadows the space or objects around it. This is a helpful tool to use in examining a concept.

To explore a concept's negative space, pay attention to what it is not. This helps minimize false assumptions and faulty conclusions. Assertiveness is not aggressiveness. Aggressiveness moves beyond assertiveness and into obtrusiveness, combativeness, and militancy. The key difference between the two is that aggressiveness leaves no room for the consideration of others' feelings, viewpoints, or objectives. Aggressiveness is about winning at all costs. The metaphor of steamrolling over someone encapsulates aggressiveness.

Assertiveness is an expressive behavior that respects others' dignity and humanity even when conveying something that might be unwelcome or controversial. Bottom line: Assertiveness is the balanced space between being a pushover and a steamroller.

WHY SHOULD I CARE ABOUT ASSERTIVENESS?

Assertiveness is our backbone, spine, spunk, or chutzpah—our ability to interact with our environment and make our voices heard! Assertiveness empowers us and helps us define ourselves to others. It feeds our sense of self-regard because we are caring for ourselves by announcing our desires, feelings, and thoughts and by clearly setting our boundaries.

While assertiveness starts in the inner realm of dealing with our own feelings and responses, it ultimately manifests in how we communicate and behave. To communicate effectively, we are often required to be assertive and to verbalize risky positions. The authors of *Skilled Interpersonal Communication* describe assertive communication in this way: "Assertive responses involve standing up for oneself, yet taking the other person into consideration. The assertive style involves . . . openly and confidently expressing personal feelings and opinions; valuing oneself equal to others; being prepared to listen to the other's point of view. . ." (Hargie & Dickson, 2004, p. 300).

Differences of opinions and conflicts are ever-present among people. To be effective in our own lives, whether at work or home, we must appropriately surface issues and deal with differences. In *The Power of a Good Fight*, Lynn Eisaguirre asserts, "We need to move toward embracing conflict as a friendly force to be directed and used, not avoided like the enemy. Leadership involves learning to value conflict" (2002, p. 5).

How much happier and more effective would we be if, in risky situations, we were consistently able to state our positions yet maintain, or even deepen, relationships? Assertiveness enables us to be true to ourselves and to respect others.

HOW CAN WE BUILD ASSERTIVENESS?

Building assertiveness usually means:

- Building it up—from reticence
- Dialing it back—from aggressiveness

First, identify where your client is on the continuum (see Figure 2.3.1). When assertiveness is required, does he or she keep silent or go into overdrive? When he or she is not being appropriately assertive does he or she always go to one end of the continuum or bounce back and forth depending on the situation? Stein and Book (2000, pp. 73–75) include a similar concept in their description of assertiveness.

Empathy and courage are requisites of assertiveness. They help us moderate our behavior at both ends of the continuum. Empathy helps us be more sensitive to others' viewpoints and helps mitigate our defensiveness. It makes it easier to treat others with respect and dignity. It will also help us consider how the information we are withholding from them could help them grow.

| Reticence | Assertiveness | Aggressiveness |

Figure 2-3.1 The Assertiveness Continuum

Courage helps us take more risks. It can stoke our spirit when we are feeling meek. It can also help us to open up and leave room for other opinions.

 ## ASSERTIVE NOT PASSIVE

Your client can shift from squirming inside because he or she did not speak up to stating his or her point of view factually and forthrightly and feeling good about it.

ASSERTIVE NOT AGGRESSIVE

Your client should stop trying to overpower or intimidate others into bending to his or her will and move to stating his or her case factually and calmly.

How does it feel to be assertive? Are you more effective?

TRANSFORMATIONAL BENEFITS

Enhanced assertiveness skills can exponentially increase our value, impact, and well-being. When we employ them elegantly, we behave neither as victims nor as instruments of mass destruction. We do not make ourselves sick from harboring ill thoughts toward others and keeping ugly feelings bottled up inside. Nor do we make others sick by exploding all over them in an offensive and caustic way. The elegant application of assertiveness makes us empowered people who face that which needs to be addressed and who can be relied on for clarity and honesty.

Organizations are more productive when managers and employees are appropriately assertive and openly share information and issues.

 # STAR PERFORMER

Dr. Martin Luther King, Jr., was a civil rights activist whose concept of "some-bodiness" symbolized the celebration of human worth and the conquest of subjugation. He gave black and poor people hope and a sense of dignity. His philosophy of nonviolent direct action and his strategies for rational and nondestructive social change galvanized the conscience of this nation and reordered its priorities" (TheKingCenter.com, 2003, p. 1).

REEL PERFORMER

Erin Brockovich is based on the life of the real Erin Brockovich (Julia Roberts plays the part, for which she won an Academy Award) and chronicles the struggles and triumphs of a profoundly tenacious person. Erin is a down-on-her-luck single mother who lands a job with attorney Ed Masry (Albert Finney). She discovers a contaminated-water incident that has caused devastating illness in a local community. Erin convinces the community to fight the company that caused the damage. She stood up for the rights of others and gave them the courage to assert themselves in a court of law. They won $333 million—the largest settlement ever paid in a direct-action lawsuit in U.S. history. The assertiveness of one person made a big difference!

Independence

WHAT IS IT?

Independence is the ability to think for oneself and not be unduly influenced by the thoughts, desires, and emotions of others. It does not mean that one is completely insensitive to the needs of other people or to societal mores. It means a person is able to sift through others' input and expectations, access his or her own beliefs and values, then reach conclusions and take actions that make sense for his or her own life.

The degree of independence considered appropriate and how it gets expressed are influenced by culture. Eastern societies value group process above individual needs, while Western cultures have a higher tendency toward independence. The timeless American icon, the cowboy, is the quintessential figure of independence.

To highlight the desirability of independence, the *Star Trek: Next Generation* television series created an alien society called the Borg. Each seemingly separate being was neurally connected to all of the others, and they operated with one mind. The concept was called the "hive mind." The power of the Borg archetype was that their complete and utter lack of independence was repulsive to the audience's Western way of thinking. Thus, it reaffirmed the Western commitment to independence.

Independence often requires courage, because a person's actions may set him or her apart from the group and raise visibility.

It can be difficult to think and act independently of others. The word "group-think" conveys the concept of conforming to the values and ethics of others. As the polar opposite of independence, groupthink does not allow for individuality.

According to Bar-On, "Independence is *the ability to be self-directed and self-controlled in one's thinking and actions and to be free of emotional dependency*. Independent people are self-reliant in planning and making important decisions. They may, however, seek and consider other people's opinions before making the right decision for themselves . . . independent people avoid clinging to others in order to satisfy their emotional needs" (2002, p. 16). The research on the EQi found a correlation between independence and assertiveness. When working with someone or a group with a strength or challenge in independence, it is important to connect both of these skill areas as well as viewing the relationships with the other fifteen factors.

Webster's defines independent as "(1) not subject to control by others: not subordinate; not affiliated with or integrated into a larger controlling unit" (1993).

WHY SHOULD WE CARE ABOUT INDEPENDENCE?

Independence is the ability to stand on one's own two feet and trust one's own judgment. It reflects self-confidence and the willingness to take risks. Independence is a key leadership trait that can enhance effectiveness whether one is the leader of a global company, supervisor of a small team, a parent, volunteer with a community organization, or the leader of his or her life.

Independence is important in a team environment, as long as it is expressed with sensitivity to the group process and is applied with a collaborative spirit. One is valued as a team member when he or she is able to take initiative to get things done while including others and contributing to the collective efforts of the group.

HOW CAN WE BUILD INDEPENDENCE?

Notice when and where in your life you are reluctant to exercise your independence. Is it in all situations or in certain circumstances with specific people? Explore what it is that makes you uncomfortable asserting your independence. Are you concerned that people will not think you're "nice"? Will others be angry? Will someone challenge your position or conclusion? Ask these same questions of your client(s).

Assess the risk of acting independently. If there is more to be gained (self-respect, confidence, and improved teamwork) by asserting independence, then map out a step-by-step plan to promote its development. If you stick with the plan, you will find that you are facing your fears about being independent and increasing your capabilities. The same can happen for your client(s) as you guide them in this direction.

 THE JOY OF INDEPENDENCE

Remember riding your first two-wheeled bike:

- At first it had training wheels, and then they were removed.
- You were left with just the two wheels and your parent holding the back of your seat while you pedaled.
- Finally, you experienced the freedom of doing it all by yourself. What a rush!!

Share this with your client and ask whether his or her confidence soared after that accomplishment.

TRANSFORMATIONAL BENEFITS

A person who uses independence effectively will have the satisfaction of knowing that he or she acts according to his or her sense of ethics and values and resists the pressure to conform in an unhealthy way. These people are not just puppets on a string. Each time a person stays true to his or her beliefs and intuition, the independence response is fortified. When the tough situations arise, he or she will have the gumption to face the challenges presented.

STAR PERFORMER

Mahatma Gandhi was a British barrister who fought for civil liberties and freedom in South Africa and in his native India. He followed his own sense of ethics and acted independently of societal expectations. His lifelong struggle was against the prejudices of creed, caste, and race. He eschewed violence and rose to prominence in the social arena on a platform of individual resistance and non-cooperation. "Gandhi had a rare combination of readiness to resist wrong and capacity to love his opponents which baffled his enemies and compelled their admiration" (www.MKGandhi.com, 2003). He was the galvanizing force that freed India from British rule.

REEL PERFORMER

In *The Matrix* we see a good example of independence in Neo (Keanu Reeves), a software techie by day and computer hacker by night. Morpheus (Laurence Fishburne) reveals the dark truth about the world—humans are the slaves of the machines they created. The humans live in pods, where their energy is harvested to run the machines. They do not resist because the machines have deluded them into thinking they live in a gleaming metropolis, when in reality they live in a virtual world, the matrix.

Neo rebels against the conventional wisdom of the matrix and fights for freedom and truth. The people in the matrix were ignorantly blissful, while the rebels faced the harsh reality. Opting for independence makes his life enormously harder, but it gives Neo a conscious life with real meaning and consequence in place of his former unconscious dream.

In *Norma Rae,* Sally Field plays a young single mother who works in an Alabama textile mill. Distaste for the deplorable conditions of the work environment and exposure to Reuben (Ron Leibman), a dedicated New York lawyer, fuels her campaign to unionize her company. This is a potentially dangerous course of action for her. The safe route is to maintain the status quo, but her fierce independence drives her to improve conditions for herself and her co-workers, even those who oppose her.

Self-Actualization

WHAT IS IT?

Bar-On presents the following definition: "Self-actualization is the process of striving to actualize one's potential capacity, abilities, and talents. It requires the ability and drive to set and achieve goals. It is characterized by being involved in and feeling committed to various interests and pursuits. Self-actualization is a lifelong effort leading to the enrichment of life" (2001, p. 89).

Psychologist Abraham Maslow was probably the first to identify the factor of self-actualization. Remember his hierarchy of needs? Writing in the middle of the 20th century, Maslow (1970) identified a hierarchy of core needs, each of which must be adequately addressed before the next step can be fully taken. The hierarchy proceeds from physiological (food, shelter, water) to safety (security, order, law) to belongingness and love needs (giving and receiving affection) to esteem needs (self-respect and the esteem of others) and finally to self-actualization.

Maslow emphasized that we must live up to our potential or we will feel dissatisfied. Self-actualization is the process of being true to our own nature and fully committed to developing our capabilities. It includes the concepts of growth, motivation, and meeting our "being" needs. Maslow later redefined self-actualization as a function of peak experiences, and it is from this aspect of the definition that some people associate self-actualization with mystical experiences. While those fortunate ones who do have mystical experiences surely are on the track of self-actualization, there are many other more common expressions of this skill to be found in daily life.

In accord with Maslow, Bar-On (2001) writes that self-actualization "is most likely the next and ultimate step after EI in the complex process of personal development. While emotional intelligence relates to being effective, self-actualization relates to doing the best you can possibly do. Or put another way, when we are self-actualized, we have gone beyond EI to achieve a higher level of human effectiveness" (p. 85).

In this 2001 article, Bar-On reports that "the best predictors of self-actualization are the following eight EI factors, listed in order of importance:

Happiness
Optimism
Self-regard
Independence
Problem solving
Social responsibility
Assertiveness
Emotional self-awareness" (p. 92)

What a profound example of the importance of building all parts of our emotional intelligence!

In this work, we are focusing on the aspects of self-motivation, which when combined with strengths in happiness and optimism, as well as the other six factors, helps us live an energized and fully engaged life. Self-actualization is a journey, not a destination. It is the place where our "doing" and our "being" modes can be joined.

Thus the key questions are

- How am I doing on this journey?
- How am I being on this journey?
- Am I happy about where am I now?
- Am I pacing myself on this journey?
- Am I motivated to be the best I can be?

WHY SHOULD WE CARE
ABOUT SELF-ACTUALIZATION?

We all have a deep inner calling to be all that we can be. For some of us this is a loud and insistent holler, while for others it may be a quiet whisper. Our current state of happiness, optimism, and the other six factors that are the underpinnings of self-actualization will influence our desire to grow this skill and our sense that it is possible. If we are inclined to be pessimistic, we limit our sense of possibility and miss many opportunities. Perhaps even the pessimist can say to him- or herself, "Well, *IF* it were possible, I would like to be. . . ." This is the path to actualizing our dreams—one day at a time.

Self-actualization is critical for today's successful businesses. Millions of dollars are spent annually in working with teams and in developing employees to help grow their motivation to be the best they can be. In this very practical sense, self-actualization is at the heart of organizational success. In fact, when Stein and Book wrote *The EQ Edge*, they conducted research using the EQ-i on nearly five thousand working people in many different occupations. They found that the first of the top five factors of overall success is self-actualization. Thus, it is one of the most important factors for organizations to highlight for employee development.

HOW CAN WE BUILD SELF-ACTUALIZATION?

Remember that self-actualization is an evolutionary journey. Be motivated to be the best you can be today. Don't get depressed that you haven't accomplished everything by today, and watch success unfold!

Pay attention to your longings and the deep messages you give yourself. Are you longing to be an artist, but you're a banker—or vice versa? This EI skill builds on eight other skills, so it's not an area of solo perfection. It's an integrated part of who one is. Use the workouts in Part Three of this book to identify your own or your client's capacities in the eight identified skill areas. It is important to notice which skills support one the most and which can be improved to help increase our self-actualization.

Pace yourself and teach your client(s) to do the same! This isn't a race; it's evolutionary. If you will intentionally move forward on a regular basis, one step at a time, keeping the vision as a possibility, you'll be able to listen to the wisdom within and enjoy much more growth than if you are always feeling bad because you "should do more." After all, the "should's" are out—they went with the last century. This is the time of possibility.

TRANSFORMATIONAL BENEFITS

Are you kidding? This is it, baby! Self-actualization can rocket a person right off the planet! The potential as one grows this skill is unlimited. Welcome the surprises.

Individually, we are much more comfortable, resilient, and fun to be with when we know we are on the right path. For most organizations, motivating employees is a key goal. Developing self-actualization is central to inspiring employees and helps everyone clarify which motivational strategies are most effective for him or her.

STAR PERFORMER

Viktor Frankl, M.D., Ph.D., the author of *Man's Search for Meaning*, was a highly inspirational psychiatrist and a professor of neurology and psychiatry at the University of Vienna Medical School. He was interned for three years at Auschwitz, Dachau, and other concentration camps. During that time he began his study of what guides us as humans. He noticed that the same horrendous conditions affected all the prisoners in the camps, yet a few were able to survive. His answer to why that occurred focused on people's individual attitudes. His teachings that no one else can ever control one's attitude, and that this is a great personal resource, have been recited across the world to inspire people in all walks of life.

REEL PERFORMER

In *Whale Rider*, the retelling of a 1,000-year-old Maori legend, a twelve-year-old girl finds the courage to challenge her traditionalist grandfather. She can't be stopped from becoming the spiritual leader she is intended to be—even though she is a girl. She demonstrates great patience throughout, somehow trusting that her gift will be recognized. Her resolute courage, accompanied by her great love for her village, her grandfather, and the whales, is a fine demonstration of listening to her calling and taking action one day at a time.

Empathy

WHAT IS IT?

Empathy is the ability to "understand, be aware of, be sensitive to, and vicariously experience the feelings, thoughts, and experiences of another," according to Webster's (1993) dictionary. The key to effectively applying this skill lies in learning how to give others accurate feedback on what they are feeling and why.

Empathy is the ability to "read" others by getting into resonance with them. The first step is to respectfully focus your attention on the person, seeking to truly listen and understand his or her actions and emotions. It requires applying the same level of awareness that you developed in building your emotional self-awareness and following with genuine curiosity the same lines of inquiry about others—What are they feeling now? How strongly? Why do they feel that way?

Our empathic capabilities begin to emerge when we first learn to distinguish between ourselves and others. As humans, we can look in the mirror and recognize ourselves. Most other animals do not have that capacity. In order to exercise our empathic skills, we must be aware of the differences between ourselves and other people. Empathy is not the same as sympathy. In sympathy we lose that critical distance and become so identified with someone else that we automatically feel the same way that he or she is feeling. If he or she is upset, we become similarly upset. If he or she is highly motivated and gung ho, so are we, and though we don't necessarily know why, it's literally because the other person is. This can be very good when we need to respond together to a common challenge, because sympathy is a critical component of loyalty and camaraderie. On the other hand, when it lacks independence, sympathy can degrade into co-dependency. We lose our objectivity, and with it goes our helpfulness.

Healthy empathy is vital to the ability to develop and maintain deep and lasting interpersonal relationships. It is also at the heart of a well-functioning workplace, community, and family. When we engage empathically, we are motivated to pay attention to other people. We attend to them by noticing their communications from multiple dimensions—by noticing what they are saying verbally as well as tonally and by noticing their non-verbal communications.

Judith Flury and William Ickes (2001, p. 114) state that the "ability to accurately infer the specific content of other people's thoughts and feelings represents the fullest expression of a perceiver's empathic skills."

WHY SHOULD WE CARE ABOUT EMPATHY?

In today's increasingly fast-paced world, empathy becomes more important every day. Paying sufficient attention to other people may take a bit more time up-front, and it definitely takes more commitment and motivation. However, being empathic pays off because it leads to dramatically more accurate communications. Productivity is enhanced and conflict is reduced. As Stein and Book state, "When you make an empathic statement, even in the midst of an otherwise tense or antagonistic encounter, you shift the balance. A contentious and uneasy interchange becomes a more collaborative alliance" (2000, p. 112).

Collaborative alliances have resiliency that elevate their strength and productivity. The first step in creating a collaborative climate is empathic interaction. Certainly, it is the beginning of building trust. When you are helping others resolve conflict, your empathic comments will open new lines of communication and bring to the discussion the flexibility that is needed to resolve any concerns. Furthermore, demonstrations of empathy are essential skills you model to the others involved in the conflict.

Scientists are exploring the connection between empathy and our evolution as humans. Natalie Angier reports in the *Denver Post* that researchers were watching the expression of empathy in chimpanzees in zoos. She writes that the "emotion most akin to gravity, the sensation that keep the affairs of humanity on track as surely as the Earth wheels around the Sun, is empathy: the power to recognize the plight of another and to take on that burden as though it were built to order" (1995, p. 2A).

In a world filled with negotiation challenges, we need all the help we can get. One powerful strategy is to use empathy in the communication. Certainly advice is more persuasive if delivered with empathy.

Each of the fifteen emotional intelligence factors we focus on in this workbook influences the others, and the extent to which our skills in empathy are developed is intimately connected with competencies such as emotional self-awareness, self-regard, reality testing, and self-actualization. As Lane (2000) states, "The ability to be aware of one's own emotions probably derives from input from others such as caregivers. Over time the representations of the experiences of the self and others become progressively differentiated from one another. With development, the ability to be accurately attuned to the emotional state of others is probably a function of the ability to draw on one's own emotional experience, which itself is a function of how these emotional experiences were represented and communicated to others in the past" (p. 184).

HOW CAN WE BUILD EMPATHY?

Learn to read body language. Attend to a person's facial expressions, breathing, posture, and tonality; then match his or her physical state in your own body and see how it feels to you! This is an easy way of getting into resonance.

A key factor in increasing our empathy includes forming an intention to pay attention to others. This calls for exercising our motivation to really listen and understand what is being expressed by those seeking to communicate with us, rather than projecting our interpretation of reality on them. This and the other strategies listed below are excellent to use with your coaching or team clients.

- Put yourself in the other person's shoes. This can be a quick interaction as a part of a conversation or you can job share, job shadow, or find another way to experience literally what is happening for the other person.
- Seek to understand the duties of others and the demands they face.
- Inquire. If someone says something that seems way off to you, say, "That's interesting, please tell me more." This can help you correctly understand what the person is seeking to communicate. It might help the other person understand him- or herself better, as well.

TRANSFORMATIONAL BENEFITS

Few of us enjoy fighting, but one of the surest ways we stir up conflict is through misunderstanding what another person intended to say. Of course, we can blame the other person, but the most effective and happiest strategy is for us to take personal responsibility for the effectiveness of the communication. Step one is to listen empathically. Not only will we get a more accurate read on what someone is seeking to tell us, but we will in all likelihood help the person to become clearer about what he or she is seeking to say.

For example, Stephanie is carefully listening to Tom describe a difficult situation with one of his customers. Periodically she gives him feedback by repeating both what she is hearing him say and how he seems to feel about it. "So they ordered two thousand units on Thursday and then called up Tuesday morning after they had shipped, to cut it down to six hundred? Man, you must have felt angry—as well as discouraged."

Tom knew he was feeling angry about this inconsiderate behavior and all the hassles it was going to cause him, but he hadn't yet acknowledged consciously that he felt discouraged because the loss in volume meant he still hadn't made his quota. Stephanie's reflection can help him develop a more effective response to his challenge because it requires different kinds of resources to rebound from discouragement than from anger.

STAR PERFORMER

This time we invite you to name someone from your life—our guess is you will find many people—who treat you with empathy. Let them be your role models and take time to acknowledge them for their care. For James and Marcia, Sherrol Horner, their officer manager at Collaborative Growth for many years, is one delightful example. Whatever trials and travails they would go through with their clients or with their own work, they knew she would give them a compassionate and clarifying ear when they talked over the situation with her back at the office.

For Bonita, it is her father, Lawrence "Chick" Patterson, who provides an inspirational example. He attentively listens and asks reflective questions that help her stay in tune with her personal ethics and values. Throughout her life, she has observed that many others have sought his counsel because he helps them to help themselves.

REEL PERFORMER

In *Terms of Endearment,* many of the actors worked empathically with the challenge of a young mother dying from cancer. Even Jack Nicholson's character, who was most inclined to be a curmudgeon, became an empathic and helpful neighbor. This greatly expanded his connection with and appreciation for life, as he was able to experience a wider variety of his own feelings more deeply.

Social Responsibility

WHAT IS IT?

Social responsibility entails recognizing and assuming responsibility for the well-being of the larger group and for the other individuals who live and operate within it. That larger group could be a business enterprise, a church congregation, a sports league, a community, and so on. One demonstrates that he or she is a constructive and cooperative member of the social group by contributing to it in a reliable manner. Typically one would give one's time, effort, participation, money, and allegiance to the group and its individual members in order to help it accomplish its collective purpose in a way that benefits all its members.

According to Bar-On (2002, p. 16), socially responsible people have "the ability to do things for and with others, accepting others, acting in accordance with one's conscience, and upholding social rules. These people possess interpersonal sensitivity and are able to accept others and use their talents for the good of the collective, not just the self. People who are deficient in this ability may entertain antisocial attitudes, act abusively toward others, and take advantage of others."

WHY SHOULD WE CARE
ABOUT SOCIAL RESPONSIBILITY?

Social responsibility is the glue that holds societies and communities together. It is the reciprocal relationship between the individual members and the group that supports them and allows groups to achieve collective goals far beyond what an individual ever could alone.

How do we ever come to identify and know ourselves as a society? We can only gain this wisdom through the reflections we receive from the world around us. In our postmodern electronic global community, those reflections increasingly come through the electronic media. Because the authentic energy of an actual person-to-person connection is not present there, it makes it more difficult for our children to develop social responsibility skills and more essential that we cultivate and model them as adults.

According to Joseph Turow (1997, p. 3), "The U.S. is experiencing a major shift in balance between society-making media and segment-making media. Segment-making media are those that encourage small slices of society to talk to themselves, while society-making media are those that have the potential to get all those segments to talk to each other."

This shift has resulted in much unconscious and conscious jostling for status between newly fragmented groups that perceive all "others" to be different. It makes developing and maintaining social responsibility all the more difficult and all the more imperative!

The cost of allowing our social responsibility to erode is perhaps best captured in the following declaration made by Pastor Martin Niemoller to the Council of the Evangelical Church in Germany, October 18, 1945. There are many versions of his remarks in circulation, but his actual statement can be found at www.christianethicstoday.com (click on #9 for the specific issue).

"First they came for the Communists, and I did not speak out—
    because I was not a Communist;
Then they came for the socialists, and I did not speak out—
    because I was not a socialist;
Then they came for the trade unionists, and I did not speak out—
    because I was not a trade unionist;
Then they came for the Jews, and I did not speak out—
    because I was not a Jew;

Then they came for me—
        and there was no one left to speak out for me."

There are two kinds of human behavior that the pendulum of history has swung between for a very long time, competition and collaboration. *Competitive* behavior produces more contents: rapid change and innovation, reduced monetary costs, more efficient manufacturing and distribution of products, and of course, winners and losers. That is because these kinds of goals tend to be linear in nature and are attainable through rational mechanistic processes led by individuals with high IQs.

Collaborative behavior produces more context: slower, system-sensitive change, reduced social and environmental costs, a more integrated and equal distribution of resources, and far fewer winners and losers. That is because these kinds of goals tend to be multidimensional, interdisciplinary in nature, and follow organic, intuitive processes led by teams with high EQ.

Rational intelligence did a great job at solving most of the problems that got our species out of the dark ages and into the 20th century, but since 1900 the number of people sharing this planet and all of its resources has increased by a factor of 3.5, and the unpaid interest on the debts that have accrued from the reductionist worldview leave us with problems too complex for it to understand, let alone resolve. In spite of all the apparent evidence to the contrary, the pendulum accelerates toward collaboration.

HOW CAN WE BUILD SOCIAL RESPONSIBILITY?

As you explore and rededicate your commitment to social responsibility, allow the words of Robert Kennedy to guide you:

"Some men see things as they are and ask 'why?'
I dream things that have never been and ask 'why not?'"

The first step in building social responsibility is to learn to value it in a new way relative to our self-interest. We must pay a new kind of attention to the cooperative advantage we sustain through communicating honestly and working together toward common goals that will genuinely benefit all of us. The economic advantage we have achieved through technology has served to weaken this awareness. When we look at the human species in comparison with all others, we notice that no other animal has an insatiable "need" for more. All other species, including the great apes, orangutans, chimpanzees, and other higher primates to which we are most biologically similar, observe a natural limit to the amount of food, territory, and so forth that they attempt to control and/or consume. Humans alone do not.

This is perhaps largely due to our ability to think symbolically, the capacity that supposedly makes us more evolved than all other animals. The downside of the "subject-object" schism is that it allows us to perceive ourselves as distinct from everything else. Our liability to this kind of misperception should be recognized for what it is and managed consciously, intelligently, and rigorously; otherwise, we can jeopardize life as we know it on the planet.

Building social responsibility means developing more relationships that explore and express our interdependency and strengthen our appreciation of that connection. In order to act in ways that bind us together rather than fragment us, we must integrate and synthesize an honest agreement about what our real needs, desires, and interests should be.

In order to build these kinds of relationships, we must re-evaluate from where we derive our sense of identity. If we see ourselves as a single isolated human body that might perish any day in an accident, or at best survive eight or nine decades before disappearing into oblivion, it could make sense to live as if "whoever dies with the most toys wins." To build socially responsible relationships we must identify with something larger than ourselves. For eight billion people to share this planet in peace and prosperity, what we value and feel a part of will need to expand to include much more of the Earth's rich diversity. Perhaps someday we will grow to feel socially responsible for all of her environment, all of her resources, all of her people.

TRANSFORMATIONAL BENEFITS

The more responsibility we take for each other and all life on the planet, the safer we will feel, the more we can achieve, the better we can care for the fragile environment that supports us. Each of us will feel a greater sense of purpose.

We will feel more valued and appreciated. We will each feel that our contribution is more meaningful, that we belong and are more fully supported in achieving our life purpose. We experience less stress when we know we are not alone.

STAR PERFORMER

George Washington Carver was a brilliant scientist whose research and scientific work resulted in the development of 325 products from peanuts and over one hundred products from sweet potatoes. These products were particularly significant in the rural economic development of the South because they provided alternatives to growing cotton that were beneficial for the farmers as well as for the soil. Carver was born a slave around 1864 and orphaned before age five. All his life he had a deep commitment to develop products that would both benefit the common people and help take care of the land.

REEL PERFORMER

In *Remember the Titans*, Denzel Washington plays Herman Boone, a Virginia football coach at a newly integrated high school in the 1970s. He must first help the young men overcome their own racial prejudice enough to bond and function as an effective football team. Then he must protect and continue to nurture their unity in the face of the community's hostility toward the coach and the African-American students. His best demonstration of building social responsibility comes when he runs his players to a Civil War battleground and helps them connect with the human pain and suffering that was common to everyone on both sides. They leave with a commitment to do their personal best to transcend those human foibles in themselves for the sake of what they all hold in common, their love of the game.

Interpersonal Relationships

WHAT ARE THEY?

Interpersonal relationships are the proving ground of emotional intelligence; they are where the rubber meets the road. Our skill in interpersonal relationships governs whether other people in our lives will feel eager to see us again or dread it. Here is where our needs, desires, and expectations are anticipated, acknowledged, appreciated, and treated with respect or where they are thwarted and ignored. The quality of our interpersonal relationships establishes the social and emotional climate in our families, neighborhoods, and workplaces. When our relationships are working well, they provide the common ground where we get to enjoy our own experience of humanness through sharing it with others.

Stein and Book (2000, p. 134) define skill in interpersonal relationships as "the ability to establish and maintain mutually satisfying relationships that are characterized by intimacy and by giving and receiving affection." The tricky part is the requirement of mutuality. Developing relationships that truly are mutually satisfying requires surrendering some of our control to another person, or to other people. But out of the natural correspondence between emotional competencies, we discover that kind of surrender is also exactly what it takes to be socially responsible! Nothing will bring our interest and attention to focus faster on the group's needs than when we surrender some of our own self-interest and have, as they say, "some skin in the game."

In order to have an authentically mutual relationship, we have to understand the other people well enough to anticipate their preferences and be able to satisfy them to some extent . . . and *they* get to be the final authority as to whether or not our attempts were successful! To make it even more complicated, there are times when almost everyone is somewhat deceptive about what they want and what they are or are not willing to give. For a relationship with real depth, we ultimately need to know the other person well enough to detect when he or she is bluffing and to constructively elicit his or her true perspective when it does matter and recognize when to let it go when it doesn't.

WHY SHOULD WE CARE ABOUT INTERPERSONAL RELATIONSHIPS?

No matter how much we might pretend otherwise, humans *must* care about interpersonal relationships because we are primates, who are by nature highly social creatures. We cannot survive long in isolation. Our ancient biology predisposes us to seek communication with others. Your brain and heart structures and the neurotransmitters that circulate throughout your body are all extensions of millions of years of behavior. You can't escape needing to be touched and held and spoken to. You can't *not* seek reflections of yourself from fellow human beings unless you suffer from some of the more extreme forms of mental illness such as schizophrenia or autism.

As the planet becomes more crowded and more of our resources have to be shared, our ability to make friends and keep them is critical to our ability to progress socially—and perhaps even to survive. Trusting, committed relationships among neighbors and community members were key ingredients in the success of the American Revolution and the settling of the frontier. It has only been as we have grown more and more affluent that we could afford to indulge in the sort of separation and fragmentedness that has now become commonplace. There are serious costs to this alienation. We harbor a vague sense of competition with our neighbors, even suspicion, and the desire not to be bothered by them.

What is surprising to those of us who have been conditioned to believe success comes out of competition and winning is that it not only doesn't cost us anything to reinvest more of our resources and concern in social responsibility, but it actually improves our stress tolerance and makes us happier. Taking a fresh, more honest look at ourselves we rediscover that we are naturally social creatures.

HOW CAN WE BUILD INTERPERSONAL RELATIONSHIPS?

 "Friendship should be more than biting Time can sever."

T.S. Elliot, *Murder in the Cathedral*

Fortunately, the skills for building durable, mutually beneficial relationships are well-known and easily practiced by those who truly want to improve this skill.

The first step is to examine honestly the level of satisfaction you currently experience. Consider the relationships that are central to your life and think about the most and least satisfying aspects. The second step is to recognize that, if you want to make new friends or improve the quality of an existing relationship, it will be *you* who does the changing. . . . It is never a useful goal to set about changing or improving the other person; rather, it is a recipe for certain frustration and failure. The third step is to start working on specific behaviors, such as improving your listening, introducing yourself to others, finding areas of common interest, reading non-verbal cues, and ending conversations in a way that encourages more contact in the future.

Certainly, there are relationships that should be abandoned rather than improved—abusive ones fall in this category. Knowing which relationships to nurture and which to let go is a separate skill, and you can find many resources on that topic. Here we are concerned with ways to start and improve healthy relationships.

TRANSFORMATIONAL BENEFITS

Improving your skills in interpersonal relationships can bring a host of benefits from stress reduction to increased productivity and creativity, as well as an expanded enjoyment of life. Celebrating your accomplishments is a key ingredient in developing happiness. To the extent you can increase the quantity and quality of your interpersonal relationships, you will have more people with whom to enjoy celebrating those achievements! As you assist your clients in building this skill, they are likely to notice more ease and success in achieving the goals that they desire.

STAR PERFORMER

Research on hair cutters has found that many have exceptional interpersonal skills. They quickly connect with each customer, remember his or her life story, empathize, and share compassionately. Marcia's family's hairdresser, Jan Eller, is a champ at building interpersonal relationships by making people feel welcome, at home, and truly valuable.

One of the characters on the television program "Friends" also worked in the personal-care industry as a masseuse. Phoebe's genuineness and straightforward manner made her easy for a wide variety of people to trust. It was obvious to everyone that she was an authentic person who was not playing a lot of deceptive games. That kind of straightforwardness helps build trusting relationships.

REEL PERFORMER

In *Something's Got to Give,* Diane Keaton and Jack Nicholson meet when she's in her fifties and he's in his sixties, having his first heart attack. Both are deeply identified with and committed to their singleness, and they defend it with strong protective shields that also "protect" them from the stability of a relationship with a life partner. However, at a deeper level it is as if their souls somehow connect and lead their personalities through a long list of lessons that produce a new and deeply rewarding relationship for both of them. It's not easy, but—wow!—is it worth it!

Stress Tolerance

WHAT IS IT?

Life is filled with stress. The sources of stress are plentiful and varied—being cut off (or flipped off!) in traffic, preparing a critical business proposal, making a presentation to the management team, preparing for a wedding, dealing with the death of a loved one, caring for a newborn child, moving to a new dream house, or getting that great new promotion. Paradoxically, stress is caused by both happy and sad situations. The stressors in our lives are inescapable.

Dealing with stress is not an *if* question, it's a question of *when* and *how often*. When it happens, EQ can help one analyze the situation and resourcefully deal with his or her feelings. The problem we face is that our primary response to stress is fight or flight. In past eras, much of our stress was due to threats to our physical safety such as being chased by a wild animal. Our bodies automatically geared up to deal with the situation, and we physically responded to the problem—stood and fought or ran like heck. When the crisis ended, our bodies returned to normal through a process called the "relaxation response."

The stress we experience today does not usually require a physical response. However, our bodies and minds still instinctively respond to perceived threat as if a wild animal is involved. We automatically gear up with the fight or flight response, but must then suppress the impulse. We often experience the never-ending pressure of chronic stress, which includes ongoing pressure at work or home, persistent financial issues, or ongoing relationship problems. Doc Childre (1994, p. 3), founder of the HeartMath Institute, asserts, "Stress stimulates the perpetual release of the hormones adrenaline, noradrenalin, and cortisol, which eventually sear the body like a constant drizzle of acid. If left unchecked, chronic stress—along with attitudes like hostility, anger, and depression—can sicken and eventually kill us."

Given the dramatic impact of unchecked stress, to remain healthy, we must expand our ability to tolerate and manage it along with all its implications.

Bar-On defines stress tolerance as:

"The ability to withstand adverse events and stressful situations without 'falling apart' by actively and positively coping with stress. . . . This ability is based on (1) a capacity to choose courses of action for coping with stress (i.e., being resourceful and effective, being able to come up with suitable methods, and knowing what to do and how to do it), (2) an optimistic disposition toward new experiences and change in general and toward one's ability to successfully overcome the specific problem at hand (i.e., a belief in one's ability to face and handle these situations), and (3) a feeling that one can control or influence the stressful situation (i.e., keeping calm and maintaining control)." (2002, p. 17)

WHY SHOULD WE CARE ABOUT STRESS TOLERANCE?

Are you kidding! The quality of one's life is profoundly impacted by his or her ability to tolerate stress. If a person cannot tolerate stress, he or she cannot live well. Being constantly stressed out leads to physical and psychological damage and negatively impacts one's effectiveness. Handling stress supports health and boosts effectiveness.

People who do not deal effectively with mounting stress often resort to self-medication—drug or alcohol abuse, tobacco use, abnormal eating patterns, or unhealthy lifestyles.

Stress increases heart attack risk. According to The Mayo Clinic, "Stress and anger may increase your risk of coronary artery disease. . ." (www.MayoClinic.com). Johns Hopkins University School of Medicine and School of Hygiene and Public Health followed a group of over 1,055 men for thirty-two to forty-eight years to study their incidence of premature heart disease compared with anger responses to stress. Those who had the highest level of anger and reported experiencing irritability and expressed or concealed anger were more than three times as likely to develop premature heart disease and over six times more likely to have a heart attack by age fifty-five (Chang, Ford, Meoni, Wang, & Klag, 2002).

Bar-On and Handley (1999) emphasize the relationship between strengths in stress management and impulse control. When we control our impulses, we reduce potential stress factors. This is one of many links that can be made between effective stress control and enhancing other emotional intelligence factors.

HOW CAN WE BUILD STRESS TOLERANCE?

 STRESS TOOLKIT—BE PREPARED

- Perfect techniques to manage the psychological and physiological impacts of stress, for example, structured breathing, visualization, and affirmations.
- Develop strategies for coping with stress so they are readily available in the heat of the situation, for example, "The next time I get a 'snippy' voicemail from Chris, I will do a brief meditation before responding."
- Get more exercise!

Who does your client know who tolerates stress well? Have your client ask that role model for tips and pointers.

Stress tolerance and optimism present us with a classic "chicken and egg" conundrum—which came first? In reality, they are very symbiotic. Strength in one area contributes to mastery in the other. As Bar-On implies, optimism and stress tolerance are inexorably intertwined. You must maintain a positive outlook and have confidence that you will successfully ride the roller coaster ride of life.

Develop strategies and techniques for preventing and dealing with stress. Research what is available, identify what seems most interesting and doable to you, and then try it out. Available approaches include exercise, meditation, visualization, deep-breathing exercises, muscle relaxation techniques, biofeedback, and massage therapy. Apply these methods as you work with your clients to choose the most appropriate strategies for their situations.

Other methods of managing stress involve reprioritizing activities and involvement. Shift from stress-producing to stress-reducing activities, including exercise, recreational activities, or mini-vacations. Diet is another key ingredient in managing stress. Eating too many unhealthy foods and not enough healthy ones creates a drag on one's body. It is saddled with processing junk and trying to maintain health with insufficient fuel.

One way to build stress tolerance is to enhance communication skills and muster some courage. Many times people avoid chronically stressful issues rather than resolve them with constructive discussion. You might urge your clients to improve their ability to talk about and resolve sensitive issues using openness and appropriate consideration while maintaining respect for themselves and others.

Finally, apply generous doses of humor. Maintain a sense of humor during difficult situations. It helps to regulate hormone levels and produces those much sought after endorphins!

TRANSFORMATIONAL BENEFITS

Success breeds success. As one improves his or her ability to deal with stress and expands his or her portfolio of stress management strategies, confidence builds because the person knows he or she can handle it. As one's confidence builds, so does one's optimistic outlook regarding managing future stressful situations.

STAR PERFORMER

Rudolph Giuliani is the former mayor of New York City. He emerged as a local, national, and international leader in the midst of the September 11, 2001, World Trade Center terrorist attack. This was one of the most stressful situations America ever faced. He personified leadership by proactively coping with stress. He visited the rescue site to console and inspire the police, firefighters, and other rescue workers. He made appearances throughout the city, answered every question, and gave numerous unscripted press conferences. In the face of his own personal shock, grief, and loss, he increased his visibility and provided comfort and encouragement to a heart-struck nation. He conveyed the gravity of the situation while reinforcing an optimistic outlook toward the future.

REEL PERFORMER

In *The Negotiator,* Lt. Danny Roman (Samuel L. Jackson) is one of the top hostage negotiators for the Chicago Police Department. The movie opens with Roman negotiating with a man who is holding his own daughter hostage and threatening to kill her unless the police bring his wife to the scene. The situation is extremely intense and it is important for Roman to keep the hostage taker's frustration level down so he won't kill the girl. To help manage the man's stress level, Roman uses humor. Almost in spite of himself, the extremely desperate man chuckles and momentarily relaxes. That stress reduction moment buys Roman valuable time to handle the situation.

Impulse Control

WHAT IS IT?

Impulses are urges that compel action. They exist beyond logic and rationality and spring from our subconscious minds with persistence and intensity. They pulsate with primal urgency and are fueled by psychological or physiological factors. Impulses can be helpful or harmful to us. We must look to the results and consequences manifest in our lives to determine how much we need to control our impulses.

Our discussion focuses on controlling impulses that diminish effectiveness. Lack of impulse control is the source of much human misery, including the recently identified peril of modern society—road rage. Road rage is an uncontrolled display of anger by the operator of a motor vehicle. As impulse control is defined in the Bar-On EQ-i®, it includes both impulse control and anger, and both aspects are addressed here and through the exercises.

Lane (2000, p. 172) describes impulse control as "not taking a particular action aimed at short-term gratification in order to avoid possible negative long-term consequences. To not act on an impulse requires that a mental representation of possible future consequences influence the behavioral expression of the impulse before it occurs. Thus, impulse control involves recognition of an incipient approach behavior and the ability to anticipate the negative consequences of that course of action. . . . Impulse control thus involves suppression of approach behavior."

Bar-On (2002, p. 18) defines impulse control as, "the ability to resist or delay an impulse, drive, or temptation to act. It entails a capacity for accepting one's aggressive impulses, being composed, and controlling aggression, hostility, and irresponsible behavior. Problems in impulse control are manifested by low frustration tolerance, impulsiveness, anger control problems, abusiveness, loss of self-control, and explosive and unpredictable behavior."

WHY SHOULD WE CARE ABOUT IMPULSE CONTROL?

The ability to control or resist harmful urges is essential to functioning at a high level of effectiveness. Let's get real—if one cannot put the bottle down, stop stuffing food into his or her mouth, or quit hitting his or her spouse, self-regard and interpersonal relationships become impaired. If one becomes demonstrably angry in the workplace, he or she may damage relationships with colleagues and customers.

Type A personalities—action oriented, constantly in motion, multi-tasking—may take a dim view of controlling their impulses. They may embrace their Type A-ness as the key to their success and see it as their competitive advantage and an essential success trait. They may not assess how much time they or others spend in cleaning up the broken glass that is left in their wake. People who don't manage impulses well *should* care because the type of impatience and free-floating hostility that can characterize their personalities increases their risk of heart disease and can be costly in the workplace.

HOW CAN WE BUILD IMPULSE CONTROL?

Building impulse control requires identifying, analyzing, and changing unproductive behavior. Controlling impulses requires emotional self-awareness and a willingness to trade the immediate satisfaction of a knee-jerk reaction for the strategic benefit of a thoughtful response. Your client must clarify the WIIFM ("What's in it for me?") and create alternative solutions that also answer the question, "What's in it for others?!"

The PCG (Polaris Consulting Group) ChangeNow™ Model we use in Workout 10.2 contains the steps necessary to build impulse control.

 IMPULSIVENESS IMPACTS RESULTS

- Think strategically and avoid impulsiveness by using effective self-talk such as "This time I will look before I leap!"
- Remember the aftermath of impulsiveness may not be worth the satisfaction of the moment!

Questions

- What satisfaction does your client derive by acting impulsively?
- What feels good about it in the moment?

TRANSFORMATIONAL BENEFITS

Controlling impulses will increase productivity and improve self-regard. It is liberating and empowering to use determination and higher-order reasoning to overcome compelling urges. When you or your clients enhance this skill, improved results in the daily challenges of life are certain to appear. New experiences could include:

- Waiting for an appropriate time to discuss an issue with an employee or co-worker, rather than "spouting off" in the heat of the moment.
- In business meetings, allowing others to complete their sentences instead of "over-talking" them.
- Emerging from the car in a reasonably relaxed state. It can happen when we do not react to every "idiot" driver who got in our way.
- Inhabiting a slimmer, more toned body.

STAR PERFORMER

Anita Hill was thrust into the spotlight when she testified at the Senate confirmation hearing of Supreme Court Justice nominee Clarence Thomas. Ms. Hill, a graduate of the Yale Law School, accused Mr. Thomas of sexual harassment when he was her supervisor at the Equal Employment Opportunity Commission (EEOC) in the 1980s. She recounted her allegations in a politically charged, highly visible environment that exposed her to extreme reactions, both positive and negative, from members of Congress and the general public.

Under intense public scrutiny, Anita Hill maintained her composure while describing uncomfortably intimate details of the alleged acts. Many believe her message had greater impact because she resisted the urge to respond emotionally.

 REEL PERFORMER

Gregory Peck plays lawyer Atticus Finch in *To Kill a Mockingbird.* It is the early 1930s in Alabama, at the height of the Depression. Racism is the order of the day. By providing legal representation for Tom Robinson (Brock Peters), a black man wrongly accused of raping Mayella Ewell, a white woman, Atticus incites the ire of Bob Ewell, Mayella's father.

What actually happened was that Mayella invited Tom into her house to repair a door. Once Tom was inside the house, Mayella made sexual advances toward him, which he rebuffed. Her father saw the interchange and told his daughter he was going to kill her. Bob was primarily infuriated because his daughter was attracted to a black man, which was a taboo of the highest order. After Tom left, Bob savagely beat his daughter. Later both Mayella and Bob claimed that she was raped and beaten by Tom. The bottom line is that Bob, in his convoluted logic, wanted the completely innocent Tom to hang because Mayella was attracted to him.

Atticus has ample opportunity to demonstrate impulse control. For example, Atticus exhibits impulse control when Tom informs Atticus of his displeasure in the most derogatory terms. Another instance is when Bob spits in his face. Bob has clearly been itching for a fight. Atticus controls his impulses and restrains himself from responding in kind.

Reality Testing

WHAT IS IT?

Our reality testing determines how clearly we discern what is actually happening in the world around us. We have learned to interpret and color our objective experience with all sorts of desires, fears, and distortions. In order to avoid mistaking our overly negative or overly positive perceptions of experience for reality, we must develop reliable processes for confirming the objective correspondence of our feelings, perceptions, and thoughts with the immediate situation.

Stein and Book emphasize an important aspect of reality testing when they point out it must occur in the "now" moment. They state that "reality testing involves 'tuning in' to the immediate situation. It is the capacity to see things objectively, the way they are, rather than the way we wish or fear them to be. Testing this degree of correspondence involves the search for objective evidence to confirm, justify, and support feelings, perceptions, and thoughts. . . . In simple terms, reality testing is the ability to accurately 'size up' the immediate situation" (2000, pp. 154–155).

It is also important to remember that in one sense we can never see reality directly; we only see it through our own perceptions. Our perceptions are learned from our experience and our society, and they give us a map of our reality, but no matter how accurate that map may be, it is never the whole territory.

improving our reality testing means verifying how well our perceptions match those of others and adding detail to that map, but in order to be as accurate as possible, it must also always honor the mystery that lies beyond all we can ever perceive.

WHY SHOULD WE CARE ABOUT REALITY TESTING?

If there is an absolute reality out there, it is very likely that no human being knows it with perfect clarity, because we have all learned to see, experience, and construct our world out of a learned perceptual bias. Because we use only three of our five senses to construct the vast majority of our experience of reality, it is always very helpful to verify that what we see, hear, and feel/sense in the world around us is accurately perceived. Likewise, it is very helpful to periodically check out our reasoning processes to confirm that the conclusions we are drawing actually follow logically from all the information that is available to us.

When we fail to do this, we are not testing reality well enough to achieve consistently the results we desire. We may avoid reality testing either because we are reluctant to engage fully in the world or because we are conditioned to expect results that are consistently better or worse than objective reality shows them to be.

HOW CAN WE BUILD REALITY TESTING?

 Be a little bit skeptical! Ask yourself:

- "What evidence am I relying on when I believe this is as it appears to be?"
- "Who wants me to believe this is reality? What are his or her motives?"

The best way to assess and develop our reality testing skills is by calling our perceptions and desires into question on a regular basis. This can be done effectively in several ways.

First, check in with your body at the sensory level—"How is my body feeling now? Hot? Warm? Cool? Centered? Upset? Out of balance?" What does that information tell you?

Then ask questions like: "What kinds of sounds am I hearing around me? Soothing? Abrasive? Scary? Angry? Seductive? Supportive? Challenging? How accurately am I seeing the situation in which I find myself? Do people really feel the way they appear to? Am I exaggerating the significance of what I perceive—either positively or negatively?"

Another way to check the quality of your reality testing is to figure out all who have a significant stake in the outcome of the situation at hand. Observe them and notice how they are responding. If it is appropriate to do so, tell them your take on the situation and ask if they concur.

TRANSFORMATIONAL BENEFITS

The benefits of developing good reality testing skills can be expressed very succinctly—these skills are what help us avoid the unexpected loss, disappointment, and bad luck that we can inadvertently cause for ourselves and others. Moreover, they help us get on the same page with everyone who is involved and keep our efforts coordinated.

 ## STAR PERFORMER

Hans Blix was in charge of the United Nations investigations in Iraq to determine the presence of weapons of mass destruction. It seemed like a constant shell game of realities—were there weapons that had been moved? Was this fresh evidence? Where were they hiding all of the armaments that we "knew" existed? Success in his mission required him constantly to verify and re-verify what his investigators were finding and what previous documentation showed. All the time he had to perform this work in the glare of the global spotlight and under the extreme pressure of the United States to produce evidence that would justify an attack.

 ## REEL PERFORMER

Matchstick Men is a movie about a con man (Nicholas Cage) who has made his living by misrepresenting reality to all his marks; and as clever as he has been in deceiving others, he has not learned how to test his own reality . . . yet.

Normally one would not have so many potential things that could appear to be one way and yet go so far wrong, but his own deceptiveness, or perhaps karma, leaves him desperately vulnerable. By the end of the movie, he has made good progress in figuring out what is valuable, what is real, and what is not.

Flexibility

WHAT IS IT?

Flexible people are resilient, able to bend when the wind starts blowing in a surprising direction. People with a strong capacity for flexibility might be compared to a willow—they can bend a long way in many directions in storms that tear the branches off harder, stouter trees. The network of deep roots that supports the willow and gives it that remarkable flexibility is similar to the deeply held core values that guide an individual or organization. When we exercise true flexibility, we must still honor our core values, because if we compromise those, we will lose the connection with the roots of our strength, our purpose, and our credibility.

Not everyone appreciates flexibility to the same degree. One worker described a colleague as "quick to adapt to new information, a skill that significantly contributes to her success." Meanwhile, another says, "Her attitudes blow with the wind or the boss's current fancy; she's unreliable, manipulative, and wishy-washy." How and why we are flexible is important; it is also important to notice if and why we judge other people when they exercise their flexibility.

Webster's (1993) defines "flexible" as "willing or ready to yield to the influence of others (tractable; manageable), and characterized by ready capability for modification or change, by plasticity, pliancy, variability, and often by consequent adaptability to new situations." Synonyms listed are elastic, resilient, springy, and supple.

Bar-On (2002, p. 17) defines flexibility as "the ability to adjust one's feelings, thoughts, and behavior to changing situations and conditions."

When they defined flexibility, Stein and Book emphasized, "This component of emotional intelligence applies to your overall ability to adapt to unfamiliar, unpredictable, and dynamic circumstances. Flexible people are . . . able to change their minds when evidence suggests that they are mistaken" (2000, p. 161).

Flexible people are often characterized as adaptable, agile, open, and tolerant of differences. Flexible people are not dogmatic, nor always convinced they are right. This is an example of how two of these fifteen factors influence one another. Happiness and flexibility often influence one another. One of our favorite questions to clients comes from *A Course in Miracles* (Foundation for Inner Peace, 1975) and we phrase it as "Would you rather be happy, or would you rather be right?" Flexible people are on the right track to choosing happiness.

Not all terms are positive; sometimes flexible people are defined as manipulative or fickle or unreliable. President Clinton was highly flexible, which brought him great success and great criticism. He would test the waters to understand how far he could take an issue, and then make a strong push in that direction. It was a strategy that valued making some progress rather than maintaining a firm ideological stance and getting nowhere. Some people praised this strategy; others decried it.

Highly flexible people may be thought of as people who will compromise their principles to please an authority. When these labels are accurate, the behavior is not emotionally intelligent. One needs clarity to exercise flexibility properly. Primarily, it must be applied with concrete reality testing, with regard for others, and without compromising our values. Thus, as with all EQ skills, flexibility must be applied in the context of the other skills. No skill is successful in a vacuum.

With true flexibility, this capacity to easily make a shift pays off when something unexpected occurs, such as when new data arrives, when circumstances change, even when we come to a new understanding of "old" information. Perhaps an "aha" has occurred and a truly better solution has finally been discovered! However, those who abuse others' flexibility sometimes manufacture phony changes in order to manipulate a situation or the people involved. For example, an employee with a flexible manager who doesn't want to do a task in the way directed may overstate obstacles to try to get out of work.

As with everything, flexibility must be applied in context. Lauren (not her real name) learned this by participating in Emergenetics® seminars. As an HR director for her city, she brought Emergenetics® to several parts of her organization and participated in several of the workshops. Lauren was the first person hired to create a discrete HR department for the city, and others in the city had many ideas as to how she and the department should operate. Lauren is quite bright, empathic, and flexible. She could see the value of most of the suggestions she received and recognized that the staff was hungry for a big menu of services.

However, she spread herself too thin, trying to make everyone happy. Lauren was working far too many hours, and her successes seemed limited because she was working on so many things at once that it took a long time for anything to be completed. One day in the middle of one of the Emergenetics workshops, she finally saw her problem. Her super-flexibility had a cost that outweighed some of the benefits. That was a turning point for Lauren's success, her happiness, and the success of her new department. Successful expression of flexibility requires boundaries as well as the willingness to change.

WHY SHOULD WE CARE ABOUT FLEXIBILITY?

Change is the greatest constant in our fast-paced world. The ability to adapt to change rapidly is a predominant characteristic of successful people. It allows them to avoid or take advantage promptly of the critical factors affecting any situation in which they are involved, rather than getting caught up in an ego-dominated struggle of how it *should* be. Inflexible people may stick to deadlines instead of the deeper goal, thus alienating co-workers rather than building up the team.

Would you rather live in a world of *should*'s, *supposed to*'s, and *wanna be*'s, or would you like to be free to *get on with the show*? While the answer is obvious, this question reflects a very real struggle that is documented by the thousands of business and self-help books written on how to deal with change. There would not be such a strong need to embrace change and demonstrate flexibility if there was not such an abundance of flux in our increasingly complex world. However, the large number of books on the topic indicates that many people struggle in numerous processes and settings to learn the wide range of appropriate ways to express flexibility.

Futurists are giving us amazingly similar forecasts—everything they are writing depicts a world of ever-increasing change, often experienced as turbulence. So we can count on the skill of flexibility remaining crucially important. This skill is particularly valuable when we feel there is too much change leading to the tendency to get rigid and *batten down the hatches* rather than to open to the new possibilities.

In Tai Chi, flexibility begins with bending the knees slightly, so we can move with the flow of energy. It's not giving up your stance but, paradoxically, strengthening it. Using flexibility in our interactions is similar. Those who will be successful in today's and tomorrow's worlds will be able to bend and flow, while applying reality testing, self-regard, and empathy.

Thus, the results from caring about strengthening your flexibility skills will certainly include:

- Enhancing your ability to work with a world changing at a radically increasing pace.
- Increasing your effectiveness as it lets you shift to use the best data instead of being caught up in saving face.
- Expanding your happiness, as you can be satisfied with what is, rather than seeking to force a reality not supported by the circumstances.

We are betting that you can add some of your own reasons. What are they?

HOW CAN WE BUILD FLEXIBILITY?

Apply brainstorming strategies when faced with a challenge. Give yourself ten minutes just to think of possibilities before you begin to look for answers.

There is a direct connection between feeling afraid and becoming less flexible. How can we help our clients expand their trust in a way that will enable them to incorporate the skills of reality testing and optimism in assessing an unfamiliar situation? Taking time to do that assessment before jumping into a dramatic response can give them resilience and expand their credibility, and others will appreciate their thoughtful response.

Notice limiting beliefs, such as "I usually make mistakes on important projects," and ego defensiveness, such as "I have to protect myself from attacks by all superiors." Are there areas your clients can work on in expanding their personal skills and the nature of their responses to help them choose greater flexibility?

TRANSFORMATIONAL BENEFITS

The benefits of increased flexibility can be astonishing—more freedom, less often needing to be right, life balance, lightened workload, less stress and defensiveness. People might even live longer and be happier because positive thoughts increase DHEA, an important hormone that supports youthfulness in the body. You can be a more successful leader and mentor. Increased flexibility translates to not sweating the small stuff, and that means more joy in your life!

STAR PERFORMER

Thomas P. "Tip" O'Neill, Jr., was a Representative to the House from Massachusetts, fondly known as "Mr. Speaker." In his many years as Speaker of the House, he gained broad respect from Democrats and Republicans alike due to the thoughtful and respectful flexibility with which he treated issues.

REEL PERFORMER

In *Lilies of the Field*, Sidney Poitier's poignant performance is a direct example of the strength and focus of flexibility. He was remarkably amenable to working with the nuns and meeting their needs, so much so that some could have thought him passive and accomplishing little. Yet, he never compromised his overall focus and intent and successfully completed his mission.

Problem Solving

WHAT IS IT?

Problem solving is the social emotional competency that calls into action our sleuthing skills, as it is very much like detective work. Problem solving requires that we be alert and observant, noticing as much as possible within the context that surrounds us. Then we must proceed in a highly logical and systematic effort to follow the clues and connect the dots that lead to a sound resolution. This requires disciplined attention and perseverance because problems do not necessarily yield to the first attempt at a solution. That is why we call them problems!

Stein and Book (2000, p. 145) define problem solving as "the ability to identify and define problems as well as to generate and implement potentially effective solutions." They describe problem solving as a multi-phasic approach; in other words, we need to break our problem-solving process into steps in order to find the best possible solution. They, as well as Dr. Bar-On, emphasize that it serves us first to understand or define the problem, next to gather facts, and then brainstorm possibilities, while considering the options and applying them to our criteria for achieving a good solution. After all these steps, we then select the best answer.

We agree that this is an important approach, especially for complex issues. We can recognize this as a solid left-brain approach, particularly calling for analytical skills. We also want to respect what is sometimes referred to as right-brain problem solving, where we might follow our intuition and go with our gut response or even get guidance from our dreams. Remember, in the fullest sense we are working with social *and* emotional intelligence, which requires both left- and right-brain applications.

As one works to develop this skill, it is valuable to notice how problems are solved now. You might ask your clients if they tend to use more of a right-brain or left-brain strategy or a hybrid approach. Evaluate a range of problems (from simple to medium complexity) that have been solved in the past and notice what kinds of solutions were achieved and the process for achieving the resolution. This direct feedback will guide your clients in evaluating whether their current strategy works well or could use some fine-tuning.

WHY SHOULD WE CARE ABOUT PROBLEM SOLVING?

Problem solving is a skill we employ constantly in our lives, from figuring how to get all our materials *and* a hot cup of coffee into the car in a single trip without spilling anything, to planning for our children's college and our own retirement. Regardless of the field in which we are employed, we are expected to solve problems and to solve them quickly, economically, and permanently. Our ability to accomplish these types of goals determines our compensation and how much leisure time and discretionary resources we have to enjoy. And guess what? If you think back to your last vacation, you will no doubt recall at least one or two significant problems you had to solve just to be able to enjoy your enjoyment!!

HOW CAN WE BUILD
OUR PROBLEM SOLVING COMPETENCIES?

 CREATE A CHECKLIST

Ask yourself if you have

- Properly defined the issue,
- Gathered all the facts,
- Brainstormed all the possibilities, and
- Incorporated all this into a timely solution.

Probably the most important component to effective problem solving is using a proven method that includes *all* the necessary steps. The Collaborative Growth Master Solve© Problem-Solving Model we use in Workout 13.1 of this book utilizes ingredients from a variety of sources, one of the most significant being neuro-linguistic programming, a powerful technology in the field of strategic communications.

TRANSFORMATIONAL BENEFITS

Improving your skills in problem solving will add to your value as a team player, make you more productive and effective regardless of the field in which you work, and, perhaps most importantly, it will make life flow more smoothly and more enjoyably.

STAR PERFORMER

William Ury is author of *The Third Win* and co-author of *Getting to Yes.* He is an internationally recognized leader in the field of negotiation and conflict resolution. As a cultural anthropologist, he has shared his wisdom on our need as a species to "change the culture of conflict within our families, our workplaces, our communities, and our world . . . to create a culture where even the most serious disputes are handled on the basis not of force and coercion but of mutual interest and coexistence" (2000, p. ix).

 REEL PERFORMER

GI Jane addresses war, one of the most intense, time-critical, and complex problem-solving settings in human experience. A female Naval officer played by Demi Moore is allowed to train with the elite Navy Seals unit in an experiment in mixed-gender combat units. The problems she is forced to solve deal not only with extreme physical demands and exhaustion, but also with political manipulators who intentionally stack the deck against her to prove the military's foregone conclusion that females cannot match the competency of males in combat.

Optimism

WHAT IS IT?

Optimists believe that good events are frequent and longlasting and that bad events are limited and temporary. Even if they have not found the solution to a problem, they're certain it is just around the corner and that they have some control over the problem.

Optimism correlates closely with success. Merely the mention of this fact gets most people to sit up and take notice! "How can growing my optimism make me more successful?" they ask. Success is directly related to how we manage our expectations. However, the kind of success we experience depends on how we define it. People often think of money first and all the things it can buy. But before long they also include the more enduring factors, such as good health, a happy family, and a safe and prosperous community. Optimism can help us achieve all of these. But what is it?

Webster's (1993) defines optimism as "a doctrine or opinion that reality is essentially good or completely good; or as good as it conceivably could be; an inclination to put the most favorable construction upon actions and happenings; to minimize adverse aspects, conditions, and possibilities, or to anticipate the best possible outcome."

Martin Seligman (1990), author of *Learned Optimism*, points out that optimistic people tend to think of defeat as a temporary setback that is not their fault. A difficult situation can be reframed as a challenge . . . an opportunity to do something novel and innovative or as a call to try harder.

Bar-On (2002, p. 18) defines optimism as "the ability to look at the brighter side of life and to maintain a positive attitude even in the face of adversity. Optimism assumes a measure of hope in one's approach to life. It is a positive approach to daily living. Optimism is the opposite of pessimism, which is a common symptom of depression."

We act optimistically when we respond to good events with a positive attitude, believing they are permanent. We give ourselves messages such as "Life is good today because I'm making sure to get enough exercise and making a conscious effort to be friendly" rather than "Life is good today, but I don't know why or what tomorrow will be like." Furthermore, we respond to bad events with a specific explanation, framing the event as temporary. Thus, we would say, "My workload is pretty heavy right now, which means I'm almost to the point of hiring some help" rather than saying, "I am so busy and tired, I will never get out of this cycle of working too much."

WHY SHOULD WE CARE ABOUT OPTIMISM?

As Seligman (2002, p. 128) writes, "Being optimistic brings about less depression, better physical health, and higher achievement, at a cost perhaps of less realism." How many of those would you like to see more of in your life? All of them? Clearly our lives will work better if we increase our optimism.

Optimists are much more likely to be survivors. Mark Jenkins (2003, p. 53) wrote about survivors, including Aron Ralston, the climber who was trapped in a slot canyon in Southern Utah and wound up cutting off his hand to save his life. Jenkins quotes Peter Suedfeld, professor emeritus of psychology at the University of British Columbia, as saying that "people under high stress are more likely to become rigid, which only decreases their chances of survival." He continues by saying that, even in a jam, "survivors are extremely adaptable people. They know how to improvise. . . . They keep an open mind, searching for options, developing strategies." Notice that this brings together the whole concept of the category in the EQi of general mood, which includes both happiness and optimism, and links it with problem solving. Certainly emotional intelligence is much more successful when our skills are well integrated!

Optimism is also linked to improved physical health, as demonstrated by an American Psychological Association report on a study in 1995 and 1996 by Martin Seligman and Gregory Buchanan. They worked with two groups of university freshmen who were inclined toward depression and volunteered to participate in the research. One group had no training; the other group participated in a workshop on cognitive coping skills. The group with training reported fewer adverse mental health concerns, as well as fewer physical problems, and was more active in getting checkups to maintain their health (American Psychological Association, 1995). The excellent results these types of studies cite are enough to inspire many to do the work it takes to develop and maintain a truly good attitude!

HOW CAN WE BUILD OPTIMISM?

 BE SOLUTION FOCUSED

- Focus on the possibilities and the answer rather than on the problem.
- Be grateful. Go out of your way to be thankful. Make sure you express gratitude at least ten times a day.

Possibly the most critical aspect of developing optimism is learning that you have a choice about your attitude. Many people think they are born optimists or pessimists and that it is something they just have to live with. Not so! Cognitive development strategies such as learning to dispute negative statements make a big difference. If your clients have a tendency to evaluate a bad event as permanent, help them learn to challenge themselves and change the message. As they will find by implementing the workouts in Part Three, they *can* change their lives by learning to give themselves more optimistic messages. Imagine the impact this attitude has on developing self-regard. Naturally, the more positive we feel about our capabilities, the more positive we feel about our selves as a whole. This is one of the many examples of the multiple connections among the fifteen factors.

Another valuable strategy is to expand gratitude. What are you grateful for right now? Stop, take a breath, and name five things. Right now! We really mean it! Stop right now before you read any further and list five things you are grateful for. We guarantee your state just changed if you did this quick exercise, as it will every time you do it! Now your attitude is more open and positive and ready to move forward with helping your clients to avail themselves of the many opportunities in this book.

TRANSFORMATIONAL BENEFITS

Increasing your optimism may very well change every part of your life—and we do not make such broad, sweeping statements carelessly! You will find data on the positive effects of optimism, for example, in *Learned Optimism* (Seligman, 1990), and much more in *Authentic Happiness* (Seligman, 2002), *The EQ Edge* (Stein & Book, 2000), the Positive Psychology Center at www.positivepsycholo-gy.org, and the EI Consortium at www.e:consortium.org. There is so much research supporting this statement that we can confidently assert that the business case for optimism is amazing. The cost-benefit ratio is as good as it gets. For very little investment, your clients can learn to change their thoughts to more positive ones, which will result in better heath and in better engagement with others. What we believe is manifested through the messages we give ourselves. Our self-talk has an enormous influence on what our future reality will become.

STAR PERFORMER

Nelson Mandela has been hailed by many as one of the most inspirational leaders in the world. Mandela was willing to be imprisoned for years if that's what it took to achieve the right result. He continually held out the possibility, even the probability, of the high-level transformation he envisioned. His undying optimism led him and his country to an entirely new way of being together with much greater respect for all. His service as president of South Africa rallied his people's optimistic belief that the hurdles handled could be successfully. He gave people the courage to show up and vote and to continue participating in their government.

REEL PERFORMER

The Wizard of Oz is a treasure of characters learning to believe there are answers to the problems they face. Dorothy is the leader. This child's "can do" optimism in the face of her own great challenge inspires the Tin Man, Scarecrow, and Cowardly Lion to face their fears and achieve what they truly desire.

After a tornado in Kansas knocks her unconscious, Dorothy finds herself in the Land of Oz. She is encouraged to be optimistic that she can find her way home by the good Witch of the North, who says she must travel to find the Wizard of Oz. On meeting Scarecrow, she draws on her growing reservoir of optimism and convinces him the Wizard will help him find what he most desires, a brain. She next inspires Lion to believe that he will find courage and the Tin Man to believe that he will find a heart.

They go through many trials getting to the Wizard just to learn that he is a phony. However, in the midst of this challenge, each one recognizes that acting as if they would get what they most wanted actually caused them to develop the desired skill on their own. If we are feeling deeply challenged, even scared, we suspect that Dorothy would advise us to remember that we just don't know the answer *yet*. If we will just act as if we are confident the problem will be resolved, our faithful action will make it so! Finally, she'd advise us to focus our intention and willingness while we click our heels and say, "There's no place like home!"

Happiness

WHAT IS IT?

We all think we know what happiness really is. But do we? Bar-On (2002, p. 18) says it's "the ability to feel satisfied with one's life, to enjoy oneself and others, and to have fun." He continues by saying that "happiness combines self-satisfaction, general contentment, and the ability to enjoy life." Most importantly perhaps, Dr. Bar-On found in doing his extensive research that happiness is a "by-product and/or barometric indicator of one's overall degree of emotional intelligence and emotional functioning."

Notice that the definition indicates that our level of happiness is an indicator of all of our emotional intelligence. Certainly one of the most important words in the definition is *satisfaction.* Our level of satisfaction with present circumstances will greatly impact our ability to be happy and the whole range of our emotional intelligence.

Webster's (1993) definition helps us notice the range in levels of happiness that are possible: "a state of well-being characterized by relative permanence, by dominantly agreeable emotion ranging in value from mere contentment to deep and intense joy in living, and by a natural desire for its continuation."

Three types of happiness are discussed by Martin Seligman (2002) in *Authentic Happiness*—"the Pleasant Life, the Good Life, and the Meaningful Life." Simple pleasures, often physical ones,

111

dominate the Pleasant Life, a concept that is also identified with hedonism. This entails a focus on maximizing pleasures such as money, food, and clothes, while minimizing pain. American consumerism is a glaring exemplar of this strategy for happiness.

Getting what we desire is central to Seligman's definition for the Good Life. This could be standard hedonism, like a great dessert, but it often goes further, such as a quest for knowledge and career advancement. Building your career may be so important to you that you are willing to endure substantial discomfort and even pain from working the long hours it takes in order to attain your goal.

Making the world a better place for others is central to the Meaningful Life. With this form of happiness we seek to give to others. It is about coming more alive through generosity.

WHY SHOULD WE CARE ABOUT HAPPINESS?

How often do we say we want to be more productive? Increased productivity means more successfully achieving our goals and fulfilling our desires. For some people these achievements are so closely identified with happiness that they become their only meaningful criteria. For others, happiness requires more abstract conditions, such as a healthy environment and inner peace.

The extensive amount of research on happiness has established the links between happiness and several factors, including health, truly rewarding career development, and being a useful and contributing member of an organization, community, and/or family. Your level of happiness affects the development and exercise of all your skills and relies on all the factors of your emotional intelligence.

HOW CAN WE BUILD HAPPINESS?

 GROW YOUR HAPPINESS

Would you rather be happy or would you rather be right?

Every day for a month notice whenever it seems like you have to be right in order to be happy. Choose to be happy and forego being right. See what happens.

Seligman (2002, p. 80) cites a traditional saying:

"If you want to be happy . . .

　　. . . for an hour, take a nap.

　　. . . for a day, go fishing.

　　. . . for a month, get married.

　　. . . for a year, get an inheritance.

　　. . . for a lifetime, help someone."

What kind of happiness do you want? What is your purpose? It is interesting how core philosophical questions become so vital to our choosing the most effective strategies in building happiness. Basic strategies to grow happiness include:

- Getting good exercise and releasing endorphins
- Reflecting—either on your own, such as through journal writing, or with a colleague
- Paying attention to your "wanting." How will you know when you have enough?
- Sharing what you have with others in need

TRANSFORMATIONAL BENEFITS

In his book *The Art of Happiness,* the Dalai Lama (1998, pp. 13–14, 20) asserts that "the purpose of life is to seek happiness. . . .[and] happiness can be achieved by training the mind. . . . [H]appiness is determined more by one's state of mind than by external events."

To experience the transformational benefits of expanding our happiness, we must pay attention to our self-talk. If we are both intentional about our quality of life and hopeful, the transformational benefits of happiness will have an expansive effect on our whole life.

As we seek happiness, particularly when we center on the Meaningful Life, we slow down and open to our inherent compassion. This brings about a chain reaction; life unfolds with a natural flow, rather than with all the fits and starts so common to our enormously fast-paced lives. This relaxation of our self-importance helps us to connect being and doing.

With increased happiness you can also experience valuable changes in your physical well-being, being more at ease and more cheerful. Happy people live longer and more fully enjoy the time they are alive.

 ## STAR PERFORMER

President Jimmy Carter smiles and speaks with a serenity and compassion that is unmistakably representative of an internal peace of mind. Through his continued efforts to help resolve conflict around the world, he demonstrates a deeply contagious happiness and productivity so remarkable that he has been awarded the Nobel Peace Prize.

 ## REEL PERFORMER

In *Love, Actually*, Hugh Grant, Emma Thompson, and many other well-known performers demonstrate the power of choosing happiness through opening to love. The movie opens with a reflection from Britain's Prime Minister, played by Hugh Grant, that, while so many are focused on the frightening challenges in our world, he refuses to let that dominate his thoughts. He says the scenes at Heathrow Airport teach him something different. Every time he is there, he sees a wide variety of people expressing love and joy as they wish fond farewells or welcome loved ones back. The end of the movie makes the point unmistakably with many heart-warming scenes of people greeting returning loved ones.

THREE

Emotional Intelligence Workouts to Build Effective Skills

Part Three contains the experiential learning scenarios we call "workouts." There are three to four workouts for each of the EI competencies discussed in Part Two. In using these workouts, it is important that you understand the EI competency you are seeking to grow, are sensitive to the potential vulnerability of your clients when addressing these topics, and understand the process of behavioral change.

BE INFORMED

We recommend you refer to the appropriate content in Part Two before using any workout. Depending on the circumstances and your knowledge about the competency, you may need to do additional reading and research. The References and Resources sections at the back of this book contain information to assist you in your developmental effort.

FACILITATOR SKILLS

Pay careful attention to the necessary facilitator skills and to the best practices recommended when working with emotional intelligence. We have indicated the level of skill usually needed for each of the workouts. However, what will be easy for some clients could be difficult for others. Thus, you will need to apply your own judgment and knowledge about the specific situation you are working in as you use these workouts.

Working in this field requires that the trainer, facilitator, coach, therapist, or manager be particularly attentive to his or her client's skills, capabilities, and needs. Fortunately, there are two excellent sources of best practices for training and development with emotional intelligence. The Consortium for Research on Emotional Intelligence in Organizations provides Guidelines for Best Practice, which are found at www.eiconsortium.org, and *Promoting Emotional Intelligence in Organizations* by Cherniss and Adler (2000) is entirely focused on this topic.

While all the points in these best practices lists are valuable, a few of the most important aspects to address include the following:

- *Provide a safe environment.* Work at a pace that is comfortable for your clients. Use strategies to empower them to influence their learning process and acknowledge their concerns and their successes.
- *Establish and observe rules governing confidentiality and disclosure.* From the first time your client(s) become aware of the work they will be doing, they should know what, why, and how any information about them will be used. Be certain that you are clear about what you will discuss and with whom after your interventions. The norm is that you will not discuss any information with anyone else. This norm creates an environment of trust that is essential for the deep work of change to be addressed successfully. If you are working with a team or group, the first ground rule is usually "What is said here, stays here."
- *Get the learning in the body.* It takes concrete experience to make change. Cognitive understanding of new concepts complements this work, but behavioral change is based on a repeatedly reinforced experiential process. Practice number 16 in the EI Consortium list correctly states: "Rely on Experiential Methods: Active, concrete, experiential methods tend to work best for learning social and emotional competencies. Development activi-

ties that engage all the senses and that are dramatic and powerful can be especially effective."

- *Pace your clients.* Just like the saying in real estate—that it's all about location, location, location—to successfully guide transformative EI development, you need to pace, pace, pace your client(s). If they are concerned about doing the work and don't have any experience, go slowly. Start with simple challenges and move to more difficult ones as understanding and trust grow. If they already have considerable experience in this area, keep your work at a more challenging level to maintain their interest.
- *Follow through.* Longlasting behavioral change happens only when there is a neuronal change. Old habits must be extinguished and new ones developed. This is possible, but it doesn't happen overnight. It takes repeated practice and reinforcement.
- *Evaluate your work.* Some of the first questions to ask when you begin working with your client(s) are, "How will you know your objectives have been accomplished?" and "What specifically will be different?" Be alert to the situations in which research on the results might be possible. The more data we can gather on the benefits of this work, the more reliable and relied on the field of developing emotional and social intelligence will become.

CHANGE

Perhaps the most critical ingredient in the work to build emotional intelligence skills is the ability to facilitate change. As discussed above, follow-through is essential to support effective change. Other key practices listed by the EI Consortium include the following:

- Build in support, such as support groups.
- Use examples of people well known in society or in the organization who exemplify the skill.
- Encourage using these skills and the language of EI on the job.
- Develop an organizational culture that supports learning. To the best extent you can, seek to have your work supported by the organization where you are working and to be role modeled by the top leadership. After all, the phenomenon of "monkey see, monkey do" is still the fundamental learning strategy for us homo sapiens.

If you are working with an assessment tool, you may be able to measure your results using that tool. For example, you could use the EQ-i or one of the other measures for a pre-test and post-test.

USING THE WORKOUTS

The workouts can be used with intact teams, groups, or individuals. The instructions are written for groups, but most activities are easily adapted for use with individuals. Where necessary, we provide additional instructions to help with the adaptation. You may also have special dynamics for your group that must be anticipated and addressed carefully. For example, if you are running a session across teams, you'll need to be aware of all the issues discussed above and work with any situations where you find differing levels of capability or buy-in. Go slowly and pay attention. This can be tricky. Further, addressing issues of confidentiality can be even more important. If you are working with a group of individuals who do not work together, you will need to address the near certainty that they will be at different levels of readiness for your work, and, again, it will take careful work to establish a safe environment so that they will open up with one another.

The first three sections of each workout—Purpose, Thumbnail, and Outcomes—explain the following:

- Purpose answers WHY you would have the people do this workout;
- Thumbnail tells you HOW participants will engage with the instructional material to generate the learning experience;
- Outcome explains WHAT your target is—the desired results they can achieve.

The workouts contain reproducible handouts (also included on the companion CD) that you may copy for your participants. Although the instructions precede the handout, it will always prove helpful to familiarize yourself with the handout before expecting to understand the instructions at the level of fine detail in which they were written!

Self-Regard

Of Thine Own Self Be Aware

Purpose

To expand recognition of the process for building self-regard.

Thumbnail

45 minutes to 2 hours

The facilitator will create a reflective process by having participants respond to a list of questions while they are given time in a quiet environment for self-reflection, followed by discussion on what is learned. There must be a high level of trust before this exercise can be shared productively among team members.

Outcome

Begin drafting a powerful map for initiating a self-exploration process that over time will build healthier positive self-regard.

Audience

- Intact team
- Individual working with a coach

Facilitator Competencies

Moderate to Advanced

Materials

- Of Thine Own Self Be Aware Handout
- Paper and pens

Time Matrix

Activity	Estimated Time
Brief background on self-regard	5–10 minutes
Self-reflection and responding to questions	30–60 minutes
Group debrief	10 minutes per member
Total	**45 minutes to 2 hours**

Instructions

1. Briefly explain self-regard and discuss the intent of the workout, which is to build awareness of self-regard and develop it by adding something of real value to participants' lives.

2. Read aloud (or to one's self if this is applied as an individual exercise):

   "In a quiet space of self-reflection, get in touch with something you want in your life. It should be something significant, meaningful, and important, not necessarily an object, although it can be. Humans tend to use objects as symbols or placeholders for values that are actually more abstract. Someone might say for instance, 'I want a new boat for water skiing,' when actually he wants the feelings of importance, success, and power he associates with people who have new ski boats. Merely getting the boat may or may not bring the feelings sought.

   "In this workout you will set a goal to feel more congruent and worthy in some aspect of your life (work, family, personal, etc.) by achieving the goal you have just identified. The process of fully accomplishing it will naturally take a more extended period of time beyond this exercise, during which you will practice new behaviors, attitudes, and expectations. The scope of this workout is to focus on clearly defining what those new conditions will need to be, how you will be able to recognize them, and how you will motivate yourself to persist in your efforts to incorporate them."

3. Distribute the handout, pens, and extra paper and instruct participants to take thirty minutes for self-reflection and consideration of the questions on the worksheet, then write down the answers. Emphasize that this is a personal exercise and the answers are only for themselves. Encourage the participants to be honest with themselves.

4. Conduct a group debriefing and encourage the participants to make a commitment to continue the learning from this exercise. *Note:* Participants should not be asked to share personal matters in a team setting unless the team is well integrated and a proven foundation of trust exists. You can still ask questions like: Was this an enjoyable exercise? Why or why not? What is the value of this kind of exercise? What sorts of questions or insights did it generate for you?

OF THINE OWN SELF BE AWARE HANDOUT

Answer the following questions in detail. Use as much extra paper as you need. This is confidential—for you alone.

1. What is something I want to accomplish in my life that, when achieved, will lead me to feel really good about myself?

2. How will I have to think about myself and my life differently to accomplish this goal?

3. What feelings about my life and myself will have to change for me to accomplish this goal?

4. How will I have to act differently?

5. What has kept me from thinking and feeling and acting in these ways up to this point?

Self-Regard

Reconciliation

Purpose

To give participants an experience of increased self-regard through a reconciliation process.

Thumbnail

35 minutes or more, depending on number of participants, plus individual working time between sessions

The participants revisit two situations—one in which they feel like they caused hurt or harm to someone else, and one in which they felt that they were harmed—and undertake to reach better resolutions. This also can be used as a self-directed practice.

Outcome

To experience the elevated sense of self-regard that comes from initiating a reconciliation process.

Audience

- Intact team
- Unaffiliated group
- Individual working with a coach

Facilitator Competencies

Advanced

Materials

- Reconciliation Handout
- Writing paper and pens

Time Matrix

Activity	Estimated Time
Facilitator explains the process of reconciliation	20 minutes
Individuals conduct steps one and two	On their own
Each individual discusses the experience	15 minutes per person
Total	**35 minutes or more + individual time**

Instructions

1. Provide writing paper and pens.
2. Distribute the handout. Tell the participants that this is an exercise on forgiveness and reconciliation, that it's not necessarily an easy process for anyone, but making apologies and repairing relationships is actually a normal and common part of human behavior. Since they are choosing the incidents to deal with, and since at least this step of it is only hypothetical, they should generally be able to handle the tension okay. Be optimistic and suggest to them that new behavior is easy once a new understanding of the situation becomes available.
3. Ask them to list three relationships in their lives where they hurt or offended someone and would like to repair things. Have them rank the incidents in order from the apparently least difficult to the apparently most difficult to repair.
4. Ask them to read Step One from the handout and then, starting with the apparently least difficult incident, ask them to write down the actual

things that they would say to the person whose forgiveness they seek. Have them write the responses they realistically anticipate they would receive in response to each of their comments.

5. Explain that this exercise provides them with an off-line opportunity to thoroughly think through the exchange of feelings and reasons they will be having with this other person—someone who may still feel like the damage cannot be undone. It's true that the facts cannot be changed, but what they mean most assuredly can be. (Ask the participants to do this with the other two incidents as well, now if they have time, or later on their own.)

6. Encourage them to follow through and actually have these conversations and remind them that much of who we think we are gets built up around our experiences of being treated unfairly, so there are likely to be some strong emotional responses from the other person as the emotional energy patterns are released.

7. Now ask them to read Step Two, list three incidents in which they felt harmed, and proceed in a similar manner.

8. Ask them to write for five or ten minutes about what they learned from this exercise and again encourage them to follow through and actually have these conversations.

9. If you have time, and wish to do so, invite participants to share some of their reflections using the kinds of questions below:
   - Was it more difficult to work with the incidents in which you are asking for forgiveness or those in which you were offering it?
   - How important was it to get into the other person's point of view to be able to complete the exercise?

RECONCILIATION HANDOUT

People benefit from conducting a reconciliation process because two kinds of emotional anchors drag on our productivity and impede our enjoyment of life—guilt and rejection. If you look carefully you will notice they are the flip sides of the same coin: When we choose not to forgive others we are putting a barrier between them and us that they cannot remove, and regardless of how justified our rejection may seem, at least at the subconscious level, we feel guilty for excluding them, just as they feel guilty for having injured us. Self-regard can't help but grow when those sorts of burdens are relieved.

Step One

First, you are going to seek reconciliation with someone you have hurt or offended or who thinks you have. Obviously, sincere humility and apology are crucial ingredients, but it does not mean you should grovel. It is important that you bring your healthiest level of appropriate self-regard with you so the other person can recognize he or she is not dealing with a needy beggar but an intact individual who sincerely wants to repair a valuable relationship. When you approach someone who feels that you have harmed him or her, expressing your vulnerability (instead of concealing it as we usually do) is generally the best defense.

Tell the person that you have been thinking about the incident a lot lately and feel that it is time to make a new effort to resolve it. Tell the person that you'd like to start off by offering a sincere apology and ask forgiveness for whatever it was you did (or he or she says you did). Sometimes people may still feel very hurt and harbor a level of hostility and resentment that causes them to try to extort a confession from you for something that you never did. It's OK. This is no longer a contest about who's right and wrong. Sincerely say the following sentence (exactly!), "I have never felt as if I did that, but if you do, then I need your forgiveness more than ever."

If the person is ready, it will unfold pretty easily and naturally from there. If he or she is not, say that you understand and that you just wanted to do whatever you could to get things started. Eight out of ten times the person will be ready. In the other two you'll have done your best and know you can feel good about it. But in that instance be careful not to start judging and blaming the person for not accepting your invitation. He or she also did his or her best. Otherwise, the good results you started may be further delayed for both of you.

Remember that much of our identity and who we think we are gets built up around our experiences of being treated unfairly, so there are likely to be some strong emotional responses from both of you as the patterns that had been holding this energy in place begin to dissolve and are released.

Step Two

The second step in this exercise is to extend reconciliation to someone who has hurt or harmed you in some way that is still unresolved. This is a little tricky because if you just walk up to someone you haven't been speaking to and say, "I forgive you for the terrible thing you did to me!" it's a bit more like a fresh accusation than a genuine attempt at reconciliation.

In fact, things will probably proceed best if you begin pretty much like you did when you were asking for reconciliation from another. Say that you've been thinking about the way things ended up and you want to do whatever you can to get your relationship into better balance. It's true that the facts cannot be changed, but what they mean to your relationship most assuredly can be.

Whether the other person shows it or not, one of his or her biggest concerns is that you are condemning him or her for what happened. However, if you maintain an open, non-judgmental attitude and posture, it will help remove this stumbling block. Whether you are standing or sitting, fold your hands loosely in front of you in a relaxed manner. Make gentle, brief but repeated eye contact in a manner that says, "Just curious . . . just wondering." Let your body seem a little tired, as if you are tired from carrying the weight of this matter.

These kinds of nonverbal cues for openness will make it easier for the person to connect at a deeper level and begin to express how he or she feels about the situation. Just to get started talking about things again will help lead toward the person's ability or desire to ask for your forgiveness.

To encourage an atmosphere of communication, you can give the person two messages that will help. Whether you say it directly or not, convey, "I don't like to have these awkward feelings between us" and "We are both losing out on something valuable as long as they persist."

If the person shows a willingness to go further, after having had a chance to say something about what it's like from the other side, you can respond matter-of-factly, "Look, it hurt, but I've been healing, and I'm not stuck on this the way I used to be." Then you will be conveying your forgiveness honestly and sincerely, whether he or she feels worthy of receiving it yet or not.

After you complete the writing assignment in preparation for each of these conversations, take some time to reflect about what you learned and how you feel about yourself, your strengths, and your shortcomings. Then follow through, have conversations, and see how much better everyone feels!

Self-Regard

Toot Your Horn and Scratch Your Back

Purpose

To encourage people to give themselves a break. To shift the focus away from all the things they need to accomplish in the future and the things they regret not accomplishing in the past. To zero in on the successes they have had—small and large. To identify what they are not giving themselves enough credit for and to celebrate their accomplishments.

Thumbnail

25 to 45 minutes

Facilitator or coach provides a list of the different roles people may play throughout their lives and asks participants to identify the areas that apply to them. They articulate the good things they have done in those areas and celebrate their accomplishments. The facilitator may need to help participants surface their successes and view them as accomplishments.

Outcomes

- Greater self-appreciation
- Enhanced self-regard

Audience

- Intact team
- Unaffiliated group

Facilitator Competencies ◯

Easy

Materials

- Aspect and Roles Handout
- Back scratchers, whistles, toy horns, or noisemakers and bags to keep them in
- Tissue paper to cover contents of bags

Time Matrix

Activity	Estimated Time
Discuss self-regard	5–10 minutes
Select areas and list accomplishments	5–10 minutes
Discussion in pairs	10–15 minutes
Debrief and celebrate	5–10 minutes
Total	**25 to 45 minutes**

Instructions

1. Have people sitting in table groups with an even number of people at each table.
2. In the center of each table have two bags
   - Bag containing back scratchers
   - Bag containing whistles, horns, or noisemakers
   Make it evident that something is being hidden to create curiosity.
3. Distribute the Aspects and Roles Handout
4. Discuss self-regard. Ask participants if they ever find themselves focusing so much on what they want to accomplish that they forget to stop and appreciate the small everyday successes they have had.

5. Ask participants to check off those categories on the Aspects and Roles Handout that pertain to them. Ask them these questions:
   - Which of these types of groups do you participate in?
   - Are you ever in any of these roles?
6. Have them select three areas and list things they have accomplished in each area. Give them examples such as the following:
   - Work—individual, project, or team success; help another employee, help your boss, help develop or coach an employee; assume a new responsibility
   - Home—clean the house, cook, do repairs, pay bills, decorate, make it safe
   - Health—exercise, watch diet, do special things to mitigate a particular disease or condition, sleep, meditate
7. Ask them to divide into pairs (or threes if necessary) and take turns sharing their accomplishments. When listening to the other person's accomplishments, each should provide positive feedback such as "great job" and "that was a lot to get done." Tell them they don't need to share anything they feel is too personal.
8. Reconvene the group and debrief by asking:
   - Did anything surprising happen? Any *aha*'s?
   - Did you realize you have been overlooking things you achieved?
9. Have them take a few moments to appreciate themselves:
   - Retrieve the back scratchers and have them scratch their own backs. An alternative would be to have them pat themselves on the back (their own backs).
   - Retrieve the whistles, horns, or noisemakers from the bag and have them toot their own horns!
10. Ask them to take their back scratchers and noisemakers with them and use them as reminders to stop and appreciate themselves.

ASPECT AND ROLES HANDOUT

____ Team   ____ Friend
____ Work   ____ Spouse
____ Home   ____ Child
____ Health   ____ Employee
____ Church   ____ Boss
____ Community   ____ Citizen
____ Parent

List your accomplishments in three of the preceding roles or areas.

1. _____ (selected area)

2. _____ (selected area)

3. _____ (selected area)

Emotional Self-Awareness

Are You in Touch?

Purpose

To demonstrate how quickly emotions can change and how seemingly insignificant things can impact emotions. The exercise also provides a technique to calm emotions and regain emotional footing.

 ## Thumbnail

25 to 40 minutes

The facilitator or coach will introduce an irritating influence to cause people to feel unsettled. The influence will cease and people will be asked to focus on how their emotions were changing during the "irritating interval." The facilitator will then lead the group through a calming visualization. Finally, the group will be asked to reflect on the entire experience and relate it to how they can manage the emotions in their lives. The facilitator needs to have a comfort level with leading a physical exercise to increase self-awareness.

Outcomes

- Increased awareness of the capricious nature of emotions
- Better understanding of how ancillary events can impact emotions
- Greater sensitivity to how changing emotions can affect human interaction
- Gain a new technique to regain emotional centeredness

Audience

- Intact team
- Unaffiliated group
- Individual working with a coach

Facilitator Competencies

Moderate to Advanced

Materials

- Are You in Touch? Handout
- Flip chart and markers
- Cacophonous music that is jarring and unsettling
    - Suggestion: James Tenney *Selected Works 1961–1969,* New World Records. www.newworldrecords.org
    - Please adhere to copyright laws when using recorded music.

Time Matrix

Activity	Estimated Time
Talk to group on a subject of interest	5–10 minutes
Debrief using the handout	5–10 minutes
Conduct Hook-Ups exercise	5 minutes
Participants record experience on handout	5–10 minutes
Review extended exercise on handout	5 minutes
Total	**25 to 40 minutes**

Instructions

1. Talk to the group or individual client about emotional intelligence (or another subject of your choosing).

2. After speaking for a couple minutes, turn on the cacophonous music. Have the music loud enough for everyone to hear but not so loud they cannot hear you. You (the facilitator) respond as if the music is not playing. You do not react in any way to the music—no wincing, twitching, eye rolling, or body stiffening.
   - If someone asks you to stop the music, calmly tell him or her you will stop it in a little while.
   - If someone asks you to turn the music down, pretend to do so, but do not change the volume.

3. At the conclusion of your brief discussion of emotional intelligence, ask the group the ten questions on the Are You in Touch? Handout. Do not distribute the handout at this time.

4. Have the group do the following physical exercise called Hook-Ups, which is designed to increase self-awareness and reduce tension. The exercise helps re-establish emotional centeredness and can be used when feeling angry, confused, or sad.

   ### Hook–Ups*

   Hook-Ups connect the electrical circuits in the body, containing and thus focusing both attention and disorganized energy. As the mind and body relax, energy circulates through areas blocked by tension.

   Part One: Sitting, the student crosses left ankle over right. Student extends arms, crossing left wrist over right. Student then interlaces fingers and draws hands up toward chest. Student may now close eyes, breathe deeply, and relax for about a minute. *Optional:* Student presses tongue flat against the roof of mouth on inhalation, and relaxes the tongue on exhalation.

   Part Two: When ready, student uncrosses legs. Student touches fingertips of both hands together, continuing to breathe deeply for about another minute.

---

*Taken from *Brain Gym* by P.E. Dennison and G.E. Dennison, 1989, Edu-Kinesthetics, Inc., Ventura, CA. Used with permission of the authors.

5. Distribute the handout and review with the group the Extended Exercise, which is at the end of the handout. Get commitment from the participants to take and record their emotional pulse in this regimented way until it becomes second nature and they find themselves automatically checking in with their emotions.

ARE YOU IN TOUCH? HANDOUT

1. How did you feel when we first started?
2. What are you feeling right now?
3. Why do you feel differently?
4. How did you emotionally react to the music? Did it impact your attitude?
5. Did it happen immediately or take a few minutes to build?
6. Did the music lead you to feel more or less open to positive interactions with others?
7. How did you feel about the facilitator or coach while the music was playing?
8. List all the ways in which you were aware of the music's effect on your emotions and attitude.
9. What did you feel when the music was turned off?
10. When the music was turned off, did any of the negative emotions caused during the time it was playing disappear automatically?
11. Think of a situation in your life in which you were feeling pretty good (or pretty bad) and some event or new information suddenly caused your feelings to change dramatically. What happened? What impact did it have on you and on the quality of your interactions with others?

Extended Exercise

Do this in the course of your normal day.

At selected times, stop and check your "emotional pulse," and write down what is happening.

- Determine the specific times during the day and evening that you will stop and check.
- Regularly record your responses to the following questions in a notebook, personal digital assistant, or appointment book:
    - What are you feeling now?
    - When did you start feeling this way?
    - Why are you feeling this way? What is the cause?

Emotional Self-Awareness

It Just Bubbles Up

Purpose

To connect with the emotions that drive unproductive behavior.

 ### Thumbnail

35 to 50 minutes

Team (or individual) identifies situations in which they regret the way they acted. They pinpoint the unproductive behaviors and recall what was going on physiologically at that point in the process.

Outcomes

- Be more in touch with changing emotions
- Build understanding of how emotions drive behaviors
- Recognize cues that emotions have changed

Audience

- Intact team
- Unaffiliated group
- Individual working with a coach

Facilitator Competencies ◯ ◑

Easy to Moderate

Materials

- It Just Bubbles Up Handout
- Flip charts and markers
- Pens

Time Matrix

Activity	Estimated Time
Identify situations, feelings, and responses	15 minutes
Discuss physical reactions	15 minutes
Debrief	5–20 minutes
Total	**35 to 50 minutes**

Instructions

1. Distribute handouts and pens to the participants.
2. Ask the team (or individual) to recall a significant situation (as recent as possible) in which they regret acting the way they did. Then ask them to write a brief description of what they regret specifically.
3. Ask them to write down in Steps 2 and 3 of the handout how they felt in the above situation, such as fearful, anxious, defensive, happy, embarrassed, and why they felt that way—for example, because they felt publicly insulted. Handout Steps 2 and 3 complete this model:

   "I felt _____ because _____."

   For example, "I felt foolish because no one volunteered when I asked."
4. In Steps 4 and 5 of the handout, have them write how they responded to those feelings.
5. Ask them to write about how they would have felt if it had gone perfectly, in accordance with Step 6 of the handout.

6. Have your participants look back and do their best to assess how others around them were feeling at the time. Did others know how they were feeling? What evidence did participants rely on to come to their conclusions? Upon reflection, do they feel they assessed the situation correctly? Did they do sufficient reality testing? Record their answers on a flip chart.

7. Ask them to evaluate their decision making from as objective a point of view as possible and record their thoughts on a flip chart. Did they feel as if they were under pressure? Could they have supplemented their emotional self-awareness with better impulse control in this situation? How?

8. Debrief the participants. Have them discuss what they are most often paying attention to instead of the sensory cues from their bodies. Write their answers on a flip chart. Most of the time at work we are preoccupied with intellectual, symbolic, verbal issues. Increasing our sensitivity to our body's internal states requires that we "shift brains," slow down, and pay conscious attention to the sensory input we generally tend to process subconsciously. Ask if anyone wants to share his or her insights with the group, but don't push anyone to share.

IT JUST BUBBLES UP HANDOUT

1. Have you recently been in a situation in which you wished you had not acted or responded in a particular way? Describe the situation.

2. What were you feeling in the above situation?
   ____ Fearful
   ____ Defensive
   ____ Anxious
   ____ Happy
   ____ Embarrassed in a positive way—for instance, someone paid you a compliment and you were glad he or she did and felt it was appropriately done
   ____ Embarrassed in a negative way—for example, you were publicly insulted
   ____ Other

3. Why did you feel that way?

4. How did you respond to those feelings listed in Step 2?
   - _____ Withdrew completely from the situation
   - _____ Stayed in the situation but tried to steer the interaction in a different direction
   - _____ Stayed in the situation and pretended you were in agreement
   - _____ Became verbally or physically abusive
   - _____ Disparaged the other person or people
   - _____ Tried to out-talk the other person or people
   - _____ Other
5. How was your body responding while you were feeling in the way you indicated
   - _____ Folded arms
   - _____ Clenched jaw
   - _____ Sweat—lip, brow, under arms, scalp, palms
   - _____ Twitching
   - _____ Tapping foot
   - _____ Drumming fingers
   - _____ Stomach clenched
   - _____ Other
6. Identify how you will act differently in the future when you notice the reactions from Step 4 or your physical cues from Step 5.

Emotional Self-Awareness

Moving Toward and Moving Away

Purpose

To help participants understand how the body's basic biological response of "moving toward" and "moving away from" influences all of their emotional activity.

Thumbnail

70 minutes

Participants will observe and explore a list of emotional scenarios that they regularly encounter, notice the distinctions among them, and describe the differences they discover.

Outcome

By exploring the suggested situations and feelings, participants will become more aware of how they respond emotionally to those issues they want to approach and those they want to avoid in their lives.

Audience

- Intact team
- Unaffiliated group
- Individual working with a coach

145

Facilitator Competencies ◑

Moderate

Materials

- Moving Toward and Moving Away Handout
- Paper and pens

Time Matrix

Activity	Estimated Time
Have participants think about which things they naturally approach and avoid	10 minutes
List specific instances for each feeling	15 minutes
Write distinctions between states	15 minutes
Ask them to notice how these emotions and states affect their choices	10 minutes
Have them explore in pairs how they actually communicate the listed feelings	20 minutes
Total	**70 minutes**

Instructions

1. Provide paper and pens, and distribute the handout.
2. Ask participants to think about how fundamental the act of moving toward and moving away from is for all life—even plants.
3. Ask them to build a list in each category under Number 1 on the handout of the kinds of things and situations that they naturally move toward and those they naturally move away from.
4. Have participants describe a specific instance for each of the feelings under Number 2 on the handout.
5. When they have responded to each of the seven different feelings, have them go back and add descriptions of how their bodies felt physically while they were experiencing those emotions.

6. Now ask the participants to recall specific instances for the different states listed in Number 3, and have them write down the physical and emotional distinctions they experience.
7. In Number 4 have them fill in the blanks.
8. Finally, ask them to work in pairs for Step 5. Here they will express the described emotional attitudes to their partners as realistically as possible, and their partners will observe and take notes of all the nonverbal components of the message. Remind them to notice tonality, volume, posture, skin tone, eye contact, and so forth. Have participants discuss what they learned.

MOVING TOWARD AND
MOVING AWAY HANDOUT

Developing this competency in emotional self-awareness increases your ability to know *what* you are feeling, *when* you are feeling it, and what *causes* those feelings in you, as well as their degree of intensity. In beginning this exercise, take a moment to reflect on the fact that human beings, along with all living organisms, share the same two fundamental responses to the events in their environment: approach or move toward, and avoid or move away from.

1. Now think about what sorts of things you naturally tend to approach and avoid, and list three or four in each category.

    Things, situations, and kinds of people I approach:

    Things, situations, and kinds of people I avoid:

2. Now, think of a *specific instance* in which you felt each of the following feelings. Address all, but you can start with whichever one seems most appealing. Describe what sort of situations and conditions and what sorts of behavior by other people has prompted you to feel. . .

Stressed

Excited and Hopeful

Frustrated

Playful

Worried

Relieved

Furious

Now go back to each category and add a few descriptions of the ways your body feels when you are experiencing each emotion. Where is there tension? Heat? Coolness? Pain? Pleasure? Weakness? What other body feedback do you notice?

3. Write down a few of the distinctions (physical and emotional) that you experience in the following states: jealousy, a job interview, expressing condolences for a death, and successfully completing a big project. Please take enough time to access real memories of specific emotional situations. It will help you be able to differentiate how strongly you feel when you experience different kinds of emotions.

4. Considering what you have learned about how you feel and the situations in which you feel that way, now make a two-column listing of what causes you to move toward some things and away from others. Use the model below:

I move toward _____ because _____.

I move away from _____ because _____.

Move Toward	Move Away

5. The way in which we communicate to others that we want them to move toward us or to move away from us is clearly a critical skill; they are two of the most important messages we ever give! So, using specific situations from memory as your reference, work in pairs to discover and describe what you do to communicate to other people that you are experiencing the following emotions:

- Enthusiasm, excitement—that you are eager to begin a new project and hope they will want to work on it with you.
- Frustrated, thwarted—that you need some new suggestions, but they'd better be good!

Emotional Self-Awareness

Grow Your Personal Power

Purpose

Groups and teams will learn the benefits of being quiet, making connections, and redirecting energy from their heads to their hearts. Within this feeling state, they can create expansively and grow their personal power.

Thumbnail

20 to 30 minutes

Participants first walk around making eye contact to and connect with each other in silence. Then the facilitator guides a discussion based on a reflection of what participants are feeling, divided into two categories: personal power and pessimism.

Outcomes

- To recognize the power of connecting with yourself and others through the noncognitive signals and feelings which emanate from the heart.
- Recognize that personal power is built from the inside out and is deeply influenced by the messages you give yourself and that you are open to receiving from others.

Audience

- Intact team
- Unaffiliated group

Facilitator Competencies ◯

Easy

Materials

- Flip chart and markers
- Paper and pens

Time Matrix

Activity	Estimated Time
Tell participants to get centered, think positive thoughts	2 minutes
Instruct them to quietly walk around, greeting one another with their eyes in silence	5–10 minutes
Ask them to return to their seats and write about their feelings	3 minutes
Use a flip chart to guide the group to list positive and negative thoughts and come to understand how to better engage their whole minds	10–15 minutes
Total	**20 to 30 minutes**

Instructions

1. Distribute paper and pens; then read the following instructions to the group*:

---

*This exercise was developed by Esther M. Orioli, M.S.Ed, president and CEO of Essi Systems, Inc., and co-creator of the EQ Map®. It is used here with the permission of Ms. Orioli and Essi Systems.

- Take a couple of minutes to get centered. Give yourself positive and peaceful messages. Think of your favorite color, one that gives you feelings of high energy, inspiration, invincibility and surround yourself in it.
- Now get up and quietly walk around the room, stopping as you come to someone when you feel mutually called to make a connection. Stop and look the other person in the eyes, don't talk or touch, silently look at one another in a moment of acknowledgment and connection. After you feel the connection, move on and stop again before another person, as it seems appropriate. Continue making silent connections until I tell you to stop. [Depending on the size of the group give them five to ten minutes.]
- Now spend a few minutes writing down some of the key words that come to you. As you write, use your body as a barometer to help calibrate how you feel.

2. Go to a flip chart and write Personal Power on top and then draw a line down the middle with one column labeled "Positive Outlook" and the other labeled "Pessimistic." Explain that personal power refers to one's own internal resources, energy, and strength. When this energy is positive, you draw on it to meet your challenges and opportunities. When the energy is negative and your outlook is pessimistic, it saps energy from you as you seek to do your work. Now ask participants to share some of the key words that they thought of or experienced during the first part of this workout. For the positive side, you're likely to get words such as alive, smiling, energized, fulfilled, being truly helpful. For the pessimistic side, you could get a few words such as helplessness, victim, dependent, isolated. However, it is more likely that the positive words will predominate.

3. Ask the group to discuss both lists. Talk with them about the value of using positive stress words that bring the energy up in your body. Then have them note the effect of negative stress words. Ask questions, such as "Which type of words is more likely to support you in getting the job done?" "Which support the type of life you would like to have?" Add further questions to fit your group's interests, and open it up for group discussion.

4. Discuss the learnings that are now coming out as a part of the new brain science. For example, the HeartMath Institute (Childre & Martin, 1999) presents substantial information on the second brain around the heart. They discuss the discoveries in the last few decades demonstrating that the heart has its own nervous system and can think on its own. This is the

basis of their advocacy that we understand the messages our hearts send our brains and work with this source of intelligence as well as our brains.

5. Point out that the group gained the opportunity to connect with the heart brain by first moving in silence and connecting with one another. The walking part gave them the opportunity to tap into their intuition and their whole brain awareness—heart and mind. Guide the discussion into talking about the development of personal power through being aware of their emotions and choosing to define themselves from the inside out. We have internal wisdom but often don't use it; instead we take our clues from others about what is happening and what is important. This compromises our own strength as we engage in work and other tasks; it depletes our personal power. When we work from our internal awareness—our personal sense of who we are—we have the opportunity to choose our own direction instead of being at the mercy of others. When this is complemented with greater understanding of our emotions, we can act with greater strength due to enhanced personal awareness and clarity.

Assertiveness

Ramp It Up

Purpose

To help build assertiveness in those who are reticent. It will push them beyond their normal comfort zones and make them stretch their capabilities.

 ## Thumbnail

40 to 110 minutes

Individuals in coaching identify areas in which they need to be more assertive and then select one specific situation from the list. To practice the skill, they then role play until they feel more comfortable. Their follow-on assignment is to be more assertive in two real-life situations. Team members identify lack of assertiveness issues that impact the group's effectiveness. They select the top two to three issues and role play to be more assertive. Their follow-on assignment is to take the learning back to the organization. The facilitator will need to be able to help more aggressive team members calm down so they use the skill of assertiveness with respect and so they model assertiveness effectively and respectfully to those who are not as assertive.

157

Outcomes

- Increased awareness of areas in which participants can be more assertive
- Overcoming barriers to being assertive
- Integrate the learning into their daily lives

Audience

- Intact team
- Individual working with a coach

Facilitator Competencies

Moderate to Advanced

Materials

- Team
  - Role-play handout to be created prior to group exercise from template provided
  - Flip charts, markers, masking tape
- Individual
  - Ramp It Up Handout

Time Matrix

Activity	Estimated Time (Individual)	Estimated Time (Group)
Discuss assertiveness	10–15 minutes	10–15 minutes
Select areas and list barriers and possible remedies	5–15 minutes	20–35 minutes
Role play	15–20 minutes	20–30 minutes
Debrief	10–15 minutes	15–30 minutes
Total	**40 to 65 minutes**	**65 to 110 minutes**

Instructions

Individual

1. As a coach, you should guide the participant through this exercise, helping identify areas for correction, discussing why some behaviors are ineffective, and implementing corrective strategies during the role play.

2. Discuss the concept of assertiveness and why a lack of assertiveness can be an issue in the workplace.

3. Give a copy of the Ramp It Up Handout to the participant. Work through each step with the participant.

4. Based on issues raised, offer to role play some scenarios with your client.

5. Review the assignment at the end of the handout.

6. Set up a time to meet again with the participant and review how the assignment went. Ask questions such as:
   - Which real-life situations did you select?
   - Were you able to be more assertive?
   - What was your comfort level while doing this?
   - What results did you get?
   - Will you do it again in the future?

Group

1. Prior to the exercise, identify those in the team who are considered to be assertive. You want the assertive people, not the aggressive ones. Ask them to help you with the exercise by sharing with the group their perspectives, techniques, and strategies.

2. With the group, discuss the concept of assertiveness and why a lack of assertiveness can be an issue in the workplace.

3. Ask participants to identify issues that impact the team's effectiveness and write what they say on a flip-chart page.

4. Ask them which of those issues listed in Step 3 may be impacted by a lack of assertiveness. Record the responses on another flip-chart page. Stimulate thought with the following examples of problems caused by lack of assertiveness:
   - A surgeon operated on the wrong body part because no one mentioned discrepancies between the documentation and the procedure that they noticed prior to the surgery.

- A company faced financial ruin partially because the people who noticed accounting irregularities did not speak up.

5. Have them discuss the benefits that could be achieved if team members were more assertive. Could problems be avoided or corrected sooner? Would morale improve because people would feel they had more of an impact on the organization?

6. List the barriers to being assertive on a flip-chart page. What stops people from being more assertive? Why do they hold back? Could they lack the skills to effectively express what they are thinking or feeling? Could they be afraid of repercussions?

7. Identify some ways to overcome the barriers. Do people need to enhance their communication skills, build confidence, or practice being assertive in a safe environment?

8. Tell the participants they will take turns role playing more assertive behavior. Ask them to form pairs and distribute the role-play handout.

9. Discuss with the entire group how everyone felt during the role plays.

10. Give the following assignment: Over the next two weeks, be more assertive in two actual work situations.

11. (*Optional*) Find a time after you have completed the assignment to review how it went with a partner or coach.

ROLE-PLAY TEMPLATE

Instructions for Facilitator

Based on the feedback from the team, select an issue similar to one from Step 3 of the team instructions and create a role play. If you are already familiar with the team's issues, you can select an issue yourself. Otherwise, you'll need to do some pre-session research to find an appropriate issue from which to create a scenario. The scenario should include elements similar to the following:

- Person A identifies a problem and brings it to the attention of someone at a higher level of authority—Person B.
- Person B is initially not happy to hear about the problem.
- Person A perseveres by asserting the benefits of addressing the issue sooner rather than later.

The following is the template to be re-created as a handout with the specifics added in for the participants.

Person A = Hunter
Person B = Jordan

There is a problem with _____*(problem area)*_____. Hunter notices it and is determined to make Jordan, the ____*(title of person in authority)*____ aware of it.

Hunter: Jordan, I'd like a few minutes of your time to talk to you about something.
Jordan (a little abruptly): Yes, what is it? I really don't have much time.
Hunter: This won't take very long
Jordan: OK, let's hear it
Hunter: I've noticed that _____*(description of problem)*_____

Jordan responds less than enthusiastically and doesn't seem to be very interested in hearing about this.

Hunter must convey to Jordan the benefits of addressing the problem now rather than waiting until later, when it will be harder to fix. He should let Jordan know that his concern is to help the organization be as effective as possible.

RAMP IT UP HANDOUT

1. Name a few specific situations in your personal or professional life when you have lacked assertiveness. It might be helpful to think of times when you regretted not speaking up.

2. Why did you lack assertiveness? What stopped you? Why did you hold back?

3. What are the barriers to being assertive? Do you lack the skills to effectively express what you were thinking or feeling? Are you afraid of repercussions? Were you conditioned as a child to be unassertive?

4. How can these barriers be overcome? Do you need to enhance your communication skills, build your confidence, or practice being assertive in a safe environment?

5. In which situations are you willing to be more assertive in your life?

Assignment

Over the next two weeks, in two real-life situations, act more assertively than you would have in the past.

Assertiveness

Dial It Back

Purpose

Help aggressive people move from aggressive behavior to assertiveness. This requires them to reduce the size of their normal comfort zone by restraining aggressive behaviors.

Thumbnail

50 to 80 minutes and follow-up assignment

A coach works with a client to identify areas in which the individual needs to be assertive rather than aggressive. They select one specific situation in which to practice dialing back the aggressiveness. To practice the skill, they then role play until the client feels more comfortable. The follow-on assignment is for the client to practice being assertive rather than aggressive in two real-life situations and then to discuss them with the coach.

Outcomes

- Increased awareness of the value of being assertive rather than aggressive
- Learning to be more aware of the intensity of aggressive behavior and dial it back so it can be expressed through appropriate assertive behavior

Audience

Individual working with a coach

Facilitator Competencies

Advanced

Materials

- Dial It Back Handout
- Paper and pen

Time Matrix

Activity	Estimated Time-Individual
Discuss assertiveness	10–15 minutes
Select areas and list barriers and possible remedies	15–30 minutes
Role play	15–20 minutes
Debrief	10–15 minutes
Total	**50 to 80 minutes**

Instructions

1. Discuss the concept of assertiveness. Zero in on situations in which the client is behaving aggressively and wants to dial it back to an appropriate level of assertiveness.
2. Give a copy of the Dial It Back Handout to your client and go through all of the steps.
3. With your help, ask the client to reenact one of the situations listed in Step 1 and role play being assertive instead of aggressive.
4. Calibrate the tipping point between being assertive and being aggressive and help your client move back and forth between assertiveness and aggressiveness until the client sees he or she can choose to behave assertively whenever he or she wants. The calibration is set by helping your client become aware of factors such as the different responses he or she receives when assertive rather than aggressive behavior is used.

5. Discuss how the client felt during the role play and which specific behaviors he or she had to change in order to accomplish the shift.
6. Give the client the following assignment: Over the next two weeks the client should commit to being more assertive rather than aggressive and practicing his or her new skills in two real-life situations.
7. Set a time for a follow-up meeting during which you and your client can discuss the results of the assignment.

DIAL IT BACK HANDOUT

1. In which specific situations in your personal or professional life have you been too aggressive? It might be helpful to think of times you regretted being overly forceful or times when people were obviously intimidated by you.

2. What do you do when you are being too aggressive? Do you raise your voice, use a condescending tone, or look angry and hostile?

3. How would you explain your aggressive behavior? Have you been angry? Do you want to win at all costs?

4. Explain what the barriers are to being assertive rather than aggressive. Do you lack the skills to effectively express what you were thinking or feeling? Are you afraid of appearing to be weak?

5. Describe how these barriers can be overcome. Do you need to enhance your communication skills, calm down, or practice being more assertive and less aggressive in a safe environment?

Assertiveness

Getting Your Point Across

Purpose

To practice different ways of communicating disagreement so that others will understand what you want, what you do not want, and why.

Thumbnail

35 to 40 minutes

In pairs, practice different styles for communicating disagreement. Then take time to understand which strategies are effective and why. In one-on-one coaching, the coach is the other person in the pair.

Outcomes

- Learn effective ways to be assertive
- Be able to disagree and still respect the other person's opinion

Audience

- Intact team
- Unaffiliated group
- Individual working with a coach

Facilitator Competencies ◯

Easy

Materials

- Getting Your Point Across Handout
- Pens

Time Matrix

Activity	Estimated Time
In pairs, practice different ways of disagreeing, taking time to reflect on the differences	15 minutes
As a group, discuss the learnings and apply to real-life situations	10–15 minutes
Individually write about a couple of challenges that require assertiveness and apply what was learned	10 minutes
Total	**35 to 40 minutes**

Instructions

1. Distribute the Getting Your Point Across Handout and review the "In Pairs" instructions.
2. Ask the group to form pairs and to complete the "In Pairs" section of the handout. Tell the pairs they will have approximately fifteen minutes to complete the role plays and pair discussions. Emphasize the need to follow the language patterns given in the models carefully.
3. After fifteen minutes, reconvene the entire group and discuss the questions in the Group Debriefing section of the handout.
4. After ten to fifteen minutes, conclude the group discussion and ask the participants to individually complete the Individual Activity section of the handout.

GETTING YOUR POINT ACROSS HANDOUT

In Pairs

Exercise 1

Working in pairs, make direct eye contact with the other person. While Person A speaks, Person B will listen, then reverse roles. In each of these scenarios, the one speaking should talk about a matter on which he or she has an opinion and state that opinion in no uncertain terms. For example: "When it comes to cutting back eligibility for overtime, the union is going to go ballistic!" Be conscious of how you are using your posture (body language) to convey this message. If you are congruent, your muscles will be more tense, your posture more angular and stiff, and your gestures will be more emphatic.

After Person A has spoken, Person B will reply by folding his or her arms across his or her chest, using a similarly confrontational tonality, and saying, "No, I disagree with you; that is not how I see this." Person B's body language will tend to mirror Person A's.

Notice how you feel, both when saying and receiving these messages. Record your observations; then switch roles and repeat. When you have each been in both roles, discuss the experience with your partner.

Exercise 2

Repeat Exercise 1, only this time Person B will stand in a comfortably relaxed posture, hands at sides, and briefly restate to the best of his or her ability what the other person has said. Then when you express your disagreement, begin with the word "and." For example, "I know you think the cut in overtime is unfair to the people who make the least money, AND I really disagree *about that* [instead of "with you"]; I'm sure there is another way for *us* to look *at* this."

Notice how you feel, both saying and receiving these messages. Record your observations; switch roles, and when you have both been in each position, discuss the experience with your partners.

Group Debriefing

Discuss how it felt to confront the other person.

- How did it feel when you were being confronted?
- Did changing the tonality and body language have much of an effect on your experience when you were receiving the communication? When you were delivering it?
- Do you feel more comfortable having rehearsed some basic assertive confrontational scenarios? Could you do this more effectively now in real life?

Individual Activity

Write about the experience and list two situations in which you will practice your new skills. Who are the specific individuals you will be disagreeing with? Describe how you anticipate they will respond, and then describe how you will respond to their response.

Independence

Cut the Apron Strings

Purpose

To move beyond uncertainty and into independent action. To surface the reason you have not been as independent as you want to be.

 ### Thumbnail

25 to 40 minutes

Participants identify the characteristics of independence. They discuss when it is easy and when it is hard to be independent. Next, they explore their current environment. They determine how they can act more independently in the current environment and practice the new behaviors.

Outcomes

- Deeper understanding of the impacts of lack of independence
- Greater comfort level with acting more independently
- Commitment to select coaches to help them rehearse their practice of independence

Audience

- Intact team
- Unaffiliated group
- Individual working with a coach

Facilitator Competencies

Moderate to Advanced

Materials

- Cut the Apron Strings Handout
- Flip charts and markers

Time Matrix

Activity	Estimated Time
Discussion of independence	10–15 minutes
Examine current environment, including personal examples	5–15 minutes
Handout steps 1–4	7-10 minutes
Debrief	3-5 minutes
Total	**25 to 40 minutes**

Instructions

1. Lead a discussion of independence. Ask participants for the characteristics of independence and write their responses on a flip chart.
2. Ask when it is easy to be independent and record participants' ideas.
3. Ask when it is hard to be independent and record participants' ideas. Use the following examples to generate discussion if responses are few. Ask what could make it hard for them to think independently in the following situations:
   - Benefits accrue to you because you are favored by these people or groups (you're in the "in" crowd):

High school—the most popular person or clique

Work—the opinion leader, the best producer, the smartest one, the boss's favorite

Community—the one with the most influence and political clout

4. Clarify the current issues in the workplace. Ask, "What are some examples where you do not believe people are acting independently?" Explain that they should not confuse contrariness with independence. Independence and rebellion are not necessarily synonymous. Ask, "What is the impact on the workplace?"

5. Ask them to think of specific behaviors that would make them more independent in the current environment. How could they exercise more initiative, be more self-directed or self-controlled? Ask them to share one of their examples if they feel safe and comfortable doing it. If no one volunteers, do not press it.

6. Distribute copies of the Cut the Apron Strings Handout, and ask participants to complete Steps 1 through 4.

7. Have them pair up with someone in the group and have each partner rehearse one of the scenarios they listed in Step 2 of the handout using the new behaviors they listed in Step 3.

8. Debrief:

   - Discuss how the rehearsal went and what they are willing to do to improve.
   - Ask them to identify someone they can ask on an ongoing basis to help them rehearse. Write that person's name in Step 5 of the handout.

CUT THE APRON STRINGS HANDOUT

1. Describe the environment (work, home, community, specific situation) you selected for this exercise.

2. List examples from your life in which it would benefit you to be more independent—have more initiative, be more self-directed or self-controlled, or less emotionally dependent.

3. Select one or two of the examples listed above and identify at least one or two specific new behaviors you would like to be able to do that would express an increased level of independence.

4. If you did the things you listed, how would it affect your confidence? Your efficiency? Your relationships with the other people in your life?

5. Find someone who is willing to work with you as a coach on an ongoing basis and set up several weekly or bi-monthly meetings in which you commit to rehearse the new behaviors. Ask the person to help you develop and practice powerful, appropriate responses to those who would challenge your independence.

Emotional Intelligence in Action

Independence

Solitary Effort

Purpose

To have participants experiment with increasing their independence by doing some activities alone that they usually do with others.

Thumbnail

20 minutes

To create the feeling of being independent, participants select an activity to do alone from a list of activities they usually do, and prefer to do, with others. In the session, they fully visualize and act out mentally what it would be like to do the activity alone. To achieve the desired level of independence, they commit to put into practice in their lives what they visualized in the simulation.

Outcomes

- Develop a method to support you in acting more independently in the world
- Increase your confidence in your ability to interact effectively when you are alone

Audience

- Intact team
- Unaffiliated group
- Individual working with a coach

Facilitator Competencies ◯

Easy

Materials

- Solitary Effort Handout
- Pens

Time Matrix

Activity	Estimated Time
List activities and select one	5 minutes
Visualization	10 minutes
Debrief	5 minutes
Total	**20 minutes**

Instructions

1. Distribute copies of the Solitary Effort Handout and review it with the group (or individual).
2. Ask everyone to complete Steps 1 and 2.
3. Have them visualize what it is like to do their selected activities alone. Ask them to close their eyes and take four deep, slow breaths. While their eyes are closed, read them the instructions in Step 3 of the handout. Play soft music in the background, such as the *Largo* CD from the Relax with the Classics® series (Various Artists, 1987). Follow copyright laws for playing recorded music.

4. Debrief the individual or team.
   - Were you able to picture yourself performing the activity?
   - Did you feel some of the anxiety you might feel if you were really doing it?
   - Did you increase your comfort with the idea of doing it alone?
5. Ask them to choose a time in the next two weeks when they will actually do this activity alone. Advise them to take a little notebook or some 3 by 5 cards and jot down notes about their experiences.
6. If you are able to meet again, schedule a time to meet in two weeks to discuss how participants felt doing the chosen activity alone.

SOLITARY EFFORT HANDOUT

1. List activities you usually do, and prefer to do, with others. These are activities that take place away from home.

2. Select from the list above one activity you will do alone in the next two weeks.

3. Visualize yourself doing this activity alone. Imagine each of the steps from when you begin to get ready until after you return home. Begin by picturing yourself:

   - At home just before the activity.
     What are you wearing?
     What are you feeling?
     If you are feeling anxious about doing this alone, imagine taking someone with you who makes you feel more comfortable and secure.
   - Approaching this activity. For example, maybe you see yourself driving to the location and/or walking up to where the activity takes place. Notice the soundscape throughout your imagined adventure. Is there music playing in the car? Do you hear people's voices? How loud or close are they? What are they saying?
   - Starting the activity. If you feel stressed, take a few deep breaths and picture yourself smiling and confident.
   - Completing the activity.
   - Leaving the activity and returning home—still smiling and confident.
   - Returning home safely.

Emotional Intelligence in Action

Independence

Going Along with the Group—Or Not

Purpose

To recognize the value of acting independently

 ### Thumbnail

30 to 45 minutes

Review the applications of independence and discern best practices.

Outcomes

- Gain perspective on the value and application of acting independently
- Identify the factors that need to be balanced to achieve real independence

Audience

- Intact team
- Unaffiliated group
- Individual working with a coach

Facilitator Competencies ◯

Easy

Materials

- Going Along with the Group—Or Not—Handout
- Flip chart and markers
- Pens

Time Matrix

Activity	Estimated Time
Discuss attached vignettes	10–15 minutes
Review examples of how they've applied independence in their own lives	10–15 minutes
Draft a 21-day development plan	10–15 minutes
Total	**30 to 45 minutes**

Instructions

1. Give the coaching client or the group the vignettes on the handout.
   - Ask them to explore how they see the exercise of independence, or lack thereof, in the examples.
   - Ask where they see healthy applications of independence and where the strategies are unhelpful.
   - Follow along this track in discussing group observations. Note that different individuals may see different applications of independence in the same vignette.
2. Ask them to discuss their own experiences with the application of independence.
   - Look for examples of both useful and unhelpful applications of the skill.
   - Work with the group or your coaching client to develop a list of criteria to consider in determining the best use of independence as a skill.
   - In your discussion of the pros and cons of behaving independently, brainstorm ways to do so successfully and tactfully.

3. Invite each individual to work with a partner (if that fits the group dynamics; if not, do so alone) to draft a twenty-one-day development plan for increasing his or her own independence. This plan includes the specific new behavior you commit to undertake for the next twenty-one days. Examples of elements of the plan follow:
   - To decide on your own two days a week when and where you want to go to lunch instead of waiting for others in your office every day
   - To speak up to authority figures in your life to present your differing view when you disagree on an important point
4. Remind them to look at the nuances of the application of independence so their behavior is respectful and furthers organizational needs as well as their own.
5. Ask each person to make a commitment to change and report back to the group or a designated person in the group in twenty-one days.

GOING ALONG WITH THE GROUP— OR NOT—HANDOUT

Read these scenarios and talk about whether each way of expressing independence was helpful to the individual and to the organization.

Scenario One

A senior management official reports to a Board that has been quite pleased with his timely and competent work. He seems to always exhibit a can-do attitude with them and reliably gets things done. It seems whatever they want, he can do, and he never complains. Needless to say, the Board members were shocked when they received the results of a 360-degree assessment with statements from his staff showing they were about to mutiny. It turned out that the senior official took whatever the Board wanted back to his staff and told them to do it, no matter what. It often meant unnecessary emergencies, late nights, and confusing assignments because they hadn't been thought through well enough. Now the Board is wondering if they can keep this employee.

Scenario Two

A few members of a seven-person team are disgruntled with their boss. The unhappiest person got the group together to develop a list of concerns that they then decided to take to their boss's boss first, without talking to their immediate boss. One member of the team refused to go along with the strategy, even though his co-workers became very angry with him. He had only been directly assigned to the team for three years, but he'd been working in the field for fifteen years and just didn't agree that this was the right way to go about it. The other team members are going ahead, and the senior boss has agreed to meet with them.

Self-Actualization

The Scavenger Hunt

Purpose

To assist participants in playing a game that requires striving to actualize some of their potential capabilities. They will need to exhibit drive and set goals to be competitive. The game will require using their underlying skills for self-actualization, including optimism, problem solving, and assertiveness.

 ### Thumbnail

80 minutes to 2 hours and 40 minutes

The facilitator will guide the group in conducting a scavenger hunt—a game that requires team action and a motivation to compete to win. The items are a challenge to find and require team problem solving and coordination. Each team, and then the group as a whole, will debrief and understand the motivational strategies they used, how they set goals, cooperated, and solved problems as a team. The group will compare their recognitions to the normal working environment and identify the specific learnings and strategies for incorporating improved motivation and engagement.

Outcomes

- Increased awareness of how the team applies its drive and sets goals
- Better understanding of how the underlying eight emotional intelligence skills impact our abilities and our accomplishments
- Take away learning on improved ways to motivate one another, problem solve, and integrate their EI skills back to the work environment

Audience

- Intact team
- Unaffiliated group

Facilitator Competencies

Moderate to Advanced

Materials

- The Scavenger Hunt Handout—one copy for each participant
- List of team assignments
- List of scavenger items and ground rules, prepared in advance (see Step 2)
- Prizes
- Flip charts, pens, and paper

Time Matrix

Activity	Estimated Time
Organize group into scavenger hunt teams	10–15 minutes
Scavenger hunt. Give prizes once all return	30–60 minutes
Team discussion with handout	10–20 minutes
Full group discussion—apply to workplace	20–45 minutes
Identify next steps for back at the workplace	10–20 minutes
Total	**80 minutes to 2 hours, 40 minutes**

Instructions

1. If you are working with an intact team and are able to do pre-work with the leaders for the team, develop learning goals for how you assign your teams. The teams should be pre-assigned to accomplish those goals. If you have assessment information from an EQ measure or other profiles, such as Emergenetics, MBTI, FIRO-B, or others, use this information to build teams with different strengths so they experience the diversity—or teams that are very similar so they experience the dynamics of similar strengths and preferences. This allows the opportunity for participants to witness the differences within and between their teams and to build intentions for how they will work together most effectively in their normal workdays. This question will be revisited in Step 6.

2. Set up the game—build expectations for great prizes and the impression that those who do better will get better prizes. Send the teams out with ground rules on when to return, how far they can go, anything else relevant to your particular group and environment, and a list of items to obtain. You will need to create the list and ground rules based on the environment you're working in and the type of teams. Here are some examples to draw from:

Scavenger Hunt Sample Items
- Snow ball
- Six-pack (they can be creative, it can be flowers, pop, etc.)
- A woman's shoe (not from anyone in the whole group)
- Something fifty years old or more
- A collage representing every color in the rainbow
- A man's tie clip
- A box of mints
- A plant
- An object from another nation
- Something that symbolically represents your team (and be prepared to tell us why)
- Other (Compile your list to represent the type of team you're working with and what might be found within the time frame for the hunt in their location.)

Scavenger Hunt Sample Ground Rules

- You must stay together as a team.
- You must be back by X (tell them the specific time).
- You cannot buy any item.
- No item can come from any member of your team.
- You may go anywhere you want.
- Other (Again, create your rules to fit the dynamics of the team you are working with. Generally, only a few ground rules are needed.)

3. After all have returned, have a lively celebration and give out prizes.
4. Give each person a copy of the handout and a pen. Direct each team to meet to talk over and write answers to questions 1 through 10. Tell them to write on the back of the handout if they need more room, or give them more paper.
5. Next have all the teams meet as a whole group to listen to one another and to discuss similarities and differences in their answers. Use the same set of questions from the handout as the small groups used, but this time record key points on flip-chart pages.
6. Instruct each person to take five to ten minutes to individually answer Question 11 on the handout.
7. Close by getting commitment from participants to implement the action steps they proposed in Item 10 on the handout.

THE SCAVENGER HUNT HANDOUT

Answer questions 1 through 10 within your scavenger hunt team first and then discuss them with the whole group.

1. Mark on the scale below to indicate your team's motivation to succeed:

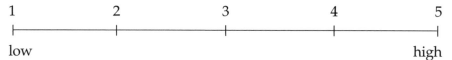

2. Mark on the scale below to rank each individual member's motivation to succeed (give each team member a number):

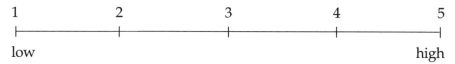

3. Discuss and write a few points about why you gave the scores for Items 1 and 2 above.

4. Take a few minutes for individual reflection. How did each of you individually define success? Is this similar to your response in the workplace? How?

5. Now work as a whole to discuss how your team defined success. Write the definition here. Is this similar to your response in the workplace? How?

6. Discuss how playing this game reflects your ability and drive to set and achieve goals.

7. Were you involved and committed to the pursuit?

Emotional Intelligence in Action

8. Self-actualization is built on many other emotional skills. Reflect on how the following factors came into play in this exercise, and then on how they are relevant to your work.

- Happiness

- Optimism

- Self-regard

- Independence

- Problem solving

- Social responsibility

- Assertiveness

- Emotional self-awareness

9. Discuss how your team worked together. Did you have different approaches or similar ones to problem solving? How well did you maximize your team's differences and similarities?

10. If your full group is an intact team, develop at least two action steps that you want to take back to your work environment based on your learnings from this exercise.

11. Complete the following item individually when instructed to do so by your facilitator:

    Take five to ten minutes, as your facilitator directs, and each person record some awareness you've gained in this workout. Do you believe you are meeting your own goals for success in life? Most people say they are meeting some, but not all of their goals. How is it for you? Based on your experience in the scavenger hunt, what two items do you want to pay attention to so you meet your own criteria for success? This is a rich topic; you may want to continue exploring your thoughts during your personal time later to enhance your own self-actualization.

Self-Actualization

Becoming All That You Can Be

Purpose

To explore what self-actualization means to each individual and to develop an action plan to enhance this skill.

Thumbnail

60 to 65 minutes

Individuals and groups work to understand what self-actualization means to them and how important it is personally and professionally. They develop an action plan.

Outcomes

- Understand the value of self-actualization in each individual's life
- Learn how others see this value through discussion (for groups only)
- Develop an action plan for increasing their self-actualization

Audience

- Intact team
- Unaffiliated group
- Individual working with a coach

Facilitator Competencies

Moderate to Advanced

Materials

- Becoming All That You Can Be Handout
- Writing paper and pens

Time Matrix

Activity	Estimated Time
Each person responds to prepared questions	10–15 minutes
Group discussion	15 minutes
Rate importance of self-actualization	10 minutes
Develop individual action plan	15 minutes
Group reflections	10 minutes
Total	**60 to 65 minutes**

Instructions

1. Distribute the Becoming All That You Can Be Handout and additional paper and pens as needed. Instruct each person to take ten to fifteen minutes to answer the questions on the handout. This guides them to begin exploring the underlying questions that lead to self-actualization.

2. Lead a group discussion (or talk with the individual you are coaching) about the questions. Bring in facts related to the importance of self-actualization. For example, Stein and Book (2000, p. 262) report in *The EQ Edge* that they found that this is the number one factor supporting workplace success.

3. Ask the group to rate, as individuals and as a group (individually only for coaching), the importance of self-actualization to them on a scale of 1 to 10. Each person should write the number down for him- or herself. Then work with the group to come up with a group answer; it may be a range. Discuss the results.

4. Now ask them to rate on the same 1 to 10 scale how self-actualized they feel their lives are now. Lead a discussion on their answers. In the discussion, the participants may give the numbers they wrote down and an explanation of why. Or they may give a more general statement, such as, "I gave myself a low score because I need to change jobs and I'm just not working on it." Ask if the score reflects that they are living within their values of meaningful success for themselves. If so, what should they keep on doing? If not, what should change? Explore whether they feel their scores reflect good alignment with their values or if change is indicated.

5. Instruct each person to take fifteen minutes to outline his or her personal action plan to achieve ongoing self-actualization. Encourage anyone who is interested to take more time to fully develop his or her plan on his or her own at a later time.

6. Wrap up with group reflections on where they would like to take this awareness. Ask them to explore ways in which they might be of support to one another.

7. (*Optional*) Have an intact team develop a group plan to enhance team self-actualization. Tell group members to take time to make the features of their collective identity explicit by exploring what values, strategies, and personal behaviors make their team unique.

BECOMING ALL THAT YOU CAN BE HANDOUT

Respond to each question below. Use as much paper as you would like.

1. Name five of your core values—in order of priority if possible—and describe why they are important to you.

2. How do you bring your values into your professional and personal lives? How good a job do you feel you are doing at living your values?

3. What really interests you? How do you (or could you) actualize your interests even more, whether at work, in a community setting, or as a hobby?

4. How much time do you set aside each week to do what truly interests you and how significant is the reward you receive?

5. What are the key skills you bring to life?

6. How fully are you able to express them at home? In the workplace? In your community?

7. Describe how well you do at accepting yourself and others unconditionally.

8. Name some circumstances where you have found yourself expressing awe and/or gratitude.

9. Briefly discuss the level of trust and depth you experience in your personal relationships.

10. When and where in your life do you feel creative or inventive?

11. Do you feel that your life path is leading you to live up to your potential?

12. What else seems important to you as a part of this reflection?

Self-Actualization

Applying Inspiration

Purpose

To help participants understand self-actualization as a process to use to answer the question *What/How/Who do I want to be?* in contrast with the process of problem solving, which tends to answer the question *What do I want to have/get/achieve?*

 ### Thumbnail

70 minutes

Participants will develop a process for building in themselves qualities, states, and behaviors that they have identified as contributing to the success of others. By following the instructions for reflective journaling in response to the selected questions, participants will be able to re-access behavioral and attitudinal resources that were originally inspired in them by others.

Outcomes

Re-connect with some of the feelings of greatness that others have inspired in you and with feelings and/or goals that you would still like to actualize.

Audience

- Intact team
- Unaffiliated group
- Individual working with a coach

Facilitator Competencies

Moderate to Advanced

Materials

- Applying Inspiration Handout
- Writing paper and pens

Time Matrix

Activity	Estimated Time
List thoughts and feelings about goals, role models, and success	20 minutes
Write what you will see, hear, feel when goals are actualized	30 minutes
Write down what has kept you from actualizing them in the past	10 minutes
Notice why it might have been appropriate to have avoided them earlier in life	10 minutes
Total	**70 minutes**

Instructions

1. Distribute paper, pens, and the Applying Inspiration Handout.
2. Ask participants to list their feelings and thoughts about Item 1 on the handout.
3. To respond to Item 2, have them explore the various aspects of what they will *see, hear, and feel* when they have accomplished their goals.
4. As directed in Item 3, ask them to discuss what has blocked their past efforts.

5. For Item 4, discuss how to develop a six-week plan using what they have discovered in this exercise and the principles of graduated goals, positive self-talk, accountability to an ally, and appropriate celebration at the end of their quest and all along the way!

APPLYING INSPIRATION HANDOUT

1. Think back to the stories you know of people who faced serious challenges and whose efforts to overcome them resulted in an inspiring success that impressed you deeply. Notice what the general similarities are between the challenges they faced and your own situation. What is it you must overcome to achieve the goals you want to accomplish? Consider what it was about those people that impressed you and why. What were some of the important qualities and abilities that you admire in them? Revisit how it felt to read or hear or watch their stories being told. List your feelings and thoughts about this in the space provided below.

2. Inspiration is the ability to behave in such a way that other people feel and believe that they too can succeed as you have and can overcome the challenges in their lives. Step 1 was designed to help you reconnect with some of the sources of "Can Do!" enthusiasm you have incorporated from your own past learning. Now imagine how it will feel when you are empowered with more of the qualities and abilities that you admire in these individuals. Write down what you will see, hear, and feel that will be different when you have actualized more of your own capacities in these areas. For instance, "When I am more assertive/expressive I will *see* looks of surprise on the faces of people who know me as shy. I will *hear* comments about how I've changed, and I will hear more people challenging me, since I will be taking a stand more often. I will *feel* scared at first but also more congruent and self-respecting, and that will be a relief."

Emotional Intelligence in Action

3. Now notice what has prevented you from expressing these qualities and skills in the past, and write down your thoughts in the space provided. Are there any useful ways in which these limits of expression have served you constructively in the past? For instance: "Expressing my opinion as a child often meant hostility and rejection. Is it still appropriate to observe those limits today? Why? Or why not?"

4. Using the thoughts and feelings that you have reactivated in your awareness during this exercise, develop a six-week plan for bringing to life more
   of what it is you truly want to be. If you have a coach, mentor, or partner
   in your workgroup with whom you are doing this exercise, review it with
   him or her, incorporate suggestions, and meet with him or her at least once
   a week to report and reinforce your progress.

Empathy

Connect Feeling with Meaning

Purpose

To build empathy skills by recognizing the importance of listening and responding to what is actually being said.

Thumbnail

35 to 40 minutes

The participants will work in pairs to practice and gain understanding of applying empathic skills through a scripted reflective exercise. Individuals work with their coaches.

Outcome

Gain understanding of a specific reflective strategy that can build their connection with others and reduce conflict

Audience

- Intact team
- Unaffiliated group
- Individual working with a coach

Facilitator Competencies

Easy to Moderate

Materials

Prepared flip chart (see instructions, Step 3)

Time Matrix

Activity	Estimated Time
Summarize empathy and describe exercise	5–10 minutes
In pairs, one person at a time talks about an uncomfortable situation—the other person reflects using the model phrases, then reverse roles	10 minutes
Group debriefing	10 minutes
2nd step optional: Repeat with pleasant situation	10 minutes
Total	**35 to 40 minutes**

Instructions

1. Describe the skill of empathy. Emphasize the importance of paying close attention to the other person. Many people think they are good at this, but are not. Such participants are likely to be lax in their efforts.

2. Ask group members to form pairs; the coach pairs up as the other partner when the workout is used with an individual. In each pair, one person will tell the other about an uncomfortable situation at work in which he or she was involved. The person listening will help him or her explore and validate the experience by reflecting both the emotions the person is feeling and the reasons he or she is feeling them.

3. Instruct the respondent to use the basic "You feel _____ because _____" model (which you should display on a flip chart). Respondents can also adapt the model to provide variety and increased accuracy with remarks such as, "Wow, that must have felt _____. It's so _____ when people behave that way."

4. Explain that the goal of the respondent is to facilitate the speaker's exploration of the situation by reflecting the feelings he or she experienced and what gave rise to them. *The respondent should not attempt to solve the problem for the speaker!* All the respondent is doing is providing the speaker with a mirror in which to see his or her behavior so he or she can gauge how to change it if a different result is desired.
5. Tell the pairs to begin.
6. After five minutes tell them to reverse roles.
7. Debrief the exercise with the group using questions such as:
   - Which was harder to identify, how the person was feeling or why?
   - How did your partner respond when your reflection was highly accurate for both the feeling and the meaning?
8. (*Optional*) Now repeat the same exercise, using a positive and happy situation (again preferably from the workplace).

Empathy

Mixed Emotions

Purpose

To give participants the opportunity to recognize that many emotions arise when someone is having a strong response to a situation and expand their skills to be empathic when this occurs.

 ### Thumbnail

60 minutes

The participants consider two situations and undertake to become aware of the complex emotions someone else is feeling. They grow their understanding of how different points of view affect someone's emotional responses.

Outcomes

- To gain an understanding of how, when a person has particularly strong feelings, he or she is often experiencing a composite of several emotions
- To recognize how much different points of view affect a situation
- To expand participants' ability to be empathic when talking with friends or colleagues while going through complex situations

Audience

- Intact team
- Unaffiliated group
- Individual working with a coach

Facilitator Competencies

Easy to Moderate

Materials

- Mixed Emotions Handout
- Paper and pens

Time Matrix

Activity	Estimated Time
Read the first scenario and discuss	25 minutes
Read second scenario and record possible feelings	15 minutes
Discuss insights and feelings as a group	20 minutes
Total	**60 minutes**

Instructions

1. Distribute pens, paper, and the Mixed Emotions Handout.
2. Ask participants to work in pairs on the first scenario. If there is an odd number of participants, the last group can contain three. Have them read the handout and proceed with the exercises as indicated.
3. After twenty minutes give them a five-minute warning, and five minutes later ask them to all begin working on the second scenario, which they will do independently.
4. After ten minutes give them a five-minute warning, and five minutes later ask the participants to discuss their experiences as a group. The following questions may be helpful:
   - In Scenario One, who had the most responsibility for improving communications?

- In Scenario Two, how might Linda's relationship with Randall have influenced the way he understood the changes in his life and how he felt about them?

MIXED EMOTIONS HANDOUT

In real life, emotions are often bundled together, sometimes with confusing contradictions, and they certainly are interpreted according to our view of a situation. Learning to recognize the implications that someone's perspective has on his or her responses, as well as the complexity of feeling multiple emotions, will greatly increase your ability to be empathic.

When you are in a conversation with someone, you can often best demonstrate your empathy by reflecting back the two critical parts of the message he or she is trying to communicate, namely the meaning and the feeling. As the situations in our lives become more and more complex, we often find ourselves adrift in a puzzling array of emotions. These feelings are chemical and electrical responses occurring in several different locations within our bodies, so they don't always announce themselves in precise words that tell us what they mean. Accurate reflection promotes clarity.

Scenario One: Ships in the Night
The Story
Imagine that your college-aged daughter leaves a message on your home answering machine saying that she has Friday off and she'll be driving home for the weekend. You expect her about noon. She arrives at dinnertime with a girlfriend, and they stay only long enough to change clothes, as they are going to the grand opening of a new dance club. They get in about three o'clock in the morning and then sleep until eleven the next day.

They go out shopping and catch lunch at the mall, getting home in time for dinner, when at last you get to talk. It's a very interesting discussion, but you have expensive tickets for a play you've been waiting to see for months, and by the time you return home they are out again. They get up when you are at church and have already left for the long drive back by the time you get home. She leaves a note saying, "Thanks, it was great to see you—I had a wonderful time." How do you feel?

Instructions
Working in pairs, take five to ten minutes to discuss how the parent could have reached out to the daughter to let her know what was going on with him or her better at the critical points during the weekend. Put yourselves in the role of

being close friends of the parent. The value of talking with close friends is that they can help us contextualize what we're going through by reflecting what they hear us saying and how they sense we feel. A good listener can serve as a multidimensional mirror for us, showing us parts of ourselves that are out of view or out of focus. One of you role play being the parent; the other be the friend talking with the parent about this scenario. Write an abbreviated list of the feelings the parent had and why in the first column below.

Now do the same thing for the daughter. Reverse the role play so that whoever was the parent last time is now the friend; the friend in the last role play is now the daughter. Discuss how you could have responded more empathically to your parents and still had the good time you were looking forward to with your best friend. List the feelings the daughter had and why in the other column.

Parent's Feelings and Why	Daughter's Feelings and Why

Here is one possible set of feelings for the parent:

After hearing her message on the answering machine you feel warm and happy and have a strong feeling of anticipation. When she's not home by three o'clock Friday afternoon, or by four o'clock or five o'clock, you feel increasingly anxious, stressed, and nauseated. When she arrives, you feel tremendously grateful and relieved, but when you realize she has a friend with her, you feel hurt and a little disappointed. This gets worse when she leaves immediately. By the time she gets home at three a.m. the next morning, you feel downright angry and used because you know she'll sleep in . . . which she does. When you finally get to see her at dinner, you feel eager and grateful to hear what she has to say, but part of you is still fuming.

Although you've been looking forward to seeing the play ever since you bought the tickets, now you wish you didn't have to go so you could spend more time with your daughter. You have a hard time paying attention because you worry that you're losing contact with her. When you leave for church in the morning you feel crestfallen, knowing that she'll probably be gone when you return. On reading the note, you feel proud of how grown-up she is and how thoughtful it was to write a nice note, but then you feel angry about how she seemed to avoid you, and then you get anxious thinking about her on the long drive back to school.

Discuss your observations in comparison with this possible rendition. Notice how your empathy for the different points of view grows. Now tell the daughter's story from her point of view from when she leaves the phone message.

Scenario Two: Complex Feelings

Instructions

Filling in the blanks as this scenario unfolds will help you recognize the complex emotions Randall and Joe felt. Working independently this time, list some of the ways that Randall might have felt and why. There are many possibilities, so provide at least two in each of the response patterns below. Use extra paper or the back of the handout if necessary.

Randall was a junior in high school in September of 2001 and was deeply upset by the World Trade Center bombings, as were all his classmates and their families.

He felt _____, because _____.
He also felt _____, because _____.
[Example: He felt furious because Americans shouldn't ever be attacked on their own soil! He also felt scared because he never thought that this could happen.]

In order to deal with some of the anger and helplessness they felt, he and his friend Joe put together a plan to graduate first semester in their senior year and join the Marines. They worked out at the gym a lot together, hung out with the local recruiter, and carefully studied the materials they were given about life in the Corps. Now Randall felt _____ because _____. Joe, who had always been recognized as a natural leader, felt _____ because _____.

Randall's birthday wasn't until August so he would not be old enough to join the Marines without his parents' permission at the semester break, and they weren't about to let him go. When it came to this, he felt _____, because _____.

Joe was old enough, and his mother was unable to influence him to stay in school and go to college, so he left according to their plan, and had everyone's attention, receiving much admiration from his classmates during the last several weeks before it was time to go. This left Randall feeling pretty _____ because _____.
Joe, on the other hand, was feeling quite _____ because _____ _____. He left for basic training the day after New Year's.

Joe's younger sister Linda started calling Randall frequently after Joe left, and they often talked for hours. It wasn't long before they started dating. About a month before Randall's birthday they learned that Joe had gone into combat; in his first firefight he had killed someone who was later identified to be a civilian.

Using a descriptive pattern similar to the model that follows, describe Randall's developing understanding of the world and how it must have felt as he moved through these stages of his life.

At first he felt _____ because _____ _____. Then he felt _____, _____, and _____, because _____ _____. Now he feels _____ because _____ _____.

Similarly, describe Joe's developing understanding of the world and how it must have felt as he moved through these stages of his life.

Even though this seems like a formula (which it is), you can still tell a pretty good story if you fill in the blanks creatively from an empathetic point of view.

Share your reflections on this process with the group.

Emotional Intelligence in Action

Empathy

Do as the Empathic Do

Purpose

To promote more meaningful connections with key people in your life.

Thumbnail

60 minutes

Working with a coach, each individual discusses the value of focused listening and how to understand another person's reality. The client will choose a specific relationship in which he or she wants to strengthen his or her connection using empathy, create a reminder card, and practice the new behaviors.

Outcomes

- Increased ability to hear what others are saying and understand what they really mean
- Enhanced capacity to respond effectively

Audience

Individual working with a coach

Facilitator Competencies

Moderate

Materials

- Do as the Empathic Do Handout
- 3 x 5 cards
- Pens

Time Matrix

Activity	Estimated Time
Value of listening discussion	20 minutes
Practice paraphrasing the meaning	15 minutes
Practice reflecting the feeling	20 minutes
Create practice card	5 minutes
Total	**60 minutes**

Instructions

1. Give the client the Do as the Empathic Do Handout, which contains a case study.
2. Ask the client to read the case study; then ask these questions:
   - Have you every experienced or observed a similar situation?
   - Does the case study solution seem actionable? Does it seem as if it is something that could be implemented?
   - Do you think something that simple could make a difference? If so, how? If not, why not?
3. Now have the client focus on his or her situation. Ask the client to select one or more of the relationships in his or her life in which he or she wants a more meaningful connection.
4. Discuss what is lacking in that relationship currently and ask the client how the other person(s) might perceive it.

Emotional Intelligence in Action

5. Ask the client to review his or her current schedule and behavior patterns and decide when in the day it will be most efficient to engage with this person(s) and give him or her the time and attention that focused listening requires.

6. To help your client learn the powerful value that paraphrasing gives to communications, compose some model statements to practice paraphrasing until he or she feels comfortable. Suggest that your client use the following types of introductions as a way to help get the hang of it: "So you're telling me. . . ." "What I hear is that you want (need). . . ." "OK, it sounds like. . . ."

7. Have your client practice suggesting how others feel about what's happening, using patterns like, "And that leaves you feeling pretty. . . . "Wow, you must feel . . . about that." "And so naturally you feel kind of. . . ." Reassure the client that if others don't feel the specific way suggested, the person will usually correct the suggestion by describing his or her actual feeling more accurately.

8. Tell the client that if he or she needs help remembering, make a card on which the new behaviors are described clearly and briefly, including who specifically the client will be practicing with and the times he or she has committed to use the new behaviors.

DO AS THE EMPATHIC DO HANDOUT

Case Study Points

- Executive manager has great leadership skills and believes she really cares about her employees.
- Employees think she is a talented manager, but they are troubled by her seeming lack of interest in them. It's beginning to affect morale.
- She is a very task-focused person and she spends her commute to work thinking about the things that need to get done that day. Since the only thing on her mind when she gets to work is getting those things done, when she arrives at work she makes a beeline to her office. She doesn't take the time to check in or touch base with her staff. She often forgets to even say hello.
- The manager becomes aware of the impact of her behavior on her employees when she receives the results of a 360-degree assessment. Subsequent discussions with her staff help her understand how they feel and how they would prefer to be treated.
- She and her coach devise a simple strategy for her to connect with her people to let them know she values them. They created a pocket card with the following reminders:
  - Stop to greet people, make eye contact, and call them by name.
  - Ask what they're working on and how its going. Stop and listen to the response!
  - Ask if there are any problems I can help with.
  - Paraphrase what I've heard and "guess" about how they're feeling— "Sounds like you're feeling skeptical about this." (Having a long list of feeling words will be helpful. Merely saying "You feel sad, mad, or glad" every day will quickly wear extremely thin.)
- She reads the card two or three times a day and rehearses the behaviors mentally at these times:
  - In her office parking lot before getting out of the car
  - Right after she gets back from lunch
  - Toward the end of the day when she will occasionally make a brief round for "Good-byes"
- Taking the time to be other-directed helped her connect with her employees and positively impacted morale.

Social Responsibility

Reflect the Best

Purpose

To shift the participants' primary focus and frame of reference away from themselves and onto the other people around them.

 ## Thumbnail

50 to 65 minutes

Participants take the time to shift their attention from the problems and deficiencies of the workplace to the resources that are currently present and available to support the people and their enterprise. This exercise draws from the theory and practice of appreciative inquiry. The facilitator must be able to model sincere appreciation and assist participants in dealing with any discomfort that this unfamiliar orientation might arouse.

Outcome

Participants will have a direct experience of the ways in which they can influence their own emotional state in the direction that will facilitate building stronger and more integrated socially responsible relationships.

Audience

- Intact team
- Unaffiliated group
- Individual working with a coach

Facilitator Competencies

Moderate

Materials

- Reflect the Best Handout
- Flip chart and markers
- Pens and paper

Time Matrix

Activity	Estimated Time
Give background on social responsibility	5 minutes
Step 1 and discussion	10–15 minutes
Step 2 and discussion	10–15 minutes
Step 3 and discussion	10–15 minutes
Group discussion of beliefs and values	15 minutes
Total	**50 to 65 minutes**

Instructions

1. Provide pens and paper.
2. Give participants a brief explanation of social responsibility and what makes it such an important quality in the workplace.
3. Distribute the Reflect the Best Handout.
4. Have the participants work through the first three steps of the exercise in pairs. Take ten to fifteen minutes for each step, including a short period for discussion.
5. For Step 4 have the entire team work together. Additional discussion time will not be necessary.

REFLECT THE BEST HANDOUT

With your partner, do your best to notice and comment on only the positive aspects of the workplace and your relationships with the others who make up your organization.

Step 1

First discuss how unusual an assignment this is and share your thoughts and feelings about undertaking this rather curious kind of communication in the workplace.

Then each person acknowledges at least three different positive things about the physical structure of your work environment that you appreciate. For example, the office is comfortable and attractive. These need to be sincere appreciations, not cleverly disguised ways of avoiding the unfamiliar and possibly uncomfortable positive orientation required by the exercise. In other words, saying, "Well, at least it doesn't smell like sewage" would not be an acceptable appreciation—unless of course it did last week and they just recently fixed the problem.

Step 2

The next step is to acknowledge to each other at least two things you appreciate about upper management.

Step 3

Now acknowledge at least one thing you sincerely appreciate about each of the other members of your team or work group.

Then begin to acknowledge the things you genuinely appreciate about your partner in this exercise. When someone offers you an appreciation, your *only* response will be to say, "Thank you."

Step 4

When we are able to consciously manage our beliefs, it is easier to improve our attitudes. When we pay attention to those attitudes and notice how we are approaching the *present* activity in our day, it is easier to manage our emotional states. When we are feeling safe, optimistic, respectful, and so on, then

Workout 7.1. Social Responsibility

managing our behavior is a much simpler task and it is easier to be intentionally supportive and appreciative of the others around us, *and* our efforts begin to generate virtuous (rather than vicious) cycles in the workplace environment.

Now the whole team together discusses the following four beliefs to see if they would be generally acceptable to the team. Be sure to explore the possible costs, downsides, and changes that would be required to adopt these beliefs and list the upsides in one column and downsides in another.

1. Simply by being alive, all people possess intrinsic value and a unique way through which they share their value.
2. There is a real bottom-line payoff in taking a little extra time to care for others.
3. Today I'm going to do my best to leave people feeling more resourceful than I find them.
4. It is good for me to give sincere praise generously. (This means looking long enough to find what is genuinely praiseworthy.)

Now fill in the list for each of the four beliefs above, noticing the pluses and minuses for the team adopting these beliefs.

	Upsides	*Downsides*
1.		
2.		

	Upsides	Downsides
3.		
4.		

Now agree to spend the rest of the day doing your best to reflect the best in everyone and see how your team blossoms!

Bonus

Some tips for managing *your* emotional state include making eye contact with the people you encounter and smiling before greeting them with a welcoming comment in a friendly tone. This is about changing your behavior, which you *can* consciously control, in order to positively affect your own emotional state (and that of others).

Social Responsibility

Who Do I Work for?

Purpose

To give participants the opportunity to explore the many expectations/demands that they experience as social beings.

 ## Thumbnail

60 minutes

Participants explore the kinds and numbers of social expectations that they experience and how to determine what the appropriate balance is.

Outcome

Experience significant insight into the different kinds of pressures and the different kinds of rewards that we experience as social beings.

Audience

- Intact team
- Unaffiliated group
- Individual working with a coach

Facilitator Competencies

Moderate

Materials

- Who Do I Work for? Handout
- Paper and pens

Time Matrix

Activity	Estimated Time
Give background on social responsibility and hand out materials	5 minutes
Ask participants to read and answer questions	40 minutes
Debrief	15 minutes
Total	**60 minutes**

Instructions

1. Distribute pens, paper, and the Who Do I Work for? Handout
2. Ask participants to read the introduction and questions and write their responses in the space provided.
3. After approximately thirty-five minutes, inform the group that they will begin to debrief in five minutes.
4. Debrief the exercise for the remaining fifteen minutes using questions such as:
    - What did you discover as you began to list all of these expectations?
    - Were the expectations of some aspects of society more concrete than others? For instance, how do you know what your community expects of you?
    - When discussing your own expectations of yourself, did you include things such as income, health, status, self-actualization, and so forth?

Emotional Intelligence in Action

WHO DO I WORK FOR? HANDOUT

To some extent we all serve some constellation of different social groups, and each group has its own expectations about what behavior constitutes an appropriate balance between acting out of self-interest and fulfilling our social responsibility. With all of these competing demands, how do you determine the right balance?

Social responsibility relates to how big a part of the world we undertake to serve. On whose behalf do you choose to employ your creativity, skills, and efforts? Are you attempting to climb the corporate ladder and be a superstar at the top? Do you discipline your behavior and tailor your communications to achieve the best that you can with your team? Respond to the following questions to explore your beliefs and feelings about social responsibility.

1. How many different kinds of expectations do I attempt to meet on behalf of the organization (or customer base) that provides my income? (Be sure to consider such things as time, skills, relationships, and so forth.)

2. In what ways are they expecting me to be productive in the workplace?

3. What is the full range of compensation and rewards I receive for my efforts in the workplace?

4. How many different kinds of expectations do I attempt to meet on behalf of my family? Consider such areas as emotions, leadership, education, discipline, morality, and so forth, along with the more obvious areas of finances, recreation, and nutrition. Discuss these expectations both in terms of the people who live under the same roof as well as those of your extended family.

5. What is the full range of rewards I receive for my efforts in the family?

6. How many different kinds of expectations do I attempt to meet on behalf of my community? Consider constituents and interests such as churches or spiritual development, schools, arts, health care, law enforcement, service groups, political parties, recreation and so forth.

7. What is the full range of rewards I receive for my efforts in my community?

8. How many different kinds of expectations do I attempt to meet on behalf of myself? (If we have no identification with some component of the social fabric—for instance Little League baseball—we won't feel or attempt to meet any expectations from that arena, so to some degree self-interest plays a role in all areas covered thus far. Instead of considering any more expectations placed on us from the outside, here is where you can explore how much you personally feel called to contribute to each of the aspects of your society.)

Social Responsibility

The Value of Volunteering

Purpose

To gain perspective on the value of volunteering and how it benefits many parts of one's life.

 ### Thumbnail

65 to 80 minutes and follow-up

Learn about social responsibility and its relationship to emotional intelligence. Participants get to reflect on their experiences of volunteering in the past and for a short time commit to a new volunteer activity. Use this workout to help the participants understand the connection between volunteering and organizational performance as well as personal well-being. Requires follow-up.

Outcomes

- Expand awareness about the value of social responsibility
- Learn at a personal level, through conducting a volunteer activity, how this connects many different areas of one's life

Audience

- Intact team
- Unaffiliated group
- Individual working with a coach

Facilitator Competencies ○

Easy

Materials

None needed

Time Matrix

Activity	Estimated Time
Discuss social responsibility and why it's important personally and to the organization. Note the connection with volunteering.	10–15 minutes
Discuss ways each individual is volunteering	10 minutes
Commit to one new volunteer activity for 21 days	15 minutes
Reflect	10 minutes
Follow up 21 days later	20–30 minutes
Total	**65 to 80 minutes**

Instructions

1. Discuss social responsibility and why it's important to the organization and to each of us personally. Note the connection with volunteering. Refer to the description of this skill in Part Two of this book.
2. Discuss the ways individuals are currently volunteering if they are. This can be done one-on-one with your coaching client, with the whole group, or in pairs, depending on the size of your group. If you do it in pairs, bring them all together afterward to discuss key points as a group.

3. Ask each person to commit to one new volunteer activity he or she will initiate and continue over the course of twenty-one days.

4. Bring the group together again after twenty-one days to discuss their experiences from the activity and how these affected their engagement with their organization. Also discuss what the activity meant to them personally.

Interpersonal Relationships

You've Got Good News

Purpose

To help participants increase their awareness of the power of affirming one another and recognize that interpersonal relationships deepen with positive interaction.

Thumbnail

50 minutes for Phase One; 80 to 110 minutes for Phase Two

This workout consists of two phases that could be coupled for a half-day team-building experience if management will really commit to participate. In Phase One, team members work in small groups on exercises that focus on affirming one another. In Phase Two they work with management to identify and affirm the group's strengths and goals. The exercise can be limited to Phase One only.

Outcomes

- Feel the experience of group reinforcement and understand the ongoing power of reflection that occurs in our day-to-day interpersonal relationships
- Experience the power of focusing on strengths as a group and recognize how that strengthens effective interactions

Audience

- Intact team
- Unaffiliated group
- Individual working with a coach

Facilitator Competencies

Moderate to Advanced

Materials

- You've Got Good News Handout
- Paper and pens
- Flip chart and markers

Time Matrix

Activity	Estimated Time (Phase One)	Estimated Time (Phase Two)
Discuss the dynamics of group affirmation	15 minutes	
Prepare personal statements on strengths and goals	15 minutes	
Practice affirming strengths	10 minutes	
Practice affirming goals	10 minutes	
Coach team members		20 minutes
Coach senior managers and supervisors; work up list of kudos		30 minutes
Managers and supervisors affirm the team together and discuss team goals in terms of future organizational direction		30–60 minutes
Total	**50 minutes**	**80 to 110 minutes**

Instructions

1. Discuss the dynamics of group affirmation, including the valuable effect that comes from receiving positive reflections from other humans in general; how the impact changes when you receive affirmation from people in your family, colleagues at work, and those with authority or prestige; and how powerfully it is magnified when it comes from *everyone* on your team.

2. Emphasize that the following exercises are designed to help the responders build the quality of generosity and enthusiasm in their responses. What they will be supplying and practicing is affirmation, not an evaluation of the person's chosen strengths or goals. Coach everyone to notice how team identification, along with understanding and respect for one another, grows as the exercise proceeds.

Phase One

1. Distribute paper, pens, and the You've Got Good News Handout.

2. Assemble the participants in groups of three; additional groups of four will work if there are one or two left over. Explain that the purpose of this exercise is to experience having a group of peers affirm what you believe (or want to believe) about yourself.

3. Review the handout, and get the groups started with Phase One by instructing each person to take up to fifteen minutes to write down three of their strongest, most valuable features and three of the goals that they would like to achieve over the next year (these can be personal or professional, but ones that they feel comfortable sharing in the group).

4. Instruct them to continue with Steps 2 and 3 of the handout.

5. Guide participants so they take up to ten minutes for affirming strengths and ten for affirming goals. Each person should participate in the small groups.

Phase Two

1. This exercise works best if you start with two separate meetings—one includes all members of the team and the second includes as many levels of the team's supervision as you can interest in the process. If you can get senior management to participate and listen to the team's direct supervisors, it will build self-regard for the supervisors and provide better engagement, insight, and understanding for the senior staff.

2. First have the coach/facilitator bring the team together and ask the members to discuss their strengths, their strongest contributions, and the key goals they want to achieve in the next year. The coach/facilitator will record their list on a flip chart.

3. Next the coach/facilitator will meet with all the supervisors who will be participating in the team exercise and instruct them on the nature of the exercise. Be certain to emphasize that this experience is designed to be empowering rather than critical. Have the supervisors compile a list of the team's greatest strengths and accomplishments.

4. After these tasks have been completed, bring the two groups together and ask the supervisors to present the list they created. Next have the team members share their lists and then guide the group in discussing their observations about each other's lists. The goal is to find everything positive and to discuss only that. Remember, *What you reinforce will be repeated!*

5. Finally, have the team present the goals they want to achieve in the next quarter/year or other selected timeframe, and ask the supervisors to be supportive with comments such as, "Yes, we can see you achieving those goals!" Have the supervisors list some of the reasons why they believe the goals are viable to the best extent possible. If a goal seems to be unrealistic, compliment the effort and work with a positive attitude to reframe it until it is viable.

6. Debrief by acknowledging the value of positive interactions and how they can enhance the interpersonal relationships within the group and, therefore, their effectiveness as a team.

Emotional Intelligence in Action

YOU'VE GOT GOOD NEWS HANDOUT

1. Write down three of your strongest, most valuable features and three of the goals that you would like to achieve over the next year (these can be personal or professional, but ones which you feel comfortable sharing in the group). Your list of three or more affirmative statements about your strengths might be something like: "I'm a good listener"; "I pay attention to detail"; or "I'm improving my handicap in golf."

2. The learner (person A) will read the first affirmative statement to the other two people (persons B and C) and both of them will smile encouragingly and say, "That's what we like about you!" enthusiastically. The purpose is to provide a person with a refreshingly congruent affirmation of him- or herself, so give the reader a chance to absorb this feedback before going on to his or her next excellent quality. Now switch roles so that B and C can each have this experience.

3. Next, Person A reads his or her goals one at a time and, after each one, B and C respond with, "Of course you can accomplish that—I can see it now." (Give the person a chance to absorb this feedback before going on to the next goal.) Each of you will read your list of three goals and receive the affirmation from your other two partners.

Interpersonal Relationships

Making New Friends

Purpose

To help people who are generally less outgoing feel comfortable beginning new friendships.

 ### Thumbnail

25 to 30 minutes

Participants in this exercise will reflect on their own lives in order to compile a set of historical events that they will feel happy sharing with anyone.

Outcome

Increased comfort in making small talk and the beginning conversations that are the foundation of basic interpersonal relationships.

Audience

Individual working with a coach

Facilitator Competencies

Easy to Moderate

Materials

- Making New Friends Handout
- Pen

Time Matrix

Activity	Estimated Time
Fill out worksheet	15–20 minutes
Discuss	10 minutes
Total	**25 to 30 minutes**

Instructions

1. Provide the client with a pen and the Making New Friends Handout.
2. Share with the client that making new friends is in part a function of our conversation skills and that this exercise will help him or her develop enough skills to begin and sustain a conversation with just about anyone who is the least bit inclined. Tell your client he or she will be gathering information from four areas of life and will learn how to share it and that the ways in which he or she listens can encourage other people to share similar stories about their lives.
3. Review the handout and ask the client to complete it.
4. After the client finishes, discuss his or her answers and reactions.

MAKING NEW FRIENDS HANDOUT

Reflect on your life and on the significant events that generally made you who you are. Some of the events will have been happy and successful; some of them will have been less so. Some of them you will enjoy sharing with everyone; some of them you may not want to discuss until you know someone can respect and appreciate that part of your life. Just remember that you have the power to choose whatever you share in the adventure of making new friends!

Write a brief note to remind yourself of at least four of these stories and record them below under the heading of Life Changes.

Life Changes

Now reflect on some background aspects of your life: where you were born and grew up, what your parents did for work, your favorite subject, sport, or hobby in school, how many siblings you have, were you the oldest, youngest, and other pertinent information. List the four or five of these facts that are the most fun for you to talk about under the heading of Background Events.

Background Events

In a third category, list two or three things you would like to achieve: finding a branch in your family tree, improving your golf or bowling or bridge score, getting your baby to sleep through the night, and so on.

Goals

In your fourth category, list a few details about each of your two most favorite vacations.

Vacations

Now you have a great foundation of supporting material to use when engaged in conversation with someone. If it ever feels like the conversation is dragging, you'll be ready to move it forward.

In addition to having these conversational tools, you will recognize that the act of talking with and listening to someone well has its own power. New friendships start most frequently when people feel that they are being listened to, not talked at! They start when you begin discovering what's interesting about another person by listening and paying attention to him or her in a way that demonstrates your respect. We all get talked at plenty. Finding someone who is patient enough and caring enough to be interested in the details of our lives is rare. We naturally want people such as these to be friends. Yet to have a balance in your friendship, you must reciprocate and tell others about yourself as well.

Starting conversations involves what is sometimes referred to as "small talk." This means very general topics of interest that affect everyone and generally benefit or offend us all equally. That's why the weather is always a great place to start. But from there it could lead to something that happened on one of their favorite vacations or to an event in your childhood.

Humans have a natural inclination to swap stories. It's a way of relating our lives together, so if you tell a story about how the weather affected your vacation, be quiet for a little while, and pretty soon someone else will probably tell you about how the weather affected something in his or her life. If silence doesn't encourage someone to talk, then maybe gently ask a general question. Then whatever sort of an answer he or she gives you, repeat it back in a paraphrase, and he or she is almost guaranteed to give you more details. For example:

> "That happened to me one time when I was down in Georgia. Worst thunderstorm I've ever seen in my life. We were about an hour out of Atlanta and the rain was up over the wheel covers."
>
> "You're kidding, 'the rain was clear up over the wheel covers'?"
>
> "Yep, and we had to drive about two miles an hour for a mile or better until the water finally went down."

Well, you get the idea.

Interpersonal Relationships

Fun and Meaningful Relationships

Purpose

To develop a keen awareness of the significant value that respectful relationships contribute to the workplace.

Thumbnail

70 minutes to 1 hour and 25 minutes

Plumb the depths of the meaning of healthy interpersonal relationships and the gifts they can bring.

Outcomes

- Expand awareness of interpersonal relationships
- Develop recognition of healthy goals and boundaries for intact teams, whether in the workplace, community, or non-profits
- Lay a foundation for expanding the skills of developing and maintaining robust interpersonal relationships

Audience

Intact teams

Facilitator Competencies

Moderate

Materials

- Flip chart and markers
- Paper and pens

Time Matrix

Activity	Estimated Time
Discuss the value of developing interpersonal relationships that emphasize respect and regard	10–20 minutes
The team defines interpersonal relationships, lists pros and cons, and lists considerations	15–20 minutes
Discuss strategies for maintaining relationships	10 minutes
Create an action plan	15 minutes
Go around the room for reflections	20 minutes
Total	**70 to 85 minutes**

Instructions

1. Lead the group in a discussion about the value of developing compassion and regard for one another, and then note how this can extend to others within the organization or community.
2. Discuss the meaning of interpersonal relationships.

    Healthy interpersonal relationships in the workplace mean taking time to listen to one another, to care that John's daughter is in ballet, that Bill's son just enlisted, that Sarah's mom went into a nursing home. It's covering for Tom so he can get to his friend's graduation from rehab, and it's helping Mary brainstorm the contents of her first presentation to the board and helping her get past her nervousness. The more in touch the members of an organization are, the less likely the chances of workplace violence, as well as many other possible challenges.

Sexual harassment is a big concern in our workplaces and is always inappropriate. Some are concerned that if we develop our interpersonal relationships, it can lead to sexual harassment. If that is a concern with your group or organization, work with them to understand the difference between respectful regard and sexual harassment.

3. Have the group:
   - Develop its own definition of healthy interpersonal relationships. As they brainstorm, write the components on a flip chart.
   - List the pros and cons of strengthening their interpersonal relationships. Help them be honest. For example some personalities and/or values don't mix well. That's OK.
   - Discuss considerations such as respecting boundaries, timing, and cultural differences.
4. Discuss what it takes to maintain valuable interpersonal relationships outside the workplace. Ask questions such as "What challenges do you experience in some of your valuable relationships because of work demands?" "What do you do to maintain the relationships?"
5. Have the team create an action plan that applies to the team as a whole and has defined check-in times to ascertain their commitment and progress toward enhancing interpersonal relationships.
6. Ask each person to reflect on the work of the team in this exercise and what it means to them individually. Go around the room and ask each person to share his or her thoughts.

Stress Tolerance

'Cause You've Got Personality

Purpose

To identify whether participants have a personality type that tends to be stressed out. To explore their reactions and select an intervening response.

Thumbnail

19 to 28 minutes

This exercise is specifically helpful for people or groups where there is a lot of highly charged, rather aggressive behavior (Type A). Participants take a personality quiz that highlights Type A behaviors. They reflect on a recent situation in which they exhibited Type A behaviors and explore how they felt and what they were thinking. They select strategies to help them calm down in those situations.

Outcomes

- Heightened awareness of reactions
- Proactive commitment to calm down and be less harsh with others, starting with using the techniques they select in the exercise

Audience

- Intact team
- Unaffiliated group
- Individual working with a coach

Facilitator Competencies

Moderate

Materials

- Personality Quiz Handout
- 'Cause You've Got Personality Handout
- Flip chart and markers
- Pens

Time Matrix

Activity	Estimated Time
Personality Type Quiz	3-5 minutes
Explanation of personality types	3 minutes
Group discussion	5–10 minutes
Calming exercise	5 minutes
Debrief	3-5 minutes
Total	**19 to 28 minutes**

Instructions

1. Distribute copies of the Personality Quiz Handout and pens. Ask the participants to complete the quiz.
2. After everyone has completed the quiz, review the scoring instructions on the second page.

3. Provide the group with an overview of the various types of behavior.

Type A Individuals

Tend to be impatient, aggressive, competitive and multi-tasking with a high need for advancement and achievement. They are often described as hard-driving. Although they are often successful in their careers, they are never satisfied. Some extreme Type A's experience "free-floating" (ever-present) hostility and frequently react with anger. The risk of heart disease may be high for Type A personalities.

Type B Individuals

Tend to be noncompetitive, consciously control anger, and express emotions appropriately. They are often described as easygoing. Although they are not driven over-achievers, they are often as successful in their professions as Type A's.

Type C Individuals

Tend to be passive and self-sacrificing, denying their own needs. They suppress anger and appease others. They are often described as bland. Extreme Type C's, not most of them, can have a profound sense of hopelessness and despair. The risk of cancer may be high for Type C personalities.

4. Lead participants in a discussion about how their bodies feel and what they are thinking when they experience the types of situations referenced in the test.
5. Ask them if they would like to be completely laid back, noncompetitive, and passive (extreme Type C). They will probably say no because they see that as being weak and not having gumption.
6. Ask them whether they can see a middle ground between where they are now, especially if that is between Type A and extreme Type C behavior. Work with the group to develop a list of more helpful alternative behavioral characteristics (Type B). Record these on the flip chart.
7. Distribute the 'Cause You've Got Personality Handout and ask participants to complete it.
8. Debrief by:
   - Asking whether they would like to share the stress reduction response they selected in Item 6 of the 'Cause You've Got Personality Handout.
   - Asking them to choose specific times in their day that they will commit to practice.

9. For an immediate experience of stress reduction that your participants can later utilize as a reference, have everyone practice a calming experience such as those listed in Item 6 of the handout.

PERSONALITY QUIZ HANDOUT

Complete the following statements by indicating whether they are true (always or usually) or false (rarely or never) for you.

Statement	True	False
1. I see myself as competitive and driving.	_____	_____
2. I hate to wait.	_____	_____
3. I work best when I'm up against a deadline.	_____	_____
4. I prefer to do more than one thing at a time.	_____	_____
5. I am often angry with others, even though it may not show.	_____	_____
6. I get irritated with people who make mistakes.	_____	_____
7. I often feel I'm in a race against time.	_____	_____
9. I set very high goals for myself, but I still get angry when I don't meet my goals.	_____	_____

SCORING SHEET

- If you have six to eight true answers, you may exhibit the behaviors of a Type A personality.
- If you have four or five true answers, you are probably more prone to Type B behavior that is balanced between the extremes of Type A and Type C.
- If you have one to three true answers, you may be rather passive and tend toward Type C behavior.

'CAUSE YOU'VE GOT PERSONALITY HANDOUT

Think of a recent interaction with others in which you felt upset, impatient, or angry. Answer the following questions about that experience.

1. How did your body feel?

2. If you felt any of the following symptoms, circle them: heart racing, sweating, twitching, breathing hard, clenching your jaw or other part of body. Did you experience other symptoms?

3. How would you characterize your thoughts about the situation? Rank them on a scale from 1 to 10 where 1 is the most forgiving and 10 is the most judgmental.

4. How did the situation work out? Were you able to reach a mutually agreeable solution?

5. Did your responses increase or decrease the level of stress in that situation?

6. Select and practice one of the following methods for calming down and relieving the pressure. Rehearse it several times in neutral situations with the intention to apply it the next time you find yourself in a stressful situation:
   - Take a deep-breathing break to release the impatience and anger. Clear your mind and concentrate fully on your breathing. Inhale through your nose slowly and deeply to a count of ten, expanding your lungs. Exhale through your nose, slowly and completely to a count of ten, contracting your chest.
   - Even it you don't feel it at the moment, act as if you have high regard for the others involved in the situation. Behave as if you want to resolve the issue *while* treating the person with respect and dignity. Call him or her by name, and make frequent eye contact.
   - Follow another method of your own design.

Emotional Intelligence in Action

7. Practice the behavior at least once and preferably twice a day for several minutes and for several days to develop the habit and perfect the technique.

Stress Tolerance

Water Off a Duck's Back

Purpose

To manage stress by anticipating issues and having coping mechanisms in place.

 ### Thumbnail

30 to 50 minutes

Participants list activities that are stressful to them and itemize the specific stressful aspects. For each aspect of the situation, they develop strategies to mitigate the stress.

Outcomes

- Enhanced ability to avoid or reduce stress through effective management
- Greater awareness of the power of planning for stressful situations

Audience

- Intact team
- Unaffiliated group
- Individual working with a coach

Facilitator Competencies

Easy

Materials

Paper and pens

Time Matrix

Activity	Estimated Time
List and select stressful activities	5–10 minutes
Outline stressful aspects	5–10 minutes
Identify stress mitigation strategies	5–10 minutes
Share with partner	10 minutes
Debrief group	5–10 minutes
Total	**30 to 50 minutes**

Instructions

1. Distribute paper and pens to each participant.
2. Ask individuals to list the three most stressful activities or situations they face on a regular basis—making a presentation, confronting a co-worker, getting through traffic, managing a heavy workload, dating someone new, attending or hosting a family gathering, and so on.
3. Ask them to select one from the list to work on. Encourage them to pick one they will be dealing with in the near future.
4. Have participants notice and write down the sequence of symptoms that indicate the onset of stress.
5. Ask your participants to write down one thing they can do to mitigate or alleviate each symptom of stress that arises in the problematic situation. The following examples may be helpful:
   - Have conversations with key people about the situation. The discussion should cover everyone's expectations and commitment.

- Climb a flight or two of stairs, taking deep breaths all the way up and back.
- Schedule extra time for unforeseen contingencies.
- Seek assistance from a friend.
- Hire a service provider to help.
- Redirect all of your attention from the external world and focus on the internal rhythm of your breath or heart beat.

6. Divide teams into pairs; individuals continue to work with their coaches. Ask the pairs to share their situations, including which aspects are stressors, and to ask their partners for ideas on some ways they would attempt to mitigate the stressors. Take up to ten minutes gathering this information.
7. Debrief the group. Ask what sorts of suggestions they heard and liked, but had not come up with on their own.

Stress Tolerance

Deep Center Breathing

Purpose

To provide simple instructions in a stress reduction technique that will enable people to get in touch with the tension they are holding in their bodies and release it.

 ### Thumbnail

13 to 18 minutes

This exercise is primarily for individuals and can be done in any comfortable location that is quiet and where one will be undisturbed. If a group of individuals wishes to undertake the experience simultaneously, there should be private or silent space available for each individual. The participant(s) practice deep breathing. The most significant competency needed in this exercise will be the facilitator's familiarity with the power and rhythms of his or her own breath. It is recommended that the facilitator practice for two or three consecutive days before attempting to coach others. The facilitator needs to have direct experience of the value this process provides in order to help the participant(s) slow down and appreciate something as intangible as breath.

Outcome

Each person who practices the Deep Center Breathing exercise will gain a greater appreciation for the power of his or her breath, the rhythms of the body, and the amount of stress that is stored in the body.

Audience

- Intact team
- Unaffiliated group
- Individual working with a coach

Facilitator Competencies

Moderate

Materials

Deep Center Breathing Handout

Time Matrix

Activity	Estimated Time
Sit comfortably in a quiet place, begin relaxing	2 minutes
Read and practice the instructions	3-5 minutes
Practice one or two rounds of the breathing exercise	6-8 minutes
Experiment with the advanced method	2-3 minutes
Total	**13 to 18 minutes**

Instructions

1. Invite participants to sit comfortably in a quiet place, relaxing to the best of their ability. Provide the participants with the handout.
2. Emphasizing that each individual's experience of breathing is as unique as their fingerprints in its depth, rhythm, frequency, tension, and cycle (and that it is regularly changing), encourage the participants to first discover just however they happen to be breathing right now.

Emotional Intelligence in Action

3. After several minutes, invite them to read the handout and practice the breathing exercises.

DEEP CENTER BREATHING HANDOUT

According to Candace Pert (2000), a leading neuroscience researcher, people who have lived in the developed world all their lives have over ninety industrial chemicals present in their bodies. Over 70 percent of our bodies' waste by-products are eliminated through our breathing and our skin. Blood, which is fully oxygenated, removes more toxins from our bodies at the cellular level and makes it more difficult for viruses and bacteria to grow in our bodies.

Deep Center Breathing is a powerful stress reduction technique that supports muscle growth and supplies the brain and body the energy they need. It can also help to relieve muscular tension and alleviate stress. Although it is simple, its value should not be underestimated! Patterns of shallow or incomplete breathing do not give the body enough oxygen, which in itself can cause stress and fatigue due to the toxic build-up of carbon dioxide. These kinds of breathing patterns are often learned and repeated unconsciously. Until some sort of conscious breathing technique such as Deep Center Breathing is employed, most people never discover the natural power of their breath. So enjoy!

Deep Center Breathing

Sitting comfortably in your chair, observe your breathing. Notice which parts of your body move with your breath; notice how often you inhale, and how deeply.

Now spread your hands across your stomach, with your thumbs just under your ribs.

Shift your breathing out of your chest down and into your belly.

Feel your lower abdomen swell as the air inflates your lungs. As you exhale, feel it shrink and grow softer.

Now draw in your abdominal muscles and empty the remaining air from your lungs. Again, feel the difference.

Now breathe in this fashion for the next three minutes, inhaling slowly to a count of four and then slowly exhaling to the same count. After you've got the hang of it, just let your hands relax comfortably in your lap. Notice what happens to your heart rate. How is it different when you inhale compared to when you exhale? After three minutes, return to normal breathing. Notice what you're thinking. Notice what you're feeling.

Do this exercise two or three times throughout the day, especially when you feel tired, or spacey, or upset. You can also do a longer version in which you build up time gradually by adding another minute every day until you reach fifteen or twenty minutes. For an additional stretch, try holding your breath for four counts when your lungs are full and again for four counts when they are empty, creating a four-part breathing pattern.

REFERENCE

Pert, C. (2000). *Your body is your subconscious mind.* Boulder, CO: Sounds True.

Impulse Control

To Impulse or Not to Impulse

Purpose

To examine the impact of impulsiveness from a fresh perspective and to show how impulsive urges can have disastrous consequences.

 ### Thumbnail

43 to 60 minutes

Group exercise uses Shakespeare's *King Lear* to illustrate the negative impact of impulsive behavior. Group members act out a portion of King Lear, Act 1, Scene 1. They identify and discuss the ramifications of impulsive behavior.

Outcomes

- New perspective on impulsiveness by looking at it through the lens of fictional history
- Increased awareness of the impacts of impulsiveness
- Utilize the learning to improve impulse control

Audience

- Intact team
- Unaffiliated group

Facilitator Competencies

Moderate to Advanced

Materials

- Facilitator Overview of *King Lear* (Step 2 of Instructions)
- Copies of *King Lear*, Act 1, Scene 1 Handout
  – OR –
- Film clip from *King Lear* showing the Earl of Kent stepping in to try to stop Lear from making a foolhardy decision regarding dividing his kingdom before his demise
- To Impulse or Not to Impulse Handout
- Pens

Time Matrix

Activity	Estimated Time
Provide overview of the Scene	3-5 minutes
Read or show film clip of *King Lear*, Act 1, Scene 1, lines 36-188	15–20 minutes
Debrief	25–35 minutes
Total	**43 to 60 minutes**

Instructions

1. Assign six people to read *King Lear*, Act 1, Scene 1, lines 36 through line 188 (from Lear's first lines until Kent's farewell after being banished). There are three male roles—King Lear, the Earl of Kent, and Albany Cornwall—and three female roles—Goneril, Cordelia, and Regan.
   – OR –
   Set up film clip.

2. Provide the group with an overview of what happens in Act 1, Scene 1, of *King Lear*, as follows.
   - King Lear is in his eighties and appears to be in good health.
   - Knowing that at eighty he is "crawling toward death," he decides to divide his kingdom now to prevent disputes after his death.

- He has already decided to divide it into three parts, one for each daughter—Goneril, Regan, and Cordelia. King Lear has a map that divides the country into thirds, reflecting his decision.
- However, instead of sticking with his plan, he declares on the spot that whichever daughter professes to love him the most will get the largest segment of his kingdom.
- He expects his youngest daughter Cordelia to win this contest.
- Cordelia has always been his favorite and she is completely devoted to her father.
- The other daughters are opportunistic and self-serving.
- His plan backfires.
  - The two older sisters flat-out lie. They profess profound love for their father.
  - Cordelia, disgusted by her sisters' hypocrisy, decides not to play this stupid game.
- Lear disinherits Cordelia and divides the kingdom between Goneril and Regan.
- The Earl of Kent, Lear's trusted advisor, loves the king and is completely loyal to him.
- Kent tries to intervene by telling Lear that he's engaging in "hideous rashness."
- For his insubordination, Lear banishes Kent from the kingdom.
- Lear should have listened to Kent's advice.
  - "By disinheriting Cordelia, Lear sets his tragedy in motion: the daughters who pledged their undying love turn on him, take away his authority, and drive his entourage from the palace and he goes mad. By the end of the play all Lear has left is Cordelia's love. And Kent's love." (Whitney & Packer, 2001, p. 81)

3. Distribute the *King Lear*, Act 1, Scene 1, Handout and have the role players read their parts.
4. Debrief, making the following points and asking the following questions:
   - Lear was in a very emotional state. He was upset about Cordelia's response. Kent was very emotional about Lear's actions.
   - Did Lear act impulsively?
     Answer: Yes, by devising that "stupid parlor trick" as the basis for dividing

the kingdom and also by deciding to ignore his original plan to divide the kingdom into thirds.

- Was Cordelia's decision to basically ignore her father's request a question of impulsiveness (the impulse to be in stark contrast to her sisters)? This is a tricky question to raise because the group may veer off into questions of ethics. Some may think Cordelia's decision to sparingly respond to Lear's request was a matter of ethics: (a) she did not want to support her sisters' hypocrisy by acting as if their statements had any validity or (b) she did not want to support their rash, and maybe unethical, behavior by participating in the charade.
- Were Kent's comments to the King measured or rash?
  Answer: Rash—he called the king's actions "hideous rashness." He did not speak to Lear in a measured way. He responded emotionally and used potentially incendiary language.
- Was Kent acting impulsively by intervening at that moment in the way in which he did?
  Answer: Many scholars and management consultants believe he acted impulsively.
- How would you have advised Kent to respond? When should he do it? What should he say?

5. Ask group members to share examples from their lives where they reacted impulsively and would have benefited from a more thoughtful and strategically sound approach.

6. Ask the group what lessons are to be learned from both Lear's and Kent's behavior.

7. Give everyone a pen and a copy of the To Impulse or Not to Impulse Handout. Ask them to respond to the questions and to record the lessons and insights that resonate with their own behavior.

KING LEAR, ACT 1, SCENE 1, HANDOUT

By William Shakespeare
(Lines 37 to 188)

King Lear

    Meantime we shall express our darker purpose.
    Give me the map there. Know that we have divided
    In three our kingdom: and 'tis our fast intent
    To shake all cares and business from our age;
    Conferring them on younger strengths, while we
    Unburthen'd crawl toward death. Our son of Cornwall,
    And you, our no less loving son of Albany,
    We have this hour a constant will to publish
    Our daughters' several dowers, that future strife
    May be prevented now. The princes, France and Burgundy,
    Great rivals in our youngest daughter's love,
    Long in our court have made their amorous sojourn,
    And here are to be answer'd. Tell me, my daughters,
    Since now we will divest us both of rule,
    Interest of territory, cares of state,
    Which of you shall we say doth love us most?
    That we our largest bounty may extend
    Where nature doth with merit challenge. Goneril,
    Our eldest-born, speak first.

Goneril

    Sir, I love you more than words can wield the matter;
    Dearer than eyesight, space, and liberty;
    Beyond what can be valued, rich or rare;
    No less than life, with grace, health, beauty, honour;
    As much as child e'er loved, or father found;
    A love that makes breath poor, and speech unable;
    Beyond all manner of so much I love you.

Cordelia

    [Aside] What shall Cordelia do?
    Love, and be silent.

Lear

    Of all these bounds, even from this line to this,
    With shadowy forests and with champains rich'd,
    With plenteous rivers and wide-skirted meads,
    We make thee lady: to thine and Albany's issue
    Be this perpetual. What says our second daughter,
    Our dearest Regan, wife to Cornwall? Speak.

Regan

    Sir, I am made
    Of the self-same metal that my sister is,
    And prize me at her worth. In my true heart
    I find she names my very deed of love;
    Only she comes too short: that I profess
    Myself an enemy to all other joys,
    Which the most precious square of sense possesses;
    And find I am alone felicitate
    In your dear highness' love.

Cordelia

    [Aside] Then poor Cordelia!
    And yet not so; since, I am sure, my love's
    More richer than my tongue.

King Lear

    To thee and thine hereditary ever
    Remain this ample third of our fair kingdom;
    No less in space, validity, and pleasure,
    Than that conferr'd on Goneril. Now, our joy,
    Although the last, not least; to whose young love
    The vines of France and milk of Burgundy
    Strive to be interess'd; what can you say to draw
    A third more opulent than your sisters? Speak.

Cordelia

    Nothing, my lord.

King Lear

    Nothing!

Cordelia

Nothing.

King Lear

Nothing will come of nothing: speak again.

Cordelia

Unhappy that I am, I cannot heave
My heart into my mouth: I love your majesty
According to my bond; nor more nor less.

King Lear

How, how, Cordelia! mend your speech a little,
Lest it may mar your fortunes.

Cordelia

Good my lord,
You have begot me, bred me, loved me: I
Return those duties back as are right fit,
Obey you, love you, and most honour you.
Why have my sisters husbands, if they say
They love you all? Haply, when I shall wed,
That lord whose hand must take my plight shall carry
Half my love with him, half my care and duty:
Sure, I shall never marry like my sisters,
To love my father all.

King Lear

But goes thy heart with this?

Cordelia

Ay, good my lord.

King Lear

So young, and so untender?

Cordelia

So young, my lord, and true.

King Lear

>Let it be so; thy truth, then, be thy dower:
>For, by the sacred radiance of the sun,
>The mysteries of Hecate, and the night;
>By all the operation of the orbs
>From whom we do exist, and cease to be;
>Here I disclaim all my paternal care,
>Propinquity and property of blood,
>And as a stranger to my heart and me
>Hold thee, from this, for ever. The barbarous Scythian,
>Or he that makes his generation messes
>To gorge his appetite, shall to my bosom
>Be as well neighbour'd, pitied, and relieved,
>As thou my sometime daughter.

Kent

>Good my liege—

King Lear

>Peace, Kent!
>Come not between the dragon and his wrath.
>I loved her most, and thought to set my rest
>On her kind nursery. Hence, and avoid my sight!
>So be my grave my peace, as here I give
>Her father's heart from her! Call France; who stirs?
>Call Burgundy. Cornwall and Albany,
>With my two daughters' dowers digest this third:
>Let pride, which she calls plainness, marry her.
>I do invest you jointly with my power,
>Pre-eminence, and all the large effects
>That troop with majesty. Ourself, by monthly course,
>With reservation of an hundred knights,
>By you to be sustain'd, shall our abode
>Make with you by due turns. Only we still retain
>The name, and all the additions to a king;
>The sway, revenue, execution of the rest,
>Beloved sons, be yours: which to confirm,

Emotional Intelligence in Action

This coronet part betwixt you.
[Giving the crown]

Kent

Royal Lear,
Whom I have ever honour'd as my king,
Loved as my father, as my master follow'd,
As my great patron thought on in my prayers,—

King Lear

The bow is bent and drawn, make from the shaft.

Kent

Let it fall rather, though the fork invade
The region of my heart: be Kent unmannerly,
When Lear is mad. What wilt thou do, old man?
Think'st thou that duty shall have dread to speak,
When power to flattery bows? To plainness honour's bound,
When majesty stoops to folly. Reverse thy doom;
And, in thy best consideration, cheque
This hideous rashness: answer my life my judgment,
Thy youngest daughter does not love thee least;
Nor are those empty-hearted whose low sound
Reverbs no hollowness.

King Lear

Kent, on thy life, no more.

Kent

My life I never held but as a pawn
To wage against thy enemies; nor fear to lose it,
Thy safety being the motive.

King Lear

Out of my sight!

Kent

See better, Lear; and let me still remain
The true blank of thine eye.

King Lear

Now, by Apollo,—

Kent

Now, by Apollo, king,
Thou swear'st thy gods in vain.

King Lear

O, vassal! miscreant!
[Laying his hand on his sword]

Albany/Cornwall

Dear sir, forbear.

Kent

Do:
Kill thy physician, and the fee bestow
Upon thy foul disease. Revoke thy doom;
Or, whilst I can vent clamour from my throat,
I'll tell thee thou dost evil.

King Lear

Hear me, recreant!
On thine allegiance, hear me!
Since thou hast sought to make us break our vow,
Which we durst never yet, and with strain'd pride
To come between our sentence and our power,
Which nor our nature nor our place can bear,
Our potency made good, take thy reward.
Five days we do allot thee, for provision
To shield thee from diseases of the world;
And on the sixth to turn thy hated back
Upon our kingdom: if, on the tenth day following,
Thy banish'd trunk be found in our dominions,
The moment is thy death. Away! by Jupiter,
This shall not be revoked.

Kent

>Fare thee well, king: sith thus thou wilt appear,
>Freedom lives hence, and banishment is here.
>[To Cordelia]
>The gods to their dear shelter take thee, maid,
>That justly think'st, and hast most rightly said!
>[To Regan and Goneril]
>And your large speeches may your deeds approve,
>That good effects may spring from words of love.
>Thus Kent, O princes, bids you all adieu;
>He'll shape his old course in a country new.
>[Exit]

Source: Shakespeare, W. *King Lear.* Available: http://www-tech.mit.edu/Shakespeare/ works.htlm

Emotional Intelligence in Action. Copyright © 2006 by Marcia Hughes, L. Bonita Patterson, & James Bradford Terrell. Reproduced by permission of Pfeiffer, an Imprint of Wiley. www.pfeiffer.com

TO IMPULSE OR NOT TO IMPULSE HANDOUT

1. What are the lessons learned from the play *King Lear*?

   - From King Lear the man?

   - From the Earl of Kent?

2. Briefly describe a time when you spoke before thinking.

3. What triggered your impulsive behavior? Is that part of a pattern for you? What could you do in the future to manage your impulsiveness?

Impulse Control

The Urge to Splurge

Purpose

To explore the motivation and results of the participants' impulsive behavior, and to chart a new path.

 ### Thumbnail

35 to 55 minutes

Participants closely scrutinize their impulses by identifying when they are impulsive, why they are impulsive, what desired and undesired results accrue, and how they can behave differently in the future.

Outcomes

- Heightened awareness due to an in-depth examination of one's own behavior
- Increased commitment to develop better impulse control
- Newly available behavioral alternatives

Audience

- Intact team
- Unaffiliated group
- Individual working with a coach

Facilitator Competencies ◖

Moderate

Materials

- The Urge to Splurge Handout
- Pens

Time Matrix

Activity	Estimated Time
Introduce concept and exercise	5 minutes
Complete PCG ChangeNow™ steps	15–20 minutes
Debrief	15–30 minutes
Total	**35 to 55 minutes**

Instructions

1. Briefly introduce the concept of impulse control. Ask the individual or group for examples of helpful impulsive behaviors:
   - Sample answer: Expressing anger (appropriately) instead of stuffing it
   - Sample answer: Impulse to flee from a dangerous situation

   Ask for negative examples of impulsiveness
   - Sample answer: Confronting someone at work about an issue publicly, when it would be better to wait until a more appropriate time
   - Sample answer: Shopping for clothes when you have scores of items in your closet you have never worn
   - Sample answer: Gaining weight due to overeating
2. Explain that this exercise will help them identify their counterproductive impulsive behavior and devise alternatives.
3. Distribute the Urge to Splurge Handout and pens and then review the PCG ChangeNow™ Model. The model explores an area in which participants are getting suboptimal results due to impulsive behavior. It asks them to analyze the circumstances in which the behavior occurs, discuss how the behav-

ior is serving them, and identify unintended consequences. The model then asks them to focus on desired results, brainstorm new behaviors that would help them achieve the desired results, surface barriers that might inhibit success, and develop strategies to overcome the barriers.

4. After reviewing the model, ask the participants to complete the handout.
5. Debrief by asking the following:
   - How did it feel to examine this behavior?
   - Were you able to identify the benefits you derive?
   - How did you feel about those benefits?
   - Did the benefits outweigh the undesired outcomes, or vice versa?
   - Were you able to move beyond the undesirable condition and achieve your desired results?
   - What alternatives to the impulsive behavior did you find?
   - Think ahead about what barriers you might encounter. What will you do when you encounter those barriers?
6. If they want to develop their skills in this area, have them notice and record their encounters with impulsiveness for one week.
   - Each day record the times you felt impulsive and how you responded.
   - During the day, catch yourself doing something right, and reward your successes with a proven stress-buster like congratulatory self-talk ("I said I was going to do it and I really did! I'm strong, I'm disciplined! I'm awesome!"), step outside for a breath of fresh air, or take a brisk walk.

THE URGE TO SPLURGE HANDOUT

PCG ChangeNow™ Model*

Current Results

1. List the areas in your life where impulsiveness is producing suboptimal results such as anxiety, unhappiness, arguments, avoidance, and so on.

Factors

2. Write down which specific impulsive behaviors are causing those results.
3. Analyze the circumstances that give rise to the impulsive behavior
   - Are the impulses localized in key areas of your life or paired with specific situations?
   - Are you operating at a generally high level of free-floating hostility that is ever-poised for an opportunity to express itself?

Benefits of Current Behavior

4. Determine how the impulsive behavior is serving you.
   - What do you get out of it?
   - What needs, desires, or habits does it satisfy?

---

*This workout is created by and used with the permission of Polaris Consulting Group.

Undesired Outcomes of Current Behavior

5. Subsequent to the initial satisfaction, what negative results do you experience?

Desired Results

6. What are the outcomes you really DO want to have—short term and long term?

Create New Approach

7. Brainstorm new behaviors that will satisfy both the positive intentions of your current approach and achieve the desired results you have not attained yet. The approaches may need to be different for each type of situation or impulse.

Barriers to Implementing Your New Approach

8. What old habits, behaviors, and unexpected conditions might highjack your new efforts and allow your previous strategies to re-assert themselves?

Strategies to Overcome Barriers

9. What will you do to overcome the barriers and resist the pull of impulsiveness?

Impulse Control

Hot Buttons

Purpose

To help people notice and modify how they respond when their self-control is starting to lose ground to their impulsiveness.

Thumbnail

60 minutes

Participants will determine whether they are triggered more easily by approach impulses or by avoidance impulses. They will learn to notice their automatic behaviors and discuss how to change them. The exercise is written so that participants can choose to improve their control over both kinds of impulses—those situations that tempt them and those situations that make them angry.

Outcomes

- Be able to anticipate and counter the effects of unconscious response patterns
- Understand the dynamics of the "move toward" and "move away from" responses

Audience

- Intact team
- Unaffiliated group
- Individual working with a coach

Facilitator Competencies

Advanced

Materials

- Hot Buttons Handout
- Paper and pens

Time Matrix

Activity	Estimated Time
Read the handout and think about how impulsiveness shows up in your life	5 minutes
Work with partner in decoding a specific impulse-control pattern in your life you'd like to change	20 minutes
Develop impulse-control plan and practice using it while partner attempts to trigger the old pattern	20 minutes
Group discussion of what people learned	15 minutes
Total	**60 minutes**

Instructions

1. Distribute pens, paper, and the Hot Buttons Handout.
2. Ask participants to get into pairs for this exercise.
3. Ask them to read the handout all the way through on their own, and then follow the directions together.
4. After twenty minutes remind them they should now begin developing their impulse control strategy.
5. After fifteen more minutes, give them a five-minute warning.
6. In five minutes begin a debriefing with questions such as, "What has changed about the way you understand your impulses now?"

HOT BUTTONS HANDOUT

Consider for a moment which type of impulses are the hardest for you to control—those that move you toward something you desire (food, shopping, alcohol, and other forms of gratification) or those that move you away from something you reject (behavior that makes you angry, kinds of people and remarks that put you off).

Once you have identified which impulses are most difficult, choose a specific example you can share with your partner in which you tried your best to consciously restrain what you said and/or did, but ended up behaving impulsively anyway. Try to identify what was happening when you first felt the impulse and, second, when your resistance was finally losing out and you actually acted on the impulse.

Carefully describe the situation to your partner, being very specific about the sequence of events that got you started. Pay particular attention to your three most commonly used senses—sight, sound, and touch. Tell your partner what you were seeing, hearing, and feeling as well as what you were saying to yourself as the specific impulse started.

Once your partner understands the pattern that initiates the sequence of impulsive behavior in this kind of situation, he or she can "argue on behalf of your impulse" by reminding you of your responses to the various environmental stimuli. For example:

> Partner: "You are seeing the beautiful coat on the rack in the store and start to feel excited as you move toward it."

Notice how your *body* responds to this description! If you are tracking down the sequence of responses of a "move toward" impulse, they may be significantly different from those that are associated with a "move away from" impulse. Eyes dilating, temperature increase, salivation, and such are common for "move toward." Tension in the face, jaws, stomach, and hands are common responses for "move away." Self-talk is typical for each type of behavior, while increased heart rate and flushing can be common responses for *both* kinds of impulses.

Now have your partner remind you of the cues that occurred at the second stage as the impulse was escalating and you were about to act. For example:

Partner: "You are seeing the beautiful color of the fabric and feeling how smooth and silky it is while you remember the fancy party you attended and hear yourself saying 'I look like a million bucks!,' and you feel that buying this coat might make everything that wonderful once again."

Notice how your *body* responds to this description! Meanwhile, practice your new strategy for resisting this impulse by seeing your credit card bill and feeling worried that you can't pay the bill, while you see all the clothes already hanging in your closet and you say to yourself, "Wait, I'm happy with who I am, not because of what I have!"

In the space below list the cues that trigger impulsiveness and the resourceful behaviors you have learned in this exercise as reminders you can use to help you notice and interrupt destructive impulse patterns in the future. Then you will be able to choose more constructive ones that serve your true goals. Use the back side of this paper if you need more space.

Reality Testing

Feel, Hear, See—Is It Reality?

Purpose

To help clarify how accurately we are assessing the correspondence between our experience and what exists objectively.

Thumbnail

60 minutes

Team members agree on one situation in the workplace that is challenging for all of them. Each person will write up an assessment of the problem, paying close attention to a list of specific factors. A group debriefing brings all the information together. Be certain to coach the participants in a manner that is highly accurate and descriptive rather than evaluative.

Outcomes

- Increase each participant's reality-testing skills
- Enhance team awareness of how they operate collectively

Audience

- Intact team
- Unaffiliated group

Facilitator Competencies

Moderate

Materials

- Feel, Here, See—Is It Reality? Handout
- Paper and pens

Time Matrix

Activity	Estimated Time
Analyze and write up assessment	15 minutes
Discuss in triads	20 minutes
Debrief in total group	25 minutes
Total	**60 minutes**

Instructions

1. Ask team members to agree on one situation in the workplace that is challenging for them.
2. Give each person paper, a pen, and a copy of the Feel, Hear, See—Is It Reality? Handout and ask them all to write up an assessment of the problem, paying specific attention to when it first began, identifying the initiating factors, how the players feel about the situation now, what it means to them, what the dangers and opportunities are, and so forth.
3. Tell the participants to get in groups of three (if need be, there can be one pair) and to discuss their assessments.
4. Reconvene the full group to debrief. Sample questions you might start with include:
   - What kinds of situations will you address best if you do more concrete reality testing?
   - Do you have any other strategies you can share that promote effective reality testing for you?

FEEL, HEAR, SEE—IS IT REALITY? HANDOUT

Answer each question individually, and then move to group discussion as instructed.

1. Describe the problem that your team has agreed to investigate. When did you first become aware of the problem?

2. How did you first become aware of it? Was it a purely cognitive recognition, an emotional recognition, or some combination of the two?

3. What specifically did you see and hear that told you how big a problem others perceived it to be?

4. How did you feel about what you saw and heard?

5. Who, if anyone, has something to gain from the way this problem is resolved? Who has something to lose? What might be gained or lost, and how motivating will that be?

6. What proof do you have to offer in support of your analysis?

7. Is there any other logical way to explain this situation, whether it seems as likely or not?

8. Have there ever been any similar situations, either in this workplace or another, that you or other team members misperceived and/or incorrectly evaluated? What was the misperception? What was the actual situation? What was the outcome?

Reality Testing

Visit Their Reality

Purpose

To increase reality testing skills by learning how to view a situation through another person's eyes.

 ### Thumbnail

40 to 45 minutes

Participants consider disagreements they are having with others in their lives (preferably something current) and explore how reality looks and works for the other person until they understand it well enough to argue the other person's side.

Outcomes

- Learn how to take someone else's point of view in order to test reality by looking at it from a different perspective
- Increase one's own empathy and negotiation skills at the same time

Audience

- Intact team
- Unaffiliated group
- Individual working with a coach

Facilitator Competencies ◯

Easy

Materials

- Visit Their Reality Handout
- Paper and pens

Time Matrix

Activity	Estimated Time
Complete worksheet	20 minutes
Practice with a partner being in the other person's shoes	10–15 minutes
Have the full group debrief the experience	10 minutes
Total	**40 to 45 minutes**

Instructions

1. Distribute the Visit Their Reality Handout and paper and pens.
2. Instruct participants to take up to twenty minutes completing the handout.
3. Have the group join in pairs and take turns so that each partner role plays being the other person in the disagreement.
4. Get the whole group together to debrief the experience. Sample questions you might begin with include:
   - Has this process helped you expand your awareness of other perspectives?
   - Where else might this process be useful?
   - How will you help yourself remember to expand your understanding of other people's reality?
5. Illustrate the difference between positions and interests by describing the situation in which two people both want the same orange. That is their position. One wants it to eat, the other wants the rind to bake cookies. Those are their interests.*

---

*This is adapted from *Getting to Yes.* Fisher and Ury (1981).

VISIT THEIR REALITY HANDOUT

Think of a disagreement you have with someone in your life. It can be at work or with friends or family, but it should be something that you are currently experiencing. It might be longstanding and not very active now, but ready to flare up if the topic is raised. By now, something has probably already come to mind.

Make a list of the reasons that you are right about your position and a list of the reasons that the other person is wrong. Be as specific as possible.

Now make a list of why he or she would say that you are wrong and he or she is right. Be as accurate and thorough as possible.

Do your best to identify the interests, goals, desires, and perceived needs that motivate the other person. Interests are distinctly different from positions. Positions are the obvious solutions we insist we must have to be happy, while interests are the deeper needs that must be met in order to really resolve the core of the problem. People usually focus on their positions and may never truly understand their interests. However, people usually can recognize their interests with some work, although that often takes someone with an impartial point of view providing assistance.

Once you have identified the other person's interests and figured out what makes him or her "tick," take the other side of the disagreement and develop the best strategy for that position. Write down the best arguments you can construct against your own position and describe why they are valid, important, and merit your consideration.

Now go back and consider your own interests. There is probably a very direct but not necessarily obvious connection between the other person's interests and your own. What are the goals, desires, and perceived needs that are motivating you? Compare the list from your point of view with the list from the other person's point of view. Where is there common ground? Where is he or she being unrealistic? Where are you being unrealistic? How would a neutral third party observing this from the "outside" perceive the situation? How have you upgraded your perception of reality by doing this exercise?

Reality Testing

Using All Three of Your Minds

Purpose

To increase the effectiveness and accuracy of your reality testing by connecting with your head, heart, and gut.

Thumbnail

60 to 80 minutes

Working with a coach or in small groups, the individuals review past and present decision making to discover the value of conducting a reality check using all three "brains." Easy references for understanding this model are listed.

Outcomes

- Discuss the idea of having three different brains, one in the head, one in the heart, and one in the gut
- Consider how participants have made decisions in the past to assess whether they used information from all three brains to connect with the whole spectrum of reality
- Apply this to future decision making and reality testing

Audience

- Intact team
- Unaffiliated group
- Individual working with a coach

Facilitator Competencies

Moderate

Materials

- Using All Three of Your Minds Handout
- Flip chart and markers (optional)
- Pens

Time Matrix

Activity	Estimated Time
Discuss using all three brains	10–15 minutes
In pairs or threes talk about prior decision-making processes, then how to make a future decision and check reality using all three brains; write about learnings	30–40 minutes
Group discussion	10–15 minutes
Reflect	10 minutes
Total	**60 to 80 minutes**

Instructions

1. Discuss the importance of reality testing and that we obtain a great deal of information from all three of our brains—those located in our head, our heart, and our gut. (Many resources about the brain address this subject, for example, Childre and Martin's [1999] *The Heartmath Solution*, www.heartmath.com, and www.mindpub.com/art411.htm have good information about the heart brain. The *Other 90 Percent*, by Cooper [2001], has some good information on the gut brain.)

Emotional Intelligence in Action

2. Distribute the handout and pens.
3. Work directly with your coaching client or organize your group in pairs (a group of three would be okay if there's an extra person) and have them follow the directions in the handout.
4. In the full group, have each person reflect on what he or she has gained from this exercise.

USING ALL THREE OF YOUR MINDS HANDOUT

In Pairs or Threes

1. Each of you tells the other(s) about a time when you made a difficult decision and what steps you took to determine what was really happening. Reflect on the details of *how* you made the decision. The issue itself is not important for this exercise, although you will discuss it some. What is important is your decision-making process. How long did you take to consider the matter? Why? How did you feel? What did you think about? Did you consider past and/or future events? Did you check in regarding each of these details with your head, heart, and gut before making a decision? If so, did you get different answers? If so, how did you decide what to do?

2. Having told each other your stories, take five minutes and make some notes for yourself about your observations.

3. In the same groups, have each person describe a pending problem that is important, but one for which no decision has yet been made. Ask yourselves all the questions discussed above. Notice what each of your brains is telling you. Answer the following:

- My head is telling me (provide details):

- My heart is guiding me to:

- My gut let me know:

Now how do you bring these three parts of you together?

4. Take time for each person to answer these questions out loud, then take five minutes and make some notes for yourself about your observations.

In Group

Reflect on what you learned and how you will take time to incorporate the wisdom of all of your brainpower in your decision making so that you connect with the full picture of reality.

Flexibility

No More Shutdowns

Purpose

To discover how to be more productive, flexible, and resilient by using positive statements to counter destructive self-talk and free our attention from disturbing, negative thoughts.

 ### Thumbnail

32 to 42 minutes

Individuals and team members will practice observing their negative, limiting thoughts and learn to substitute more positive ones. As they notice the difference from using the more flexible statement, they will be motivated to give themselves the type of messages that will increase their flexibility. Team members will observe how negative self-talk influences others, thus decreasing flexibility and the power to deal effectively with change. They will list the negative, fearful messages they hear themselves saying and will practice countering them by substituting more positive phrases.

Outcomes

- Learn how the way we think about an issue impacts us, and particularly focus on the consequences of flexible thinking

- Discover the value of clarifying statements and requests before jumping to *"No!"* or *"It won't work!"* and similar comments that shutdown options for resourceful responses

Audience

- Intact team
- Unaffiliated group
- Individual working with a coach

Facilitator Competencies

Moderate

Materials

- List of negative thoughts and positive counters. You may use the No More Shutdowns Handout or create your own list to meet the specifics of your individual's or team's situation
- Paper and pens

Time Matrix

Activity	Estimated Time
Brief introduction of flexibility	5 minutes
Participants read and discuss the concept of positive "can do" thoughts; make a commitment to change	7 minutes
Individually, or in pairs, practice the different negative messages followed by the positive messages	10–15 minutes
Discuss and apply to real-life examples	10–15 minutes
Optional: Set a strategy for repeating the process on their own and then reporting back if possible	Up to the discretion of the trainer
Total	**32 to 42 minutes**

Instructions

1. Give a brief introduction to the topic of flexibility. Refer to the discussion in Part Two of this book on flexibility for guidance.

2. Distribute the No More Shutdowns Handout (or your own list) and pens. Explain that the participants will be working with the statements in the handout, first making a negative comment that will then be followed by a positive comment intended to open up possibilities.

3. Ask the participants to get into pairs.

4. Tell participants to begin practicing the statements with their partners, noticing how they feel when they say or receive shutdown statements, as compared to opening statements of possibilities.

5. After ten to fifteen minutes, reconvene the entire group and debrief with a focus on what occurred and why. Notice multiple areas of response. How did it feel to say no, or to hear no? How did it feel when new possibilities were invited using the positive statement? Connect feelings with the meanings.

6. Lead the group or individual in a discussion about how to apply this learning in the workplace.

NO MORE SHUTDOWNS HANDOUT

Moving from Shutdown (SD) to Possibility (P)

Four areas of comments are listed in the following chart. Expand the categories or add new ones as meets your needs.

Change

SD (Shutdown)	I've always done it this way and it keeps me safe. I don't want to change.
P (Possibility)	I think I'll explore how well this is thought out. Perhaps I should give it a chance.
SD	Every reorganization we've tried has been meaningless. This will be just the same, so I'm not going to try.
P	I know they have worked hard on this reorganization, so, while I'm skeptical, I'll give it a chance. (Bonus: I'll help them be successful by using my skills.)

About Me

SD	It seems like I never finish my work as it is; there's no way I can join the office softball team.
P	I've heard that getting exercise helps people do their work faster. I'll join the team for the six-week season and give it a try.

Others

SD	Sally is always making big changes; she must never get her work done.
P	I'm curious about all those changes Sally makes. I'm going to ask her how that helps her get her work done.

Work

SD	When I go to work, I have to follow my routine to get my work done. Otherwise, I'm derailed and the day is pointless.
P	I like to follow my routine at work. But some of what is on my plate just isn't getting done. I need some new tools or strategies. What have I got to lose looking in a new direction?

SD	All these changes hurt my friends; no one is looking after their interests.
P	I wonder what these changes will mean for my friends and others here? I'm going to help everyone consider what is happening very seriously.
SD	I just know they haven't considered all the facts in developing this new plan. I oppose it.
P	I'll give this a chance and along the way find out what data they have looked at. Maybe I can help them consider all the critical factors.

Flexibility

Yes, No, Maybe So

Purpose

To recognize the value of flexibility in responding to life's endless challenges. To note how our choices relate to other emotional intelligence skills such as reality testing and stress tolerance.

Thumbnail

40 minutes

Participants discuss what it means to be flexible and recognize that judgment is required for effective application of this skill. They also discuss the rich connection to other emotional intelligence factors in determining the consequences of their flexibility.

Outcomes

- Gain awareness of the value of flexibility and of specific applications in our lives
- Recognize that using flexibility requires judgment; it is not a black-and-white world

Audience

- Intact team
- Unaffiliated group
- Individual working with a coach

Facilitator Competencies ◯ ◑

Easy to Moderate

Materials

- Yes, No, Maybe So Handout
- Flip chart and markers
- Range of Response Continuum (see Step 2 in instructions)
- Pens

Time Matrix

Activity	Estimated Time
Discuss pros and cons of flexibility	5 minutes
Review a range of responses to challenges	5 minutes
Discuss scenarios	20 minutes
Pull together with a list of key points	10 minutes
Total	**40 minutes**

Instructions

1. Review the reasons why we tend to be inflexible. Notice that there are many personal differences. Some seem to go with the flow; others want it just so. Each can have strengths at different times. However, we know that our world is dramatically impacted by continuous changes and we can't fight against too many of them and still survive. Note the need to pull in additional emotional intelligence elements in determining how to respond to many situations. Reality testing is often key: "Is this worth resisting?" Optimism can be critical: "Even though this seems like a setback, we know we can find a good solution. We just don't know it *yet*."

2. In order to gain perspective, instruct the individual you are coaching or your group to consider the following range of responses to opportunities to use their flexibility. (The following range should be on a flip chart to which you can point.)

Don't Change	Moderate Change	Go for It

3. Ask what pros and cons they see to the different responses. Then lead the group in a discussion of how to choose and how to be flexible in degrees. Can they say yes to aspects of a change and help find win/win answers? Record key strategic points they make in the discussion.
4. Distribute the Yes, No, Maybe So Handout and pens and ask participants to read through the scenarios. If you wish, supplement this list with examples of your own choosing or actual examples from participants' experiences.
5. As a group, discuss a variety of responses, noting the ways to build flexibility. Help them grow to understand the value of flexibility in their lives and to recognize that it's not about giving up values. Show them that there are times to say "Yes!" and times to say "No!" and times to say, "Maybe, let's see."
6. To conclude, have participants list the key points they have discovered. Then have each take a few minutes to think of a recent time in his or her life when he or she would have benefited by being more flexible.

YES, NO, MAYBE SO HANDOUT

1. Your assistant has just made a passionate presentation on the value of changing your computers from PC's to Mac's. It's the first thing he's ever really advocated, and he spent a lot of time researching this proposal, although you had no idea he was working on such a plan. Your whole office uses PC's, and you've never touched a Mac.

2. Your boss wants you to give up flex hours. She says it's just too confusing and reduces productivity to not have a five-day work week. Currently you work ten hours a day for four days. This fits your childcare needs perfectly.

3. You manage a section with fifty people and have four direct-report first-tier supervisors. They're begging you to moderate your highly flexible strategy with the staff. You allow people to set their own hours and trust that they worked those hours if they accomplish their goals.

4. Your colleague keeps a messy office and seems to love it that way. He says he can find things and he loves to have lots going at once. You strongly prefer a neat, orderly office. Your files are put away at the end of the day. (His never are!) You work best on one project at a time. The two of you have started getting on one another's nerves because you work in close quarters and share data. It's becoming a stress for everyone so you have both agreed to discuss your different styles and see whether you can find a way to reduce the tension.

5. Your daughter just took up drums and practices religiously for an hour, starting just when you get home from work and need quiet time.

6. You have been working diligently to get a favorite project done; however, every time you take it to the review committee, they ask for more changes.

7. The City just added a turn light at the intersection near your home. It seems like it takes forever to go through it and get home.

8. Getting through security at the airport takes three times as long as it used to, and you just don't have that much time.

Flexibility

Flex Time

Purpose

To begin the process of increasing flexibility by committing to do at least one flexibility enhancing activity.

Thumbnail

30 to 35 minutes

Participants or individuals discuss the negative impacts of not being flexible. They brainstorm to create a list of things they can do to increase flexibility. Each person selects one or two activities to do in the next week. If they are meeting in an ongoing forum, they report back to the group at the next meeting and share their experiences.

Outcomes

- List of activities to develop flexibility
- Commitment to use at least one tool to increase flexibility and report back to group or coach

Audience

- Intact team
- Unaffiliated group
- Individual working with a coach

Facilitator Competencies ◯

Easy

Materials

- Flip chart and markers
- 3 x 5 cards
- Pens

Time Matrix

Activity	Estimated Time
Discuss impacts of lack of flexibility	10 minutes
Develop list of activities	10 minutes
Create pocket card	10–15 minutes
Total	**30 to 35 minutes**

Instructions

1. Ask the participants to think of recent situations in which they believe they should have been more flexible.
2. Ask the group to share negative impacts of not being more flexible, and capture the responses on a flip chart.
3. Say to the group, "What could you have done to be more flexible? One of the biggest obstacles to increasing our flexibility is that we don't want to!" Have the group list three reasons that people don't want to be more flexible; discuss why and what we can do about it. Capture the information on a flip chart.

4. Next, ask participants to develop a list of things they can do differently that would require them to be more flexible. Record the list on a flip chart. If the group has trouble getting started, use items from the following list to jumpstart the process:
   - Eat a kind of food you've never eaten before
   - Drive a different route to work
   - Listen to a different type of music
   - Read something outside of your usual area—biography, mystery, history, art, science
5. Tell participants to select at least one or two of these specific changes to incorporate into their lives and to make a written commitment to do so—including when and how.
6. Distribute the 3 x 5 cards and pens. Tell participants that they will be creating pocket cards.
   - On one side, they are to list the specific behavior to change.
   - On the reverse side, they should write why it is important to be more flexible and list the specific times of day and the number of days they will refer to the card to reinforce the commitment.
7. (*Optional*) In the next meeting or coaching session, share experiences and select another activity to increase flexibility.

Problem Solving

Using the MasterSolve Model©
for Teams

Purpose

To give participants a real-life emotional intelligence problem-solving experience in which they receive real feedback about their success.

 ### Thumbnail

65 to 85 minutes

A team will work with a sample problem taken from a situation they share. They will be required to put their differing information together to find the full nature of the problem and then to collaborate on the solutions.

Advanced Version: Facilitator introduces a new set of variables and changes that occur after the first solution has been implemented, and the team must craft a second response to the new problem. This can be repeated up to four times, continuing the fifteen-minute deadline for each new iteration.

Outcomes

- Experience a "real-life" problem-solving scenario and get "real" feedback
- Expand awareness of problem-solving capabilities
- Learn to combine the joint dynamics of considering the problem well while meeting a deadline
- Boost problem-solving skills

Audience

Intact teams

Facilitator Competencies

Moderate to Advanced

Materials

- MasterSolve Model for Teams Handout
- Sample Scenario for facilitator
- Problem scenarios prepared for each participant (see Step 3 and Sample Scenario)
- Timer or clock
- Flip chart and colored markers

Time Matrix

Activity	Estimated Time—Group
Brief introduction to problem solving	5–10 minutes
Participants read and discuss the MasterSolve Model	10 minutes
Develop a general hypothesis on the nature of the problem	5–10 minutes
Read the case scenarios and collaboratively plug data into the problem-solving formula	20 minutes
Create response	15 minutes
Debrief	10 to 20 minutes
Total	**65 to 85 minutes**

Instructions

1. Give a brief introduction to problem solving.
2. Distribute the MasterSolve Model© for Teams Handout. Read and discuss the model.
3. Distribute the problem scenario sheets (prepared in advance by the facilitator). Each participant receives the same background statement and the unique information about the problem of which he or she alone is aware. This creates a puzzle effect, so the group has to work together to know the whole problem. If your group is too large for the situation, you can break into subgroups and have multiple groups solve the same scenario. The problem scenarios should be prepared in advance by the facilitator. A sample situation is included at the end of the instructions. Review it to ensure you understand the type of problem to which you will apply the process.
4. Instruct the participants to read their handouts; tell them that they will then be working together to solve the problem, given the information that they have. Instruct participants to develop a group hypothesis about the general nature of the problem.
5. Direct the group members to work collaboratively to plug all the facts into the MasterSolve formula to create a detailed model of the problem. Strictly enforce a twenty-minute deadline on this step.
6. Based on the model, have them create and report their potential solutions to you in fifteen minutes or less! Failing to respond in that amount of time results in a fatal crisis (created by the facilitator and relevant to the particular problem scenario developed for the team—the buyer withdraws the offer, the airplane departs without them, etc.). The solutions must directly reflect how they have used the steps of the model.
7. Debrief the process. Questions you might ask to get the discussion started include:
   - How well were you able to integrate all the facts to develop the whole picture of what is happening?
   - What was your process and experience as you applied Step 2 of the model to create awareness of the factors leading to a good solution?
   - What was the impact of the strict time rules? How is this like situations at work when it seems you are working on tight deadlines? How would you suggest meeting those deadlines while staying creative and resourceful?

Sample Scenario

Note to Facilitator: When creating the problem sheets, the top part of each sheet should contain the same scenario. The bottom part of each sheet, however, should contain a different role so that only the person playing that role receives that information.

Success with this exercise requires that you use a factual situation similar to those your team struggles with. The following sample would work for a group of city or county employees. If your team is a different type of group, you will need to create a more relevant problem scenario.

In this example, the information under Cozy Coffee vs. National Biggie would appear on the top of each of the handouts that you create.

Emotional Intelligence in Action

COZY COFFEE VS. NATIONAL BIGGIE

Scenario: Your team works for the City of Hope and Well-Being. Despite your very positive name, which city leaders bestowed in a surge of zest and optimism, the city's tax base has been declining. Actually, it's an up-and-down affair. The city looks pretty good, but appearances can be deceiving. It's a struggle to keep up the good appearance. Now there's an opportunity to add a reliable storefront presence on Main Street, but there seem to be as many citizens against bringing in a national brand franchise coffee shop as there are for it. The city's team in the Planning and Zoning Department is convening to discuss the issue and attempt to provide leadership to turn dissension into a collaborative and positive result for the city.

Each staff member has focused on the dynamics and positions of one particular group (Cozy Coffee, National Biggie, neighborhood groups, college students, other downtown businesses, or the city council itself). Now you are coming together to understand the different perspectives and to problem solve so the city council can provide the leadership that is so important. National Biggie would like a zoning variance to remodel the store to meet its preferred format, but they could make it work without the variance. Therefore, the only explicit control the city has is in the decision, which will be made by the director of the department, on whether or not to issue the variance the national chain franchise coffee shop has requested. The team includes the people from the planning department who have met with each of the different groups as described below.

Note to Facilitator: The bottom part of each sheet would then contain one of the following role descriptions, with each team member receiving a different sheet.

National Biggie

You have spoken with representatives from National Biggie and found them very eager to open a store in your downtown area. The location is picked out, the franchise is ready to be signed. They think it should be a cakewalk for this to come to fruition. The citizen opposition is annoying, but they don't want to deal with it. After all, National Biggie is not inclined to take time building relationships with the community. You know this attitude will be at their peril, but you're not sure who to even talk to about the situation in this big, faceless corporation.

Cozy Coffee

Cozy Coffee has been a true neighborhood coffee shop and deli for thirty years. All the locals hang out there; the college kids love it and convene for late evening discussions; and you and your spouse drop by on Sunday mornings for the croissants and coffee while you read the paper. They've begun talking of expanding and adding an Internet café, but now their plans are on hold because they fear the influence of a large chain just down the block. They've heard about what happens to local businesses when a national chain comes in, and they're concerned that Cozy Coffee will be put out of business. They see it as the beginning of a negative trend, so they're certainly not in favor of allowing National Biggie to take over. Is there any leadership in this town to protect local charm and integrity? You are concerned about what you can raise on their behalf as a member of the local government planning team.

Neighborhood Groups

You have been contacted by a local neighborhood group, Vigorous Defense, which is up in arms about this potential insult to the charm and quaint aspects of your beautiful little town. They have asked you to fight this! They are sure you should help them as a part of your planning role. You want to be helpful but balanced. They argue that if this chain comes in, they are sure that many of the city's locally owned businesses are in peril, not just Cozy Coffee, and they are fighting this tooth and nail! You know they do have a good point.

College Students

Students at a nearby college tend to congregate at Cozy Coffee before, between, and after classes. They don't buy much, and may even be taking seats from paying customers. You have met with this group of enthusiastic students, and are concerned about whether they will be well organized or just introduce a chaotic element. However, your children both attended this college, and they have also protested to you that it's wrong to let a national chain take over what is one of the last sacred spaces on the planet. It's a cozy, beautiful community, and the students assure you that they are not going to sit idly by and see it destroyed. You have heard that they are going to stage a protest at the council hearing and also attempt to fight the chain with a nationwide boycott. You know there's a lot of agitation on campus about this topic right now, and these small, private colleges do have many moneyed backers.

Downtown Businesses and the Chamber

Representatives of other downtown businesses and the Chamber of Commerce have bent your ear on this topic. They are a small but progressive group, determined to make sure the town turns into the city it's supposed to be. They are tired of the unreliable tax base and of businesses either closing or always being close to closing. They believe that the presence of a national chain is the beginning of good times. What's the fuss? Just let the coffee shop go in. Merchants you've spoken with want you to talk to the planning and zoning decision maker and make sure the right decision is made. Progress is critical, they say, or the town may just whither and die.

City Manager

This is a tricky situation. The Council is split about whether the new coffee shop should go in or not. There are so many questions. About half the Council members want to build this community into a new progressive city. The other half wants the cozy community we've always had. Some of the Council members are confused about who should be making the decision. You will have to work with them to help them understand the limits of their authority.

MASTERSOLVE MODEL FOR TEAMS HANDOUT

The Collaborative Growth MasterSolve©
Problem-Solving Model*

1. Construct your best understanding of the problem:
   - Decide what specifically you want to have happen
   - Observe in detail what is happening instead
   - Notice at what point(s) in the sequence does/did the problem appear
2. Concretize the solution in sensory based descriptions:
   - When the problem is completely resolved, what difference will people
     See: (stable customer list, smiling faces, etc.)?
     Hear: (familiar voices calling in regular orders, optimistic remarks and pleasant tonalities in the workplace)?
     Feel: (safe and welcomed on arriving at work)?
     Know: (interpersonal relationships are key to our productivity)?
3. Determine what is preventing the desired result from occurring now.
4. Brainstorm and record as many possible solutions as you can in an appropriately limited amount of time.
5. Analyze and test options to find the best one and rank order them, noting possible advantages and drawbacks for each one.
6. Confirm that the best one will produce the sensory-based results generated in Step 2; if not, make whatever adjustments are needed.
7. Enact the chosen solution and carefully monitor what happens.
8. Re-enter the new data into this process and run it again if the desired result hasn't yet been achieved.

---

*This workout was created by and is used with the permission of Collaborative Growth, LLC.

Emotional Intelligence in Action. Copyright © 2006 by Marcia Hughes, L. Bonita Patterson, & James Bradford Terrell. Reproduced by permission of Pfeiffer, an Imprint of Wiley. www.pfeiffer.com

Emotional Intelligence in Action

Problem Solving

Win-Win Negotiating

Purpose

To apply the key criteria for win-win negotiation that promote good problem solving.

Thumbnail

60 minutes

The team will explore four criteria that lead to win-win negotiation and practice them in a role play.

Outcomes

- Learn the four criteria for effective negotiation
- Recognize the many ways these can be used in effective problem solving, whether considered a negotiation or not

Audience

- Intact team
- Unaffiliated groups

Facilitator Competencies

Moderate

Materials

Win-Win Negotiating Handout

Time Matrix

Activity	Estimated Time
Discuss connection between problem solving and negotiation and four key criteria	30 minutes
Role play application of the criteria	20 minutes
Debrief	10 minutes
Total	**60 minutes**

Instructions

1. Help the group understand that there is a close connection between problem solving and negotiation. Excellent examples of good problem-solving skills are those addressed by Fisher and Ury (1981) in *Getting to Yes*. The authors emphasize interest-based bargaining and break the key skills into four parts:
   - Separate the people from the problem
   - Focus on interests rather than positions
   - Expand options
   - Develop criteria

   Discuss these criteria with the group. Ask for an example of a good problem-resolution strategy. When has the strategy worked for them? When hasn't it? Does the strategy include the use of these skills?
2. Divide the group into pairs and distribute the Win-Win Negotiating Handout.
3. Have the pairs role play the problem scenario/negotiation in the Win-Win Negotiation Handout and use these four skills. You can change the scenario, if desirable, to a problem they are more likely to encounter.
4. Bring the group back together to discuss the role play and their application of the four criteria. Reflect on the value of following these options when they are problem solving.

WIN-WIN NEGOTIATING HANDOUT

In the following role play, do your best to apply the four criteria for problem solving as articulated by Fisher and Ury in *Getting to Yes* (1981):

1. Separate the people from the problem.
2. Focus on interests rather than positions.
3. Expand options.
4. Develop criteria.

Scenario

One of you is the boss, one an employee. The employee is asking for a 5 percent raise in salary. The boss would like to give the raise but is somewhat offended that the employee, not the boss, raised the issue and defensive that the profitability of the company just doesn't allow the raise at this time. The employee is aware that he or she has brought more customers in than anyone else in the last two years. The employee really likes the company, but his or her kids are going to college soon, and he or she just must have more money.

Both people would both like this to resolve well, but don't want to compromise, initially at least. They are hopeful and apprehensive at the same time.

REFERENCE
Fisher, R., & Ury, W. (1981). *Getting to yes: Reaching agreement without giving in.* Boston, MA: Houghton Mifflin.

Problem Solving

Let's Cover Our Bases

Purpose

To provide a logical problem-solving method that incorporates the four major thinking components.

 ### Thumbnail

60 to 165 minutes

Using the Emergenetics® model, participants will solve a real-life problem with which they are struggling. (For more information on Emergenetics, see www.cgrowth.com; www.polarisconsulting.biz; and www.emergenetics.com.)

Outcomes

- Expanded portfolio of problem-solving tools
- Increased confidence in problem-solving skills
- Better understanding of thinking styles

Audience

- Intact team
- Unaffiliated group
- Individual working with a coach

Facilitator Competencies

Moderate to Advanced

Materials

- Let's Cover Our Bases Handout
- Flip charts and markers

Time Matrix

Activity	Estimated Time
Define problem to be solved	20 minutes
Discuss Emergenetics model	10 minutes
Use the model to create solutions	15–120 minutes
Debrief	15 minutes
Total	**60 to 165 minutes**

Instructions

1. Ask participants to identify some problems they are having with the goals they need to achieve within their team or workplace. List these on a flip chart.
2. Have them select one from the list to work on in this session.
3. Ask, "How do we know it is a problem?" "What are the indicators?" Record their responses on the flip chart.
4. Distribute the Let's Cover Our Bases Handout and ask participants to read about the Emergenetics® Problem-Solving Model. Give them ten minutes.
5. Discuss the Emergenetics® Problem-Solving Model. (For background information on the model refer to the websites referenced under the Thumbnail.)
   - Discuss the thinking modes—Conceptual, Analytical, Structural, and Social.
   - Discuss how different behaviors can impact the group dynamics and task assignments.
6. Discuss solutions to the problem by examining the contributions of each aspect of the Thinking Attributes segment of the model in order—Con-

Emotional Intelligence in Action

ceptual (concepts and ideas), Analytical (logic, purpose, and strategy), Structural (control and status quo), and Social (people and relationships). Capture these ideas on the flip chart.

- Ask the participants to use the Conceptual part of their brain to brainstorm solutions to fix the problem. Their behaviors will guide them in doing this.
- Have them use the Analytical, Structural, and Social parts of their brains to evaluate the potential solutions.
- Select the best solution and develop implementation steps.

7. In some cases, two sessions will be needed to complete the solution design, with an assignment to be completed by the participants between sessions. Here are some sample assignments:
- Market research
- Cost research
- Find a politically well-placed champion for the solution. Assertiveness behavior influences how it will be done and by whom.

8. Debrief the process by asking questions such as:
- What differences did you notice when you worked with the seven different parts of the model? Which ones did you relate to best?
- Does the model address all aspects of solving a problem?
- How can you incorporate the awareness of these seven components into your work or personal lives?

9. (*Optional*) In Step 4, with the entire group, use the Conceptual part of the model to brainstorm solutions to fix the problem. Then divide the group into three teams—Analytical, Structural, and Social—and ask each team to evaluate the potential solutions using their assigned attribute. Have each group prepare a flip-chart presentation to share its work with the group. Reconvene and have each team report back to the entire group. Select the best solution and develop implementation steps.

LET'S COVER OUR BASES HANDOUT

The Emergenetics® Problem-Solving Model*

This handout provides a summary of the seven components of the Emergenetics model:

Conceptual   Expressiveness
Structural   Flexibility
Analytical   Assertiveness
Social

Thinking Attributes

Conceptual—Concepts and Ideas (Brainstorm Solutions)

- What is the ideal vision of success for this situation?
- How can we not just fix the problem but improve the situation so the problem does not reoccur?
- What would we do if we were working with a clean slate with no restrictions or boundaries?

Analytical—Strategy and Logic (Evaluate Proposed Solutions)

- Will it resolve the problem?
- What is the strategic value?
- What are the benefits?
- What are the costs?
- How do we research this? What data do we gather?
- Have we analyzed it enough?

Structural—Control and Status Quo (Evaluate Proposed Solutions)

- Who will be in control?
- What's the timeline?
- Will it move us outside of our comfort zone?
- Will this be too much of a change for us?
- What are the rules and guidelines for what to include?
- What is the implementation process?

---

*This information is used with the permission of Geil Browning, The Browning Group International.

Social—People and Relationships (Evaluate Proposed Solutions)
- Who will be involved?
- Are enough people involved?
- Are the right people involved?
- How will others be affected?

Behaving Attributes

Behavior attributes are expressed in terms of being in the first, second, or third segment of the behavioral continuum. The first third (1/3) means that a person demonstrates the behavior to a very little degree. The second third (2/3) indicates a moderate display of the behavior, and the third third (3/3) is a definite and strong manifestation of the behavior.

Expressiveness—The Amount of Social Interest People Show for Others and the World Around Them

1/3	quiet and reserved and may enjoy working with *things* more than with *people*
3/3	interacts easily with others and may easily express emotions

Assertiveness—Amount of Energy Invested in Expressing Thoughts, Feelings, and Beliefs

1/3	passive and accepting and may not want to express an opinion
3/3	likes a fast pace and may have a strong desire to convince others of a point of view

Flexibility—Willingness to Accommodate the Thoughts and Actions of Others

1/3	likes unchanging situations and may support the status quo
3/3	easily handles ambiguous situations and may be open to suggestions from others

Optimism

Be Solution-Focused

Purpose

Individuals and teams will learn the benefits of being solution-focused and expressing positive messages rather than staying stuck in the problem.

 ### Thumbnail

17 to 25 minutes

Participants working in pairs, or individuals working with a coach, will read the problem scenarios and seek to fully focus on the problem (*not* on the solution). Then they will shift to a solution-focused approach using positive statements to stimulate a hopeful, optimistic attitude. This helps the participants directly experience the difference between the two styles.

Outcome

To recognize the power of beginning the decision-making process with an upbeat, solution-focused approach, as it supports better decisions and generally leads to making them more quickly.

Audience

- Intact team
- Unaffiliated group
- Individual working with a coach

Facilitator Competencies

Moderate

Materials

Be Solution-Focused Handout or design scenarios to meet your specific situation

Time Matrix

Activity	Estimated Time
Review the practice scenarios focusing on the problem.	3-4 minutes
Discuss how participants feel when their attention is fully on the problem	3-4 minutes
Repeat both steps above and discuss this time with a focus on the solution	6-7 minutes
Facilitator presents a brief discussion on optimism, linking it to solution-focused thinking and behavior	5–10 minutes
Total	**17 to 25 minutes**

Instructions

1. Distribute copies of the Be Solution-Focused Handout and ask the participants to form pairs. If appropriate, develop an alternative list of scenarios to the ones provided here that better match the circumstances facing your individual or group.
2. Tell participants to review the practice scenarios with a focus that emphasizes the problem. Participants are *not* to solve the problem, but rather to figure out all the issues and just how difficult they are.

Emotional Intelligence in Action

3. Next ask participants to discuss how they are feeling when the focus is fully on the problem. This may be done in pairs or as a group.

4. Repeat Steps 2 and 3 with a focus on the solution and follow with group discussion. Encourage the group to notice any negative expectations and to set them aside in a willingness to generate more open, "can do" responses.

5. Present a brief discussion on optimism, linking it to solution-focused thinking and behavior. Take questions from the participants.

BE SOLUTION-FOCUSED HANDOUT

Sample Problem Scenarios

With your partner, discuss how to solve the following scenarios using a strategy that focuses intensely, if not exclusively, on the problem, making sure to notice all the issues and just how difficult they are.

1. You work in an organization where you provide assistance to several "bosses." Boss A asks you to complete an assignment in two weeks, and you say, "No problem." Then another assignment comes in from Boss B that is due in twelve days. It is much more interesting than the first assignment, and the deadline is much more solid; the first one could be extended. However, it is just about impossible to get them both done. Boss A is out of town until the day the assignment is due. What do you do?

2. Jamie needs a ride to soccer at the same time that Terry needs a ride to dance lessons. They cannot take a bus and there is no other family member to help out.

3. You're really tired of working on the weekends and committed to balancing your life better, but you also have a creative project under way that you have wanted to do for many years. It's finally started up. The best way to get time for the project—which is work, just more creative—is to get caught up on work so you can work on the project, but that requires working on the weekends. What do you do?

4. You will have a lot less stress in your life if you get your bills paid off, but you really want to help your son and daughter go to college. Paying for college will only increase your debt, but. . . .

5. You have four managers reporting to you. Only one is a woman and she is convinced that you put her down. The last survey from her staff is reflecting increasing disgruntlement with her, and her productivity is down. She reports that she's doing more than ever and thinks her staff highly respects her. What do you do?

After some discussion, you will repeat this activity when the facilitator instructs you to do so. You will be given new directions.

Optimism

See a Positive Resolution

Purpose

To learn how vividly imagining a problem as well-resolved generates the positive energy to help us move more rapidly toward an effective resolution.

Thumbnail

50 minutes

Discussion of how our beliefs affect our optimism and why it's valuable, and then some reflective time to allow new associations to surface. Next a discussion of an issue in each person's life that doesn't have a readily apparent answer and pairs work to imagine the details of a positive result.

Outcomes

- Expand awareness of the consequences of thinking pessimistically, as contrasted with thinking positively
- Make a commitment to guide thinking for more positive results

Audience

- Intact team
- Unaffiliated group
- Individual working with a coach

Facilitator Competencies

Easy to Moderate

Materials

None needed

Time Matrix

Activity	Estimated Time
Discuss connection between optimism, values, and beliefs	10 minutes
In pairs, or with coach, discuss value of optimism	10 minutes
Take some quiet, reflective time to allow new associations to develop	5 minutes
In pairs, discuss an issue in each person's life that doesn't have an answer and then imagine a positive result. Learn the details of the resolution	15 minutes
Discuss learnings and set commitments for practicing optimism	10 minutes
Total	**50 minutes**

Instructions

1. Discuss the relationship between optimism and the belief in positive outcomes. What we believe will happen has a powerful effect on the outcomes we experience. One example of this result is that optimistic salespeople are the most effective at their jobs.

2. Ask the individual you are coaching or the team members to discuss their perceptions of the value of optimism in their lives with a partner. Then discuss the topic as a group. Ask how much value optimism contributes to their lives.

3. Ask people to share what they do when they find themselves in a pessimistic state. How soon do they notice? Does it creep up on them so they don't even notice when they are feeling fairly depressed and discouraged?

4. One way to counter the pessimism is to change thoughts such as: "I am overwhelmed and don't think this can work out well" to "I know there's a good result to this concern; I just don't understand what it is *yet*."

5. Have participants choose partners to work with and announce that the first step in the following learning process is to remain silent for four minutes. Acknowledge that it may seem like a long time, but that you will watch the clock carefully and tell them as soon as the time's up. Ask them to sit comfortably, breathe deeply, and let their minds rest. When thoughts come up, they will just let them go and redirect their attention to the sound of their breathing or the sensations they feel in their bodies.

6. At the end of the time, ask them to bring their attention back into focus in the room and to turn to their partners. One person will go first and tell the other about a situation that he or she believes won't work out well and over which he or she feels a lack of power. (*Note:* Guide the level of difficulty of the issue you raise based on your familiarity and expertise in expanding emotional intelligence skills and the nature and skills of your group or the individual with whom you are working. You can keep this simple by instructing participants to think of a meaningful but moderate challenge. This skill can be expanded as they take on new issues, having mastered the process at less challenging levels.)

   - Now that the first person has described the situation, the other should be instructed to say: "I understand that you don't know the answer yet, but let's work together to imagine that somehow a miracle happened, and the issue is now completely resolved. Notice everything that is different. What do you feel, what do you see, what do you hear? What else do you know now that this change has occurred?"
   - The person in the listening role works with the other for four or five minutes to develop as detailed a positive resolution as possible.

- Tell them to reflect with their partners about the difference between feeling like they don't have the answer yet, but recognizing that it will appear at some time, and just feeling powerless because they don't know the answer.
- Ask the pairs to switch roles and repeat the process.

7. Reconvene the entire group and discuss the activity. Ask participants to commit to practicing optimism by remembering this day and this group and this process when a new problem arises, and to remind themselves in such situations: "I just don't know the answer *YET*." Questions you might ask in debriefing include:
   - What do you feel in your body when you are feeling pessimistic as compared to feeling optimistic?
   - On a scale of 1 to 10, how important is optimism to you?
   - How might you influence others to be more optimistic?

Optimism

The Optimistic Explanation

Purpose

To help participants explore the way they explain the events that happen to them in life and to understand how that dynamic affects their optimism and, ultimately, their success.

 ### Thumbnail

25 to 30 minutes

Each participant will read the brief scenarios in the hand-out and do his or her best to imagine that what happened in the vignette actually happened. Participants will then write explanations of why each point in the story occurred the way it did and be given a key for analyzing the significance of their responses.

Outcome

This exercise will teach participants how their explanatory style influences their optimism and how it can be modified to change the results they get in the world.

Audience

- Intact team
- Unaffiliated group
- Individual working with a coach

Facilitator Competencies

Moderate

Materials

- The Optimistic Explanation Handout
- Paper and pens

Time Matrix

Activity	Estimated Time
Explain optimism using handout	5 minutes
Scenario One	5 minutes
Scenario Two	5 minutes
Group discussion or individual reflection	10–15 minutes
Total	**25 to 30 minutes**

Instructions

1. Provide participants with paper, pens, and The Optimistic Explanation Handout.
2. Explain optimism, drawing on the explanation in Part Two of this book and the analysis section of the handout.
3. Instruct the participants to read the two scenarios and write their explanations of what caused the events as if they really happened to them.
4. Convene the full group to debrief the experience. Sample questions you might begin with include:
   - What was your experience as you worked with the two scenarios?
   - What did you learn that would benefit your work and life as a whole?
   - Do you find that when you're more optimistic, that it is easier to solve problems?

Emotional Intelligence in Action

THE OPTIMISTIC EXPLANATION HANDOUT

Analysis

The explanations of causality that we offer hinge on three critical dynamics, and these ultimately determine how optimistic or pessimistic a person is. This concept is discussed by Martin Seligman (1990) in *Learned Optimism*. We explain these three concepts as follows:

1. *Permanence*—We perceive the causes of events in our lives to either be *temporary* or *permanent*. "I never remember to fill my gas tank" is permanent. "I forgot to fill my tank yesterday" is a temporary explanation.

2. *Pervasiveness*—"People who make *universal* explanations for their failures give up on everything when a failure strikes in one area. People who make *specific* explanations may become helpless in that one part of their lives, yet march stalwartly on in the others" (Seligman, 1990, p. 46).

3. *Personalization*—When bad things happen, humans either attribute the cause to other people or circumstances (externalization) or we attribute it to ourselves (internalization). When we blame ourselves it tends to erode our self-esteem. When we blame others or external circumstances we don't lose self-esteem, but persistent blaming of others can become problematic in itself because it is inherently disempowering, and other people will begin to reject us if we never take responsibility for the effects we cause. Appropriate reality testing is an excellent tool for helping maintain the desired balance.

Here is the formula for optimism: When you are explaining *positive* events, you want them to be permanent, universal, and internal. For example, "*All* the good things that happen in my life are *always* a result of *my faith* (internal) in our Creator." When you are explaining *negative* events you want them to be temporary, specific, and external. For example," The flat tire I had *today* (specific) was the result of some *nails that were spilled on the highway* (external)." Contrast that with, "I *always* (permanent) get flat tires because *I* (internal) can *never* (permanent) avoid all the road hazards out there."

How do these kinds of explanations compare with the ones you usually use to explain what happens in your life? If you want to be more optimistic, and hence more successful, practice changing the way you use these three dynamics when you explain the causes of both the positive and negative events in your life.

Read the two scenarios that follow and explain the causes that contributed to each step in the story as if they happened to you. Apply the three dynamics of optimism you just reviewed as you make up your explanations.

Scenario One

1. You are reading an article in the newspaper and see a display ad that says "Wanted . . . Good Problem Solvers."
2. Although you already have a job, you call them, and they sound like they are interested in you right away.
3. You schedule an interview and find the office where you apply to be friendly, well-appointed, and easy to get to. When you find out what kind of work they do, it's almost like a dream come true!
4. The pay is significantly better than your current job, so you accept the position and begin to have the best work experience of your entire life.

Make up an explanation of why each step happened the way it did as if this story actually happened to you. In number 1, for example, you might write: "I've always been a curious person who follows up on unusual things that catch my eye . . . like an ad for "Good Problem Solvers." Write your answers below.

1.

2.

3.

4.

Scenario Two

1. You are on the way to meet someone you're really interested in for a date, and your car runs out of gas.

2. You manage to get a ride to a gas station and call the restaurant, leaving a message that you will be about half an hour late. It takes a long time to get back to your car and it's closer to an hour when you finally arrive.

3. Your date is still there, but obviously not too happy. The conversation drags and you can't seem to stop apologizing.

4. When the check comes, you insist on paying as the least you can do, and your date finally chuckles and seems to lighten up.

5. Unfortunately, the waiter returns saying your credit card has been declined and their policy, as the signs clearly state, is "Absolutely no checks!" You have only three dollars in cash, and your date ends up paying the bill.

Make up an explanation of why each step happened the way it did as if this story actually happened to you.

1.

2.

3.

4.

Examine the explanations that you made for the causes of each event in the two scenarios. Were they permanent or temporary? Universal or specific? Internal or external? Do you feel more optimistic?

REFERENCE

Seligman, M. (1990). *Learned optimism.* New York: Pocket Books.

Happiness

Growing My Happiness

Purpose

For participants to notice how happy they are, how happy they would like to be, and develop a strategy to get there.

Thumbnail

35 to 45 minutes

Participants assess their current level of happiness, connect it with circumstances in their lives, and then develop action plans to live with the level of happiness they prefer. The total time could be expanded in order to have an advanced version.

Outcomes

- Increased understanding of some of the attitudes and conditions in life that influence happiness
- Enhanced ability and willingness to influence how happy one is

Audience

- Intact team
- Unaffiliated group
- Individual working with a coach

Facilitator Competencies

Moderate

Materials

- Growing My Happiness Handout
- Paper (could be a journal) and pens

Time Matrix

Activity	Estimated Time
Introduce the topic and exercise	5 minutes
Each individual writes in response to provided questions	5 minutes
With coach or in groups of two or three, discuss what was written	10 minutes
Conduct individual assessment and write action plan	5 to 10 minutes
With coach or in small groups, discuss the plan and commit to implementation	5 minutes
Debrief group	5 to 10 minutes
Total	**35 to 45 minutes**

Instructions

1. Distribute paper and a pen to each participant.
2. Discuss what happiness means. You can draw on the material in Part 2 of this book on happiness for information.
3. Each participant, or the coaching client, should develop a list of responses to the following statements:
   - I'm content about:
   - I'm worried/frustrated about:
4. Now instruct each participant to write a few paragraphs observing and connecting these two factors as they are currently playing out in the participants' lives.

5. If working with a team, have them get together in groups of two or three and discuss what they wrote. Each person should take three to four minutes. Individuals should discuss their responses with their coach.

6. Distribute the Growing My Happiness Handout and instruct participants to use the handout to assess their current level of happiness and then develop action plans.

7. Discuss what they wrote in their small groups or with their coaches and make a commitment to follow through with improving their happiness through heightened awareness and commitment.

8. Debrief as a group. Potential questions you might ask include:
   - Who are some of the happiest people you know? Do you want to be like them?
   - What does happiness mean to you?
   - How important is happiness in your life?

9. *Advanced Version:* Take more time and be more comprehensive with each step. For example, for Step 2, participants could do a comprehensive inventory of the positive and negative life conditions affecting their lives. Expand each of the other steps accordingly. Meet again to follow through with a discussion on complying with commitments.

GROWING MY HAPPINESS HANDOUT

Personal Assessment

This is similar to the Fordyce Emotions Questionnaire discussed in Seligman (2002, p. 15).

____ 1. On a scale of 1 to 10 (10 is highest), how happy am I?

____ 2. On the same scale, how unhappy am I?

____ 3. On the same scale, how neutral or checked out am I?

____ 4. How happy would I like to be? (Make it an amount you are willing to strive toward accomplishing in your life.)

My Happiness Action Plan

In order to accomplish my intention and heartfelt desire to be happy at a . . . level, I commit to take the following actions. Be specific so you can measure your success. (*Note:* Use the information from your reflections at the beginning of this exercise so that you connect with your current state of happiness. You may find a need to add much more information about your current life conditions to fully develop this action plan. You are encouraged to add in further reflections as you have more time.)

REFERENCE

Seligman, M. (2002). *Authentic happiness.* New York: The Free Press.

Happiness

Pay It Forward with Gratitude

Purpose

To recognize that gratitude is contagious, feels good, and expands our resourcefulness.

Thumbnail

50 minutes (can be expanded or contracted)

After discussing the power of gratitude, individuals working with a coach and teams or groups working in pairs review five or more items for which they are grateful. They develop a commitment to pay it forward so when they receive a statement of gratefulness, they reach out to expand the attitude.

Outcomes

- Feel happier
- Know how to keep and increase happiness even with just one strategy
- Recognize that there are many more great ways to enhance happiness

Audience

- Intact team
- Unaffiliated group
- Individual working with a coach

Facilitator Competencies

Easy to Moderate

Materials

None needed

Time Matrix

Activity	Estimated Time
Discuss research on the power of gratitude	10 minutes
In pairs, take turns reviewing five things for which each person is grateful; the other listens attentively	15 minutes
As a whole group, discuss what they have recognized	10 minutes
Group discussion to increase awareness	10 minutes
Develop commitment to pay it forward	5 minutes
Total	**50 minutes**

Instructions

1. Discuss with the group, or the person you are coaching, that there is now research on the power of gratitude. Refer them to www.authentichappiness.com to take the gratitude questionnaire and learn more about how gratitude works in their lives. (*Note:* This can also be an assignment before the group or individual come to this session. If so, have them print out and bring in their results.)

2. Say to the group, "Fortunately, the benefits of gratitude are becoming well-recognized. The *New York Times Sunday Magazine* included Seligman's 'Gratitude Visit' in its annual list of '100 Great Ideas.' The strategy is described as follows:

"You think of a person in your life who has been kind to you but whom you've never properly thanked. You write a detailed 'gratitude letter' to that person, explaining in concrete terms why you're grateful. Then you visit that person and read the testimony aloud. According to Seligman, the ritual is powerful. 'Everyone cries when you do a gratitude visit,' he says. 'It's very moving for both people.'" (Pink, 2004, pp. 2–3). Ask your participants if any have done a gratitude visit. Recommend that it can serve them well.

3. For this exercise, have each person pair with someone else and tell him or her five things for which they are grateful. If you are coaching, the individual will tell you. The coach/listener should listen attentively and then ask questions. Help the individual become clear about why he or she is grateful. Then switch and the coach/listener will identify about five items for which he or she is grateful and tell the partner, who will help to clarify why the person feels grateful.

4. As a group, or with your client, discuss what you experienced during this process. If you are working with a group, time permitting, ask for people to move and create new pairs and repeat the process. You can repeat this as often as fits your group and the time available.

5. Conclude with everyone discussing how they are feeling having just spent this time on gratitude. Apply this awareness to work. Ask:
   - What happens when someone genuinely thanks you?
   - How do you feel?
   - How do you engage with your work when you return to it?

6. Take gratitude a step further by building in a pay-it-forward commitment. The gratitude visit, Seligman believes, can be an effective way to "increase the intensity, duration, and frequency of positive memory" (p. 3). We can expand this benefit by returning gratitude every time someone expresses gratitude to us, but only if we truly received their gift first.

7. Ask the partners to commit to pay gratitude forward at least twice a day for one week. Then have the pairs agree to commit to a time when they will get together at the end of that week to revisit their commitment and discuss how it is working. Hopefully, they will agree to renew the commitment for another week. Emphasize that change happens only with practice; therefore, the amount of diligence they give this benefit will have a direct impact on their success.

REFERENCE

Pink, D. (2004, January 24). The AHC gratitude visits. *New York Times* Sunday magazine's 100 great ideas. *Authentic Happiness Coaching Newsletter, 2*(1).

Happiness

Attitude of Gratitude

Purpose

To experience how an attitude of gratitude and expectation expands the palette of possibilities for creating hope and happiness.

 ### Thumbnail

30 to 50 minutes

The team or individual focuses on what he or she is good at and what has been done successfully. Participants "dream" of what they can do to build on what they've done well. (It will be helpful if the facilitator has an awareness of the appreciative inquiry process.)

Outcomes

- Greater self-appreciation
- Increased confidence
- Expanded happiness

Audience

- Intact team
- Unaffiliated group
- Individual working with a coach

Facilitator Competencies

Easy to Moderate

Materials

- (Team) Flip chart and colored markers
- (Individual) Paper and pens

Time Matrix

Activity	Estimated Time
Discuss concept of an appreciative approach	5–10 minutes
Share occurrences of excellence	5 minutes
Envision future	5 minutes
Discuss how they feel	5–10 minutes
Reconvene and debrief (team only)	5–10 minutes
Actions after session and wrap-up	5–10 minutes
Total	**30 to 50 minutes**

Instructions

1. This exercise is based on appreciation, as understood through the appreciative inquiry process. Discuss with the group the power of focusing on the positive. Discuss these points:
   - When the focus is on problems—"Where do they exist?" and "How many are there?" and "How do we fix them?" With this approach, you will always find problems. In fact, you find more and more of them. The focus on problems can exacerbate them or make them seem more dire.
   - Appreciative inquiry research has shown that highlighting and sharing instances of excellence ignites its proliferation. (Refer to the article *What Is Appreciative Inquiry?* www.thinbook.com/chap11fromle.html for more information.)
2. Hand out paper and pens. Ask participants to remain silent for three minutes and think in detail about:

Emotional Intelligence in Action

- (For a team) When the team or organization was at its best.
- (For an individual) When you were at your best.

3. Ask the group or individual to share the information. Record the details about what was excellent about the situation in terms of what event or behavior made it significant. Discuss the impact and the meaning. How did it look? How did it feel? What were people saying? Record their responses on the flip chart.

4. Ask them to envision a positive future based on past or current successes. Record responses.

Team Questions

- What would the organization be like if the type of peak moments we just discussed were the norm instead of the exception?
- How would it look different?
- What would it mean to be part of it?
- What would people be saying?
- How would you feel being part of that organization?
- How would you behave in that organization?

Individual Questions

- What would it mean if peak moments were regular daily occurrences in your life?
- How would it look different?
- What would it mean to be part of it?
- What would people be saying?
- How would you feel about your life?
- How would you behave differently in the workplace? At home with family or friends?

5. Work with the individual or divide the team into groups of two to five to discuss how they feel. Have them respond to these questions:
- Did focusing on the valuable things that have already been done make you feel more hopeful? Why or why not?
- Did you feel happier knowing that greatness is present now and ready to manifest in you, the team, or the organization? Why do you think you felt that way?

6. If working with a team, reconvene and debrief. Ask them to share what they discussed. Capture responses. If working with an individual, capture responses as part of Step 5.

7. Ask what they can do beyond this session to expand their focus on creating more positive situations and outcomes and minimize emphasis on looking for and fixing problems. For example, when a problem surfaces, ask, "When has the organization done this correctly and what were the conditions of that positive situation?" Or, if working with an individual, ask, "When have you done this correctly and what were the conditions of that positive situation?"

8. Gain commitment from the individuals or team to experiment further with this positive approach.

Resources

AUTHORS' CONSULTING SERVICES

Collaborative Growth
Marcia Hughes, President
James Terrell, Vice President
P.O. Box 17509
Golden, CO 80402
303.271.0021
contact@cgrowth.com
www.cgrowth.com

Polaris Consulting Group
L. Bonita Patterson, President
1617 Coalton Road, PMB 200
Superior, CO 80027
info@polarisconsulting.BIZ
www.polarisconsulting.BIZ

ASSESSMENTS

The following is contact information for the four assessments covered
in this book:

Bar-On EQ-i®
EQ-360™
Multi-Health Systems, Inc.
P.O. Box 950
North Tonawanda, NY 14120–0950
800.456.3003
customerservice@mhs.com
www.mhs.com

ECI 360
EI Hay Group
877.267.8375
http://ei.haygroup.com

EQ Map®
Essi Systems, Inc.
70 Otis Street
San Francisco, CA 94103
800.252.3774
www.essisystems.com

MSCEIT™
Multi-Health Systems, Inc.
P.O. Box 950
North Tonawanda, NY 14120–0950
800.456.3003
customerservice@mhs.com
www.mhs.com

RESEARCH AND TOOLS

The following are some of the many sites that provide research and tools for developing EI.

Brain.com
Offers an array of software, music, and books on various aspects of the brain.
19782 MacArthur Boulevard, Suite 310
Irvine, CA 92612
866.623.7460
www.brain.com

Brain Connection
Provides information and education on the brain and how people learn.
A web resource of Scientific Learning Corporation
300 Frank H. Ogawa Plaza, Suite 600
Oakland, CA 94612–2040
www.BrainConnection.com

Brain-Mart
Supplies brain models and anatomical charts. An Internet division of Red Reef Publications.
P.O. Box 244286
Boynton Beach, FL 33424–4286
www.brain-mart.com

Collaborative Growth
Sponsor of the EQ Symposium. Provides EQ certification for organizations and trainers.
www.cgrowth.com

Creative Therapy Associates, Inc.
Produces materials that address the mental health and social issues of children and adults
7709 Hamilton Avenue
Cincinnati, OH 45231–3103
800.448.9145
www.ctherapy.com

Dr. Pearson's Wonderful Toy Company, Inc.
Provides emotional intelligence toys for children.
www.wondertoy.com

EI Consortium
The Consortium for Research on Emotional Intelligence in Organizations aids the advancement of research and practice related to emotional intelligence in organizations.
www.eiconsortium.org

EI World
A center for the research and development of emotional intelligence.
www.eiworld.org

EQ Alliance
An association of emotional intelligence practitioners and allies.
www.nexusEQ.com/assoc

EQ Directory
Presents a consolidated web directory of emotional intelligence resources. Founded by Joshua Freedman and contributed to on a volunteer basis.
650.685.9880
www.eq.org

EQ University
Offers online EI assessment and training.
www.equniversity.com

Institute of HeartMath
Conducts research and supplies education on finding the balance between mind and heart in life's decisions.
14700 West Park Avenue
Boulder Creek, CA 95006
831.338.8500
www.heartmath.org

Multi Health Systems
Distributes EQ, MSCEIT, and supporting products.
Ordering:
3770 Victoria Parke Avenue
Toronto, Ontario M2H 3M6
Contact:
P.O. Box 950
North Tonawanda, NY 14120–0950
www.MHS.com

National Professional Resources
Distributes professional development materials for teachers and others who work with learners of all ages who have differing abilities.
25 South Regent Street
Port Chester, NY 10573
800.453.7461
www.nprinc.com

Six Seconds
Brings emotional intelligence into practice in schools, families, organizations, and communities. Founded the Nexus EQ conferences.
316 Seville Way
San Mateo, CA 94402
650.685.9885
www.6seconds.org

Talent Smart
Provides EI training and products.
www.talentsmart.com/

References

BOOKS AND ARTICLES

American Psychological Association. (1997). *"Learned optimism" yields health results.* Available: http://health.discovery.com/centers/mental/articles/optimism/optimism.html.

Angier, N. (1995, May 14). Society's glue: Science explains empathy's role for man, beast. *Denver Post.*

Ashkanasay, N.M., Hartel, C.E.J., &. Serbe. W.J. (2000). *Emotions in the workplace: Research, theory, and practice.* Westport, CT: Quorum Books.

Bar-On, R. (2000). Emotional and social intelligence: insights from the emotional quotient inventory. In R. Bar-On & J.D.A. Parker (Eds.), *The handbook of emotional intelligence.* San Francisco, CA: Jossey-Bass.

Bar-On, R. (2001). EI and self-actualization. In J. Ciarrochi, J. Forgas, & J. Mayer (Eds.), *Emotional intelligence in everyday life.* New York: Psychology Press.

Bar-On, R. (2002). *Bar-On emotional quotient inventory (EQ-i) technical manual.* Toronto, Ontario: Multi-Health Systems, Inc.

Bar-On, R.,& Handley, R. (1999). *Optimizing people: A practical guide for applying EQ to improve personal and organizational effectiveness.* New Braunfels, TX: Pro-Philes Press.

Bennett-Goldman, T. (2001). *Emotional alchemy.* New York: Three Rivers Press.

Caruso, D.R., & Salovey, P. (2004). *The emotionally intelligent manager.* San Francisco, CA: Jossey-Bass.

Chang, P.P., Ford, D.E., Meoni, L.A., Wang, N., & Klag, M.J. (2002). Anger in young men and subsequent premature cardiovascular disease. In *Archives of internal medicine.* Available: http://archinte.ama-assn.org.

Cherniss, C. (2004). *Emotional intelligence.* In Speilberger, C. (Ed.), *Encyclopedia of applied psychology.* San Diego, CA: Academic Press.

Cherniss, C., & Adler, M. (2000). *Promoting emotional intelligence in organizations.* Alexandria, VA: American Society for Training & Development.

Cherniss, C., & Goleman, D. (2001). *The emotionally intelligent workplace.* San Francisco, CA: Jossey-Bass.

Childre, D. (1994). *One minute stress management freeze frame.* Boulder Creek, CA: Planetary Publications.

Childre, D., & Martin, H. (1999). *The heartmath solution.* San Francisco, CA: Harper.

Ciarrochi, J., Forgas, J.P., & Mayer, J.D. (2001). *Emotional intelligence in everyday life.* London, England: Taylor and Francis.

Collaborative Growth's EQ Symposium. (2004). *Power tools: Connecting theory and action.* www.cgrowth.com

Cooper, R. (2001). *The other 90 percent.* New York: Three Rivers Press.

Cooper, R., & Q-Metrics. (1996). *The EQ map interpretation guide.* San Francisco, CA: AIT and Essi Systems, Inc.

Crum, T. (1987). *The magic of conflict.* New York: Simon & Schuster.

The Dalai Lama & Cutler, H. (1998). *The art of happiness.* New York: Riverhead Books.

Damasio, A. (2003). *Looking for Spinoza.* Orlando, FL: Harcourt.

Dennison, P.E., & Dennison, G.E. (1989). *Brain gym* (teacher's ed. rev.) Ventura, CA: Edu-Kinesthetics, Inc.

Eisaguirre, L. (2002). *The power of a good fight.* Indianapolis, IN: Alpha.

Feldman, D.A. (1999). *The handbook of emotionally intelligent leadership: Inspiring others to achieve results.* Falls Church, VA: Leadership Performance Solutions Press.

Fisher, R., & Ury, W. (1981). *Getting to yes: Reaching agreement without giving in.* Boston, MA: Houghton Mifflin.

Flury, J., & Ickes, W. (2001). Emotional intelligence and empathic accuracy. In J. Ciarrochi, J. Forgas, & J. Mayer, *Emotional intelligence in everyday life.* New York: Psychology Press.

Foundation for Inner Peace. (1975). *A course in miracles.* Tiburon, CA: Foundation for Inner Peace.

Frankl, V. (2000). *Man's search for meaning.* Boston, MA: Beacon Press.

Goleman, D. (1995). *Emotional intelligence: Why it can matter more than IQ.* New York: Bantam.

Goleman D. (1998). *Working with emotional intelligence.* New York: Bantam.

Goleman D., Boyatzis, R., & McKee, A. (2002). *Primal leadership: Realizing the power of emotional intelligence.* Boston, MA: Harvard Business School Press.

Gowing, M.K. (2001). Measurement of individual emotional competence. In C. Cherniss & D. Goleman (Eds.), *The emotionally intelligent workplace.* San Francisco, CA: Jossey-Bass.

Government of India. (1987, March). *Gandhi's life in 5000 words.* Available: www.mkgandhi.org/bio5000/bio5index.htm

Hargie, O., & Dickson, D. (2004). *Skilled interpersonal communications.* New York: Routledge.

Hughes, M. (2004). Success and EQ. www.cgrowth.com.

Jenkins, M. (2003, August). The hard way: Aaron Ralston—between a rock and the hardest place. *Outside Magazine, 28*(8).

Kapadia, M. (2004). *Emotional intelligence: A workbook for beginners.* New Delhi: BPI PVT LTD.

The King Center. (2003). *Biographical outline of Dr. Martin Luther King, Jr.* Available: www.thekingcenter.com/mlk/bio.html.

Lane, R.D. (2000). Levels of emotional awareness: Neurological, psychological and social perspectives. In R. Bar-On & J.D.A. Parker (Eds.), *The handbook of emotional intelligence.* San Francisco, CA: Jossey-Bass

Maslow, A. (1970). *Motivation and personality* (2nd ed.). New York: Harper & Row.

Mayer, J.D., Salovey, P., &. Caruso, D.R. (2000). Emotional intelligence as zeitgeist, as personality, and as a mental ability. In R. Bar-On & J.D.A. Parker (Eds.), *The handbook of emotional intelligence.* San Francisco, CA: Jossey-Bass.

Mayer, J.D., Salovey, P., &. Caruso, D.R. (2001). *MSCEIT™ personal summary report.* New York & Toronto: Multi-Health Systems, Inc.

Mayer, J.D., Salovey, P., &. Caruso, D.R. (2002). *MSCEIT™ users manual.* New York & Toronto: Multi-Health Systems, Inc.

Orme, G. (2001). *Emotionally intelligent living.* Glasgow, Scotland: Crown House.

Pearman, R. (2002). *Introduction to type and emotional intelligence.* Palo Alto, CA: CPP, Inc.

Pert, C. (1997). *Molecules of emotion.* New York: Simon & Schuster.

Pert, C. (2000). *Your body is your subconscious mind.* Boulder, CO: Sounds True.

Pink, D. (2004, January 24). The AHC gratitude visits. *New York Times* Sunday magazine's 100 great ideas. *Authentic Happiness Coaching Newsletter, 2*(1).

Salovey, P., & Sluyter, D. (1997). *Emotional development and emotional intelligence.* New York: Basic Books.

Seligman, M. (1990). *Learned optimism.* New York: Pocket Books.

Seligman, M. (2002). *Authentic happiness.* New York: The Free Press.

Shakespeare, W. *King Lear.* Available: www-tech.mit.edu/Shakespeare/works.html.

Stein, S., & Book, H. (2000). *The EQ edge: Emotional intelligence and your success.* Toronto: MHS.

Turow, J. (1997). *Breaking up America: Advertisers and the new-media world.* Chicago, IL: University of Chicago Press.

Ury, W. (2000). *The third side.* New York: Penguin Books.

Various Artists. (1987). *Largo.* San Francisco, CA: LIND Institute. Available: www.relaxwiththeclassics.com/pages/ordering.htm.

Webster's third international new dictionary. (1993). Springfield, MO: Merriam-Webster, Inc.

Weisinger, H. (1998). *Emotional intelligence at work.* San Francisco, CA: Jossey-Bass.

Whitney, J., & Packer, T. (2001). *Power plays.* New York: Simon & Schuster.

WEBSITES

www.authentichappiness.org
www.cgrowth.com
www.christianethicstoday.com
www.eiconsortium.org
www.heartmath.com
www.mconsolion.org
www.mindpub.com/art411.htm
www.MKGandhi.org
www.polarisconsulting.biz
www.positivepsychology.org
www.TheMayoClinic.com
www.thinkbook.com/chap11fromic.html

About the Authors

Marcia Hughes is president of Collaborative Growth, L.L.C., and serves as a strategic communications partner for leaders and teams in organizations that value high performers. She weaves her expertise in emotional intelligence throughout her consulting work, facilitation, team building, and workshops to help people motivate themselves and communicate more effectively with others. Her keynotes are built around powerful stories of how success can grow when people work collaboratively. Businesses, governmental agencies, and nonprofits have all benefited in such areas as team and leadership development, strategic design, and conflict resolution from her proven formula for success.

Marcia is a certified trainer in the Bar-On EQ-i and EQ 360. She certifies senior HR leaders, coaches, and consultants to utilize these measures with the people they lead. She provides Train the Trainer training and coaching in powerful EQ delivery. Her inspiration and persistent efforts led the development, promotion, and hosting of Collaborative Growth's International EQ Symposium in 2004 and attracted participants from nine nations. It focused on distilling effective strategies for behavioral change from the theory and research on emotional intelligence.

Her efforts to improve productivity in the workplace through strategic communications grew out of a distinguished career in law where her firm specialized in complex public policy matters. There again her leadership and communication skills enabled Marcia's team to effectively address controversial environmental, land use, and water development matters involving numerous stakeholders that included federal, state, and local governments along with the general public.

As an assistant attorney general she served the Department of Public Health and the Environment, she clerked on the 10th Circuit Court of Appeals for the Honorable William E. Doyle and served with the Environmental Protection Agency in Washington, D.C. Marcia is author of *Life's 2% Solution.*

L. Bonita Patterson is president of Polaris Consulting Group, an organizational effectiveness firm. She offers keynotes, executive coaching, consultation, facilitation, and workshops to improve bottom-line results by strategically aligning behaviors with business intent. She works with a broad array of corporate, government, and non-profit clients in the areas of communications, emotional intelligence, values alignment, strategic planning, leadership and team development, and management retreats.

Her ability to transform organizations to enhance competitive advantage was honed during her years in senior management. Her experience includes fifteen years in management and leadership with IBM in the areas of sales and marketing, training and development, and systems engineering; vice president of a leadership development company; and division manager of training and development for the Department of Energy/Kaiser-Hill nuclear weapons plant closure project at Rocky Flats. She has managed a business development center that generated $100 million in revenue in an eighteen-month period; designed and facilitated an organizational change effort to revitalize a flagging organization; facilitated a post-merger transition to a new operating model; and developed executive leadership programs leveraging world-class educators, executives, and researchers to enhance leadership capabilities of senior management in global organizations.

James Bradford Terrell is vice president of Collaborative Growth, L.L.C., where he applies his expertise in interpersonal communication to help a variety of public and private sector clients anticipate change and respond resiliently. He coaches leaders, teams in transition, and senior management, using the Bar-On EQi®, among other measures. He also works as a contract mediator for federal agencies.

James gave his insight and enthusiasm to assist in developing, promoting, and hosting Collaborative Growth's successful 2004 International EQ Symposium and is leading the development of future Symposiums. He provides Train the Trainer training and coaching in delivering powerful EQ results.

He worked as a psychotherapist in private practice for many years, seeing primarily clients who were seeking to resolve conflict in relationships—with their spouses, children, parents, employers, and/or co-workers. For three years, he was executive director of the Syntropy Institute, a not-for-profit research organization investigating how communication training impacts human effectiveness. He also served as the director of training for the Metro-Denver Mutual Housing Association, an early developer of cooperative housing.

In a previous life, he was the owner/operator of Integrity Building Systems, a construction company specializing in residential and commercial renovation and served as a project coordinator on a wide variety of projects including Denver International Airport and the National Digital Cable Television Center.

Index

A

Adaptability EQ, 18, 19, 20. *See also* Flexibility competency
Adler, M., 116
Aggressiveness, 50, 52
American Psychological Association, 107
Angier, N., 66
Aniston, J., 43
Applying Inspiration (workout/handout), 201–205
Are You in Touch? (workout/handout), 133–137
The Art of Happiness (Dali Lama), 113
Assertiveness competency: described, 19, 38, 49–50; differences between aggressiveness and, 50, 52; how to build, 51–52; importance of, 50–51; relationship between independence and, 56; star and movie exemplifying, 40*t*, 52–53; transformational benefits of, 52
Assertiveness Continuum, 51*fig*
Assertiveness workouts/handouts: Dial It Back, 163–166; Getting Your Point Across, 167–170; Ramp It Up, 157–162
Attitude of Gratitude (workout/handout), 367–370
Authentic Happiness (Seligman), 108, 111

B

Bar-On EQi: impulse control defined in, 87; learning about fifteen skills defined in, 15; overview of, 18–20. *See also* EQ-360; EQ-i

Bar-On, R.: Bar-On EQi developed by, 18; "emotional quotient" coined by, 11; on flexibility, 96; on happiness, 111; on impulse control, 88; on independence, 56; on optimism, 106; on problem solving, 101; on relationship between optimism and stress tolerance, 83; on relationship between stress management and impulse control, 83; on self-actualization, 59, 60; on self-awareness, 46; on self-regard, 41, 42; on social responsibility, 71; on stress tolerance, 82; *Technical Manual* by, 20
Be Solution-Focused (workout/handout), 343–346
Becoming All That You Can Be (workout/handout), 193–199
Blix, H., 40*t*, 93
Body language, 67
Book, H., 45, 49, 51, 61, 66, 77, 91, 96, 101, 108
Boyatzis, R., 20, 21, 46
Brain: emotional intelligence as synthesis of heart and, 13–14; emotional responses processed in the, 12–13
Brainstorming strategies, 98
Buchanan, G., 107

C

Cage, N., 93
Carter, J., 40*t*, 114
Caruso, D. R., 11, 12, 22, 24
Carver, G. W., 40*t*, 75
Case Western Reserve University, 20

'Cause You've Got Personality (workout/handout), 255–263

Chang, P. P., 83

Change facilitation, 117–118

Cherniss, C., 7, 116

Childre, D., 13, 82

Cognitive development strategies, 107

Cognitive intelligence, 11

Collaborative behavior, 73

Communication: empathy and, 66, 67, 68; of feelings, 45; reading body language, 67. *See also* Language

Competitive behavior, 73

Conflict: EI role in resolving, 14, 15; as friendly force, 51

Connect Feelings and Meanings workout, 207–209

Consortium for Research on Emotional Intelligence in Organizations, 20, 108, 116, 117

Cooper, R., 24, 25

Cortisol, 13

Council of the Evangelical Church (Germany, 1945), 72

Courage/assertiveness relationship, 51, 52

A Course in Miracles (Foundation for Inner Peace), 96

Cozy Coffee vs. National Biggie, 329–331

Cross-Reference Matrix, 27t–35t

Cut the Apron Strings (workout/handout), 171–174

D

Dalai Lama, 40t, 43, 113

Damasio, A., 13

Deep Center Breathing (workout/handout), 269–273

Denver Post, 66

Desire motivation, 10

DHEA, 13, 99

Dial It Back (workout/handout), 163–166

Dickson, D., 51

Do as the Empathic Do (workout/handout), 219–222

E

ECI 360: Cross-Reference Matrix for, 27t–35t; description and measurements of, 21; four

domains and eighteen competencies of, 21–22; origins of, 20–21

EI Consortium, 20, 108, 116, 117

Eisaguirre, L., 51

Eller, J., 80

Elliot, T. S., 79

Emergenetics seminars, 97

Emotional intelligence: benefits of exploring and developing, 9; brain role in governing, 12–13; developing competence in, 15; four domains of, 11; heart role in governing, 13–14; intelligence defined within concept of, 12. *See also* Intelligence

Emotional Intelligence (Goleman), 21

Emotional intelligence tests: Bar-On EQi, 15, 18–20, 87; described, 12; ECI 360, 20–21, 27t–35t; EQ Map, 7, 24–26, 27t–35t; EQ-360, 7, 18–20; EQ-i, 7, 18–20, 27t–35t, 61; MSCEI, 7, 11–12, 22–24, 27t–35t

"Emotional quotient," 11

Emotional Quotient Inventory Technical Manual (Bar-On), 41

Emotional Self-Awareness competency: described, 18, 19, 21, 38, 45–46; how to build, 46; importance of, 46; mood shifts and, 47; overlap between self-regard and, 42; star and movie exemplifying, 40t, 47–48; transformational benefits of, 47

Emotional Self-Awareness workouts/handouts: Are You in Touch?, 133–137; Grow Your Personal Power, 153–156; It Just Bubbles Up, 139–143; Moving Toward and Moving Away, 145–152

Emotional self-control, 21

Emotions: biochemistry of, 10; described, 10, 12; processes in the brain, 12–13; self vs. other identification and, 14; visualizing, 11. *See also* Feelings

Emovare (to move), 10

Empathy competency: communication and, 66, 67, 68; described, 18, 19, 21, 38, 65–66; how to build, 67–68; importance of, 66–67; relationship between emotional self-awareness and, 45–46; as requisites to assertiveness, 51; star and movie exemplifying, 40t, 68–69; transformational benefits of, 68

Empathy workouts/handouts: Connect Feelings and Meanings, 207–209; Do as the

Empathic Do, 219–222; Mixed Emotions, 211–217

Encyclopedia of Applied Psychology (Cherniss), 7

The EQ Edge (Stein & Book), 61, 108

EQ Map: Cross-References Matrix for, 27t–35t; description and measurements of, 24–25; locating workouts for, 7; origins of, 24; scales used by, 25–26

EQ-360: locating workouts for, 7; multi-rater format of, 18; scoring method used by, 18–20; straightforward presentation of, 20. *See also* Bar-On EQi

EQ-i: Cross-Reference Matrix for, 27t–35t; locating workouts for, 7; research on self-actualization using, 61; scoring method used by, 18–20; straightforward presentation of, 20. *See also* Bar-On EQi

Erin Brockovich (film), 40t, 53

Essi Systems, 24

F

Facilitating thought domain, 11

Fear motivation, 10

Feel, Hear, See—Is It Reality? (workout/handout), 297–300

Feelings: aggressiveness lack of consideration for other's, 50; assertiveness as ability to express, 49; emotional self-awareness and communication of, 45; fear, 10; symbolic meanings of, 11. *See also* Emotions

Field, S., 58

Fight-or-flight response, 13, 14

Finney, A., 53

Flex Time (workout/handout), 321–323

Flexibility competency: brainstorming strategies to improve, 98; described, 19, 20, 39, 95–97; how to build, 98–99; importance of, 97–98; star and movie exemplifying, 40t, 99; transformational benefits of, 99. *See also* Adaptability EQ

Flexibility workouts/handouts: Flex Time, 321–323; No More Shutdown, 311–315; Using the MasterSolve Model for Teams, 325–332; Yes, No, Maybe So, 317–320

Flury, J., 66

Ford, D. E., 83

Foundation for Inner Peace, 96

Frankl, V., 40t, 62

"Friends" (TV show), 40t, 80

Fun and Meaningful Relationships (workout/handout), 251–253

G

Gandhi, M., 40t, 57–58

Gardner, H., 11

General Mood EQ, 18, 19, 20

Getting to Yes (Fisher & Ury), 14, 103

Getting Your Point Across (workout/handout), 167–170

GI Jane (film), 40t, 104

Giuliani, R., 40t, 84–85

Going Along with the Group—Or Not (workout/handout), 179–182

Goleman, D., 20, 21, 46

The Good Girl (film), 40t, 43

Gowing, M., 24

Grant, H., 114

Gratitude: Attitude of Gratitude, 367–370; Pay It Forward with Gratitude, 363–365; relationship to happiness, 108

Groupthink, 56

Grow Your Personal Power (workout/handout), 153–156

Growing My Happiness (workout/handout), 359–362

Guidelines for Best Practice (EI Consortium), 116

H

Handley, R., 83

Happiness: being right vs., 112; defining level of, 111; three types of, 111–112

Happiness competency: described, 19, 20, 39, 111–112; how to build, 112–113; importance of, 112; star and movie exemplifying, 40t, 114; transformational benefits of, 113–114

Happiness workouts/handouts: Attitude of Gratitude, 367–370; Growing My Happiness, 359–362; Pay It Forward with Gratitude, 363–365

Hargie, O., 51

Health/optimism relationship, 107

Heart: electromagnetic signal sent to brain from, 13; emotional intelligence as synthesis of brain and, 13–14

HeartMath Institute, 82
Hill, A., 40*t*, 89–90
Hippocampus, 13
Horner, S., 40*t*, 68–69
Hot Buttons (workout/handout), 293–296

I

"I-ness," 14–15
Ickes, W., 66
Identity/emotions relationship, 14–15
Impulse Control competency: described, 19, 20, 39, 87–88; how to build, 88–89; importance of, 88; PCG (Polaris Consulting Group) ChangeNow Model to improve, 89; relationship between stress management and, 83; star and movie exemplifying, 40*t*, 89–90; transformational benefits of, 89
Impulse Control workouts/handouts: Hot Buttons, 293–296; To Impulse or Not to Impulse, 275–286; The Urge to Splurge, 287–292
Independence competency: described, 18, 19, 38, 55–56; how to build, 56–57; importance of, 56; relationship between assertiveness and, 56; star and movie exemplifying, 40*t*, 57–58; transformational benefits of, 57
Independence workouts/handouts: Cut the Apron Strings, 171–174; Going Along with the Group—Or Not, 179–182; Solitary Effort, 175–178
Institute of HeartMath, 13
Intelligence: within concept of emotional intelligence, 12; developing theories on nature of, 11–12. *See also* Emotional intelligence
Interpersonal Relationship competency: described, 18, 19, 38, 77–78; importance of, 78–79; scoring, 18; star and movie exemplifying, 40*t*, 80; transformational benefits of, 79–80
Interpersonal relationships: Bar-On EQi defined skills used in, 15; building social responsibility linked to, 74; healthy empathy as vital to, 66; learning to value our, 16
Interpersonal Relationships workouts/handouts: Fun and Meaningful Relationships, 251–253; Making New Friends, 245–249; You've Got Good News, 239–243
Intrapersonal EQ, 18

IQ tests, 11
It Just Bubbles Up workouts/handouts, 139–143

J

Jackson, S. L., 85
Jenkins, M., 106
Johns Hopkins University School of Hygiene and Public, 82–83
Johns Hopkins University School of Medicine, 82–83

K

Keaton, D., 80
Kennedy, R., 73
King Lear, Act 1, Scene 1 (Shakespeare), 279–285
King, M. L., Jr., 40*t*, 52–53
Klag, M. J., 83

L

Lane, R. D., 87
Language: body, 67; semantic, 11. *See also* Communication
Learned Optimism (Seligman), 105, 108
Leibman, R., 58
Let's Cover Our Bases (workout/handout), 337–341
Lilies of the Field (film), 40*t*, 99
Love, Actually (film), 40*t*, 114

M

McKee, A., 21, 46
Making New Friends (workout/handout), 245–249
Managing emotions domain, 11
The Manchurian Candidate (film), 40*t*, 48
Mandela, N., 40*t*, 108
Man's Search for Meaning (Frankl), 62
Martin, H., 13
Maslow, A., 59–60
Matchstick Men (film), 93–94
The Matrix (film), 40*t*, 58
Mayer, J. D., 11, 12, 22, 24
The Mayo Clinic, 82

Meaning: achieving dreams that give life, 16; of feelings, 11

Meoni, L. A., 83

Mixed Emotions (workout/handout), 211–217

Molecules of Emotion (Pert), 10

Mood shifts checking, 47

Moore, D., 104

Moving Toward and Moving Away (workout/handout), 145–152

MSCEIT (Mayer-Salovey-Caruso Emotional Intelligence Test): abilities hierarchy of, 22–23*fig*; Cross-References Matrix for, 27*t*–35*t*; description and measurements of, 11–12, 22; locating workouts for, 7; scoring used for, 23–24

Murder in the Cathedral (Elliot), 79

N

National Institute of Mental Health, 10

Negative space, 50

The Negotiator (film), 40*t*, 85

Neo-cortex, 13

Nicholson, J., 69, 80

Niemoller, Pastor M., 72–73

No More Shutdown (workout/handout), 311–315

Norma Rae (film), 58

O

Of Thine Own Self Be Aware (workout/handout), 119–122

1-5-15 method of scoring, 18

O'Neill, T. P., Jr., 40*t*, 99

"Oprah Winfrey Show" (TV show), 47

Optimism competency: being solution focused to improve, 107; described, 19, 20, 39, 105–106; how to build, 107–108; importance of, 106–107; relationship between stress tolerance and, 83; star and movie exemplifying, 40*t*, 108–109

Optimism workouts/handouts: Be Solution-Focused, 343–346; The Optimistic Explanation, 351–357; See a Positive Resolution, 347–350

The Optimistic Explanation (workout/handout), 351–357

Orioli, E., 24

Orme, G., 15

The Other 90 Percent (Cooper), 24

Other, 14

P

Patterson, L. "Chick," 40*t*, 69

Pay It Forward with Gratitude (workout/handout), 363–365

PCG (Polaris Consulting Group) ChangeNow Model, 89

Peck, G., 90

Perceiving emotions domain, 11

Personal Competence (ECI 360), 21

Personality Quiz Handout, 259

Pert, C., 10

Peters, B., 90

Phoebe ("Friends" character), 40*t*, 80

The Pleasant Life, 112

Poitier, S., 40*t*, 99

Positive Psychology Center, 108

The Power of a Good Fight (Eisaguirre), 51

Primal Leadership (Goleman, Boyatzis, & McKee), 20, 21

Problem Solving competency: creating checklist to improve, 103; described, 19, 20, 39, 101–102; how to build, 103; importance of, 102; star and movie exemplifying, 40*t*, 103–104; transformational benefits of, 103

Problem Solving workouts/handouts: Let's Cover Our Bases, 337–341; Win-Win Negotiating, 333–335

Promoting Emotional Intelligence in Organizations (Cherniss & Adler), 116

Q

Q-Metrics, 24, 25

Q-Metrics Approach, 26

Quality of life, 15

R

Ralston, A., 106

Ramp It Up (workout/handout), 157–162

Reality Testing competency: described, 19, 20, 39, 91–92; how to build, 92–93; importance of, 92; skepticism use to improve, 92; star and movie exemplifying, 40*t*, 93–94; transformational benefits, 93

Reality Testing workouts/handouts: Feel, Hear, See—Is It Reality?, 297–300; Using All Three of Your Minds, 305–310; Visit Their Reality, 301–304

Reconciliation (workout/handout), 123–128

Reeves, K., 58

Reflect the Best (workout/handout), 223–227

Relationship Management (ECI 360), 21–22

Remember the Titans (film), 40*t*, 75

Roberts, J., 53

Role-play template, 161

Rutgers University, 20

S

Salovey, P., 11, 12, 22, 24

Satisfaction, 111

The Scavenger Hunt (workout/handout), 183–191

See a Positive Resolution (workout/handout), 347–350

Self identification/emotions relationship, 14

Self-Actualization competency: best predictors of, 60; described, 18, 19, 38, 46, 59–60; how to build, 61–62; importance of, 61; as journey, 60; star and movie exemplifying, 40*t*, 62–63; transformational benefits of, 62

Self-Actualization workouts/handouts: Applying Inspiration, 201–205; Becoming All That You Can Be, 193–199; The Scavenger Hunt, 183–191

Self-Awareness, 18, 19, 21

Self-confidence, 21

Self-Management, 21

Self-Regard competency: described, 18, 19, 38, 41; how to build, 42; importance of, 41–42; overlap between emotional self-awareness and, 42; star and movie exemplifying, 40*t*, 43; transformational benefits of, 43

Self-Regard workouts/handouts: Of Thine Own Self Be Aware, 119–122; Reconciliation, 123–128; Toot Your Horn and Scratch Your Back, 129–132

Seligman, M., 105, 106, 107, 108, 111, 112, 113

Semantic language, 11

September 11, 2001, 84

Shakespeare, W., 279

Skepticism, 92

Skilled Interpersonal Communication (Hargie & Dickson), 50–51

Social Competence, 21

Social Responsibility competency: described, 19, 38, 71; how to build, 73–74; importance of, 72–73; star and movie exemplifying, 40*t*, 75; transformational benefits of, 74–75

Social Responsibility workouts/handouts: Reflect the Best, 223–227; The Value of Volunteering, 235–237; Who Do I Work for?, 229–233

Solitary Effort (workout/handout), 175–178

Something's Got to Give (film), 40*t*, 80

Star Trek: Next Generation (TV show), 55

Stein, S., 45, 49, 51, 61, 66, 77, 91, 96, 101, 108

Stress: cortisol secreted during times of, 13; fight-or-flight response to, 13, 14

Stress Management EQ, 18, 19–20

Stress management techniques, 83–84

Stress Tolerance competency: described, 19–20, 38, 81–82; how to build, 83–84; importance of, 82–83; relationship between impulse control and, 83; relationship between optimism and, 83; star and movie exemplifying, 40*t*, 84–85; transformational benefits of, 84

Stress Tolerance workouts/handouts: 'Cause You've Got Personality, 255–263; Deep Center Breathing, 269–273; Water Off a Duck's Back, 265–267

Stress toolkit, 83

Suedfeld, P., 106

Survivor characteristics, 106

T

Technical Manual (Bar-On), 20

Terms of Endearment (film), 40*t*, 69

Thalamus, 13

The Third Win (Ury), 103

Thomas, C., 89, 90

Thompson, E., 114

To Impulse or Not to Impulse (workout/handout), 275–286

To Kill a Mockingbird (film), 40*t*, 90

Toot Your Horn and Scratch Your Back (workout/handout), 129–132

Total EQ score, 18

Turow, J., 72
Type A personalities, 88

U

Understanding emotions domain, 11
The Urge to Splurge (workout/handout),
    287–292
Ury, W., 14, 40*t*, 103–104
Using All Three of Your Minds
    (workout/handout), 305–310
Using the MasterSolve Model for Teams
    (workout/handout), 325–332

V

The Value of Volunteering (workout/hand-
    out), 235–237
Visit Their Reality (workout/handout),
    301–304

W

Wang, N., 83
Washington, D., 75
Water Off a Duck's Back (workout/handout),
    265–267
Websites: EI Consortium, 20, 108, 116; The
    Mayo Clinic, 82; MKGandhi, 58; Pastor
    Niemoller's remarks on Christian ethics,
    72; Positive Psychology Center, 108
Weisinger, H., 49
Weschler, D., 11
Whale Rider (film), 40*t*, 62–63
Who Do I Work for? (workout/handout),
    229–233

WIFM (What's in it for me?), 88
Win-Win Negotiating (workout/handout),
    333–335
Winfrey, O., 40*t*, 47–48
The Wizard of Oz (film), 40*t*, 109
Working with Emotional Intelligence (Gole-
    man), 21
Workout best practices: evaluate your work,
    117; follow through, 117; get learning in
    the body, 116–117; pace your clients, 117;
    provide safe environment, 116
Workout categories: Assertiveness, 157–170;
    Emotional Self-Awareness, 133–156;
    Empathy, 207–222; Flexibility, 311–315;
    Happiness, 359–370; Impulse Control,
    275–296; Independence, 171–182; Interper-
    sonal Relationships, 239–253; Optimism,
    343–357; Problem Solving, 333–341; Reali-
    ty Testing, 297–310; Self-Actualization,
    183–205; Self-Regard, 119–132; Social
    Responsibility, 223–237; Stress Tolerance,
    255–273
Workouts: Cross-Reference Matrix on,
    27*t*–35*t*; described, 115; facilitating change
    through the, 117–118; facilitator
    skills/practices recommended for,
    116–117; locating the, 7; using the, 118;
    what to read before using, 115
World Trade Center terrorist attack, 84

Y

Yes, No, Maybe So (workout/handout),
    317–320
You've Got Good News (workout/handout),
    239–243

How to Use the CD-ROM

SYSTEM REQUIREMENTS

PC with Microsoft Windows 98SE or later
Mac with Apple OS version 8.6 or later

USING THE CD WITH WINDOWS

To view the items located on the CD, follow these steps:

1. Insert the CD into your computer's CD-ROM drive.
2. A window appears with the following options:

   Contents: Allows you to view the files included on the CD-ROM.

   Software: Allows you to install useful software from the CD-ROM.

   Links: Displays a hyperlinked page of websites.

   Author: Displays a page with information about the Author(s).

   Contact Us: Displays a page with information on contacting the publisher or author.

   Help: Displays a page with information on using the CD.

   Exit: Closes the interface window.

If you do not have autorun enabled, or if the autorun window does not appear, follow these steps to access the CD:

1. Click Start -> Run.
2. In the dialog box that appears, type d:<\\>start.exe, where d is the letter of your CD-ROM drive. This brings up the autorun window described in the preceding set of steps.
3. Choose the desired option from the menu. (See Step 2 in the preceding list for a description of these options.)

IN CASE OF TROUBLE

If you experience difficulty using the CD-ROM, please follow these steps:

1. Make sure your hardware and systems configurations conform to the systems requirements noted under "System Requirements" above.
2. Review the installation procedure for your type of hardware and operating system.

It is possible to reinstall the software if necessary.

To speak with someone in Product Technical Support, call 800-762-2974 or 317-572-3994 M–F 8:30 a.m.–5:00 p.m. EST. You can also get support and contact Product Technical Support through our website at www.wiley.com/techsupport.

Before calling or writing, please have the following information available:

- Type of computer and operating system
- Any error messages displayed
- Complete description of the problem.

It is best if you are sitting at your computer when making the call.

Pfeiffer Publications Guide

This guide is designed to familiarize you with the various types of Pfeiffer publications. The formats section describes the various types of products that we publish; the methodologies section describes the many different ways that content might be provided within a product. We also provide a list of the topic areas in which we publish.

FORMATS

In addition to its extensive book-publishing program, Pfeiffer offers content in an array of formats, from fieldbooks for the practitioner to complete, ready-to-use training packages that support group learning.

FIELDBOOK Designed to provide information and guidance to practitioners in the midst of action. Most fieldbooks are companions to another, sometimes earlier, work, from which its ideas are derived; the fieldbook makes practical what was theoretical in the original text. Fieldbooks can certainly be read from cover to cover. More likely, though, you'll find yourself bouncing around following a particular theme, or dipping in as the mood, and the situation, dictate.

HANDBOOK A contributed volume of work on a single topic, comprising an eclectic mix of ideas, case studies, and best practices sourced by practitioners and experts in the field.

An editor or team of editors usually is appointed to seek out contributors and to evaluate content for relevance to the topic. Think of a handbook not as a ready-to-eat meal, but as a cookbook of ingredients that enables you to create the most fitting experience for the occasion.

RESOURCE Materials designed to support group learning. They come in many forms: a complete, ready-to-use exercise (such as a game); a comprehensive resource on one topic (such as conflict management) containing a variety of methods and approaches; or a collection of like-minded activities (such as icebreakers) on multiple subjects and situations.

TRAINING PACKAGE An entire, ready-to-use learning program that focuses on a particular topic or skill. All packages comprise a guide for the facilitator/trainer and a workbook for the participants. Some packages are supported with additional media—such as video—or learning aids, instruments, or other devices to help participants understand concepts or practice and develop skills.

- *Facilitator/trainer's guide* Contains an introduction to the program, advice on how to organize and facilitate the learning event, and step-by-step instructor notes. The guide also contains copies of presentation materials—handouts, presentations, and overhead designs, for example—used in the program.

- *Participant's workbook* Contains exercises and reading materials that support the learning goal and serves as a valuable reference and support guide for participants in the weeks and months that follow the learning event. Typically, each participant will require his or her own workbook.

ELECTRONIC CD-ROMs and web-based products transform static Pfeiffer content into dynamic, interactive experiences. Designed to take advantage of the searchability, automation, and ease-of-use that technology provides, our e-products bring convenience and immediate accessibility to your workspace.

METHODOLOGIES

CASE STUDY A presentation, in narrative form, of an actual event that has occurred inside an organization. Case studies are not prescriptive, nor are they used to prove a point; they are designed to develop critical analysis and decision-making skills. A case study has a specific time frame, specifies a sequence of events, is narrative in structure, and contains a plot structure—an issue (what should be/have been done?). Use case studies when the goal is to enable participants to apply previously learned theories to the circumstances in the case, decide what is pertinent, identify the real issues, decide what should have been done, and develop a plan of action.

ENERGIZER A short activity that develops readiness for the next session or learning event. Energizers are most commonly used after a break or lunch to stimulate or refocus the group. Many involve some form of physical activity, so they are a useful way to counter post-lunch lethargy. Other uses include transitioning from one topic to another, where "mental" distancing is important.

EXPERIENTIAL LEARNING ACTIVITY (ELA) A facilitator-led intervention that moves participants through the learning cycle from experience to application (also known as a Structured Experience). ELAs are carefully thought-out designs in which there is a definite learning purpose and intended outcome. Each step—everything that participants do during the activity—facilitates the accomplishment of the stated goal. Each ELA includes complete instructions for facilitating the intervention and a clear statement of goals, suggested group size and timing, materials required, an explanation of the process, and, where appropriate, possible variations to the activity. (For more detail on Experiential Learning Activities, see the Introduction to the *Reference Guide to Handbooks and Annuals*, 1999 edition, Pfeiffer, San Francisco.)

GAME A group activity that has the purpose of fostering team spirit and togetherness in addition to the achievement of a pre-stated goal. Usually contrived—undertaking a desert expedition, for example—this type of learning method offers an engaging means for participants to demonstrate and practice business and interpersonal skills. Games are effective for team building and personal development mainly because the goal is subordinate to the process—the means through which participants reach decisions, collaborate, communicate, and generate trust and understanding. Games often engage teams in "friendly" competition.

ICEBREAKER A (usually) short activity designed to help participants overcome initial anxiety in a training session and/or to acquaint the participants with one another. An icebreaker can be a fun activity or can be tied to specific topics or training goals. While a useful tool in itself, the icebreaker comes into its own in situations where tension or resistance exists within a group.

INSTRUMENT A device used to assess, appraise, evaluate, describe, classify, and summarize various aspects of human behavior. The term used to describe an instrument depends primarily on its format and purpose. These terms include survey, questionnaire, inventory, diagnostic, survey, and poll. Some uses of instruments include providing instrumental feedback to group members, studying here-and-now processes or functioning within a group, manipulating group composition, and evaluating outcomes of training and other interventions.

Instruments are popular in the training and HR field because, in general, more growth can occur if an individual is provided with a method for focusing specifically on his or her behavior. Instruments also are used to obtain information that will serve as a basis for change and to assist in workforce planning efforts.

Paper-and-pencil tests still dominate the instrument landscape with a typical package comprising a facilitator's guide, which offers advice on administering the instrument and interpreting the collected data, and an initial set of instruments. Additional instruments are available separately. Pfeiffer, though, is investing heavily in e-instruments. Electronic instrumentation provides effortless distribution and, for larger groups particularly, offers advantages over paper-and-pencil tests in the time it takes to analyze data and provide feedback.

LECTURETTE A short talk that provides an explanation of a principle, model, or process that is pertinent to the participants' current learning needs. A lecturette is intended to establish a common language bond between the trainer and the participants by providing a mutual frame of reference. Use a lecturette as an introduction to a group activity or event, as an interjection during an event, or as a handout.

MODEL A graphic depiction of a system or process and the relationship among its elements. Models provide a frame of reference and something more tangible, and more easily remembered, than a verbal explanation. They also give participants something to "go on," enabling them to track their own progress as they experience the dynamics, processes, and relationships being depicted in the model.

ROLE PLAY A technique in which people assume a role in a situation/scenario: a customer service rep in an angry-customer exchange, for example. The way in which the role is approached is then discussed and feedback is offered. The role play is often repeated using a different approach and/or incorporating changes made based on feedback received. In other words, role playing is a spontaneous interaction involving realistic behavior under artificial (and safe) conditions.

SIMULATION A methodology for understanding the interrelationships among components of a system or process. Simulations differ from games in that they test or use a model that depicts or mirrors some aspect of reality in form, if not necessarily in content. Learning occurs by studying the effects of change on one or more factors of the model. Simulations are commonly used to test hypotheses about what happens in a system—often referred to as "what if?" analysis—or to examine best-case/worst-case scenarios.

THEORY A presentation of an idea from a conjectural perspective. Theories are useful because they encourage us to examine behavior and phenomena through a different lens.

TOPICS

The twin goals of providing effective and practical solutions for workforce training and organization development and meeting the educational needs of training and human resource professionals shape Pfeiffer's publishing program. Core topics include the following:

Leadership & Management

Communication & Presentation

Coaching & Mentoring

Training & Development

E-Learning

Teams & Collaboration

OD & Strategic Planning

Human Resources

Consulting

What will you find on pfeiffer.com?

- The best in workplace performance solutions for training and HR professionals

- Downloadable training tools, exercises, and content

- Web-exclusive offers

- Training tips, articles, and news

- Seamless on-line ordering

- Author guidelines, information on becoming a Pfeiffer Affiliate, and much more

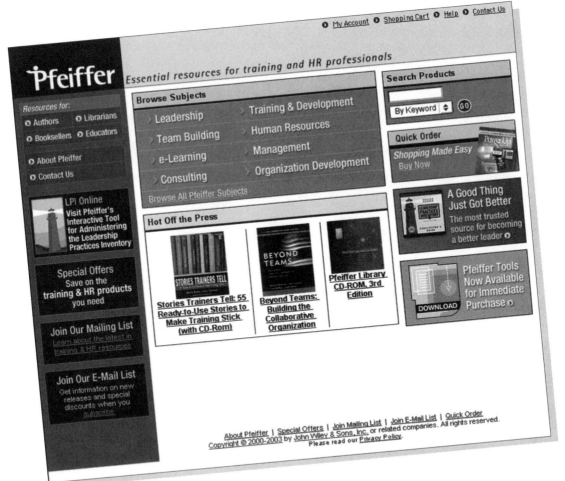

Discover more at www.pfeiffer.com